Old Jamestown Across the Ages

Highlights and Stories of Old Jamestown, Missouri

Compiled by Peggy Kruse

Front Cover: Sioux Passage Park looking toward Missouri River with Pelican Island at upper left
  Drone photo taken by Chan Mahanta
Back Cover: Google Earth Map of Old Jamestown, Larger Image: Map 1-1, Chapter 1

OLD JAMESTOWN ACROSS THE AGES
Highlights and Stories of Old Jamestown, Missouri

Permissions to include content in this book came with specific conditions. Please do not copy any quoted or adapted material without getting your own permission from the source.
Content correction or questions should be sent to Peggy Kruse, mopeaceweavers@aol.com

First Edition, April 15, 2017
Self Published by Peggy Kruse (Peace Weavers, LLC)
Printed by CreateSpace, an Amazon.com Company
Copyright © 2017, All rights reserved.
ISBN-13: 978-1544741918, ISBN-10: 154474191X

OLD JAMESTOWN ACROSS THE AGES

Highlights and Stories of Old Jamestown, Missouri

Contents

Preface	8
Chapter 1 – Overview -- Old Jamestown Across the Ages	9
Attraction of Old Jamestown	10
Major Themes	11
Across the Ages: The Tunstall-Douglass House	16
Chapter 1 Photos and Maps	17
Chapter 2 – American Indians and Explorers	18
Attraction of Old Jamestown	18
Sioux Passage Park – Cahokia satellite community	18
Other American Indian presence near Old Jamestown	21
American Indian Travel	21
Explorers on the Missouri River	22
Lewis and Clark Expedition	24
Zebulon Pike Expedition	25
Chapter 2 Photos and Maps	27
Chapter 3 – Land Grants and Early Settlers (1)	30
Attraction of Old Jamestown	30
James Richardson	33
Guy Seeley	34
John N. Seeley	34
Carrico Family	35
Charles Desjarlais	35
Brown Family	36
Elisha Herrington/James B. Hart	36
Farquar McKensie	36
James Family	36
Sarah James – Ferry	37
Phinehas James – James' Town	38
Morris James	41
Benjamin Franklin James	41

James James... 42
    Cumberland James... 42
  Chapter 3 Photos and Maps.. 43
Chapter 4 – Land Grants and Early Settlers (2) – Hodges Family 47
  Hodges Family.. 47
    Captain Edmund Hodges.. 48
    Ebenezer Hodges... 51
    Gilbert Hodges... 52
    Rachel Hodges (m. Benjamin Franklin James) 53
    Julie Hodges (m. Charles Desjarlais) 53
    Daniel Hodges.. 53
    Samuel Hodges.. 53
  Chapter 4 Photos and Maps.. 55
Chapter 5 – Land Grants and Early Settlers (3) – Patterson Family 56
  Patterson Family.. 56
    John Patterson, Jr. 56
    William Patterson... 58
    Elisha and Lucy Patterson.. 59
    Hume Family.. 60
    Later residents on Patterson land grants.. 62
  Chapter 5 Photos... 64
Chapter 6 – Musick's Ferry Area 66
  Attraction of Old Jamestown.. 66
  Musick's Ferry and Inn... 67
  Musick Family.. 70
  Warren Family.. 70
  Desloge Estate... 72
  Boeing Leadership Center.. 72
  Stories from Musick's Ferry 72
  Steamboats 76
  Halls Ferry Road.. 77
  Chapter 6 Photos and Maps.. 79
Chapter 7 – Very Early Schools, Churches, Cemeteries 83
  Cemeteries... 83

Cold Water Cemetery	83
New Coldwater Burying Ground Memorial Park Cemetery	84
Churches begun on Cold Water Cemetery ground	85
Rev. John Clark – Protestant in Spanish Catholic Times	86
Coldwater Church	87
Salem Baptist Church	87
African American Church and School on New Coldwater Burying Ground	88
Schools	88
Brown School	88
Coldwater School	89
Vossenkemper School	90
Student Memories from the Early Schools	91
Chapter 7 Photos and Maps	95
Chapter 8 – Farmers, Immigrants	98
Attraction of Old Jamestown	98
Farming in Old Jamestown area	98
Rosenkoetter Family	99
Ruegg – Portland Cement Company Town	101
Others	102
Robbins	102
Veale/Vaile	102
Buenger	103
Meyer	104
Wehmer	105
Thompson	107
Gerling/Albers	108
Leber	109
Lange	109
Niehaus	111
Slavery and Divided Loyalties during Civil War	111
Chapter 8 Photos	113
Chapter 9 – Prominent Residents	117
Attraction of Old Jamestown	117
Desloge Family -- Vouziers Mansion	117

- Shelby Curlee -- Curlee Clothing Company ... 118
- Mesker Family ... 119
- McNair Family – St. Louis Cold Drawn Steel ... 120
- Evarts Graham, M.D. ... 120
- Alexis Hartmann, Sr., M.D., and Alexis Hartmann, Jr., M.D. ... 122
- Vilray Blair, M.D. ... 122
- Ellis Fischel, M.D. ... 123
- Episcopal Bishop William Scarlett ... 124
- Henri Chomeau ... 124
- Oscar Hammer ... 125
- Adela R. Scharr ... 126
- Behlmann Family ... 127
- Zykan Family ... 128
- Christian and Jennifer Welch Cudnik ... 129
- Eddie Moss ... 129
- "Bubbleheads" ... 129
- Chapter 9 Photos and Maps ... 131

Chapter 10 – Land/Water (Environment) ... 135
- Attraction of Old Jamestown ... 135
- Karst – Old Jamestown Association Efforts to Protect ... 135
- Missouri River – Changes over the years ... 137
- Quarries ... 138
- Laclede Gas Underground Storage Facility – OJA Efforts ... 139
- Parks – Sioux Passage, Briscoe, Champ ... 141
- Pelican Island ... 142
- Coldwater Creek Cancer Issues ... 143
- Residents' Environmental Efforts ... 144
  - Combatting Soil Erosion in 1947 ... 144
  - Cultivating Native Plants ... 145
  - Waier's Geothermal Heating/Cooling ... 146
- Chapter 10 Photos and Maps ... 147

Chapter 11 - Current Organizations ... 150
- Attraction of Old Jamestown ... 150
- Nonprofits ... 150

    Governments 152

    Businesses 153

    Boeing Leadership Center 155

    Churches... 155

    Residents 157

    Chapter 11 Photos and Maps 158

Appendices.. 159

    Appendix 1 - Old Jamestown Association History and Activity 159

    Appendix 2 - Old Jamestown Geographic Features 163

    Appendix 3 - Living with the Sinks – Missouri Resources Magazine 165

    Appendix 4 - Newspaper Article – Early Days in Missouri 169

    Appendix 5 - Congressional Testimony – Election Judge at Musick's Ferry 173

    Appendix 6 - Occasional Crime at Musick's Ferry 177

    Appendix 7 - Vincent Family – New Coldwater Burying Ground 179

    Appendix 8 - Baptist Friends to Humanity 182

    Appendix 9 – Slavery and Civil War... 183

    Appendix 10 - Ralph Wehmer's Stories and Photos 189

    Appendix 11 – Desloge Family & Vouziers Mansion... 195

    Appendix 12 – Timeline 202

End Notes... 204

Bibliography 218

    Family Histories.. 218

    Old Jamestown Area History.. 218

    St. Louis Area History 219

    Missouri History 220

    Magazines.. 220

    Newspapers.. 221

    Government Documents 221

    Web sites.. 222

Acknowledgements 225

Index... 228

Preface

My first experience of the Old Jamestown area was in the mid 1950s when, as a pre-teen, I went with two friends to Triple C (Coldwater Community Club) 4-H meetings and events. We were driven there by our parents, past many farm fields, from our north St. Louis City homes. At that time the Triple C Club was led by Hilda Albers whose home was on New Halls Ferry near the Desloge Mansion. Many of the meetings and events I remember were near Salem Baptist Church on Old Jamestown Road.

When my husband and I began looking for land to build a new home in 1984, we found a 4-1/2 acre lot on Old Jamestown Road, within sight of Salem Baptist. After we moved to our home in 1986, I often wondered whether American Indians and early explorers had a path along Old Jamestown, but did not go further than wondering.

Little did I know the many fascinating stories that were available from longtime residents and online sources. In response to a July 2011 question from Don Zykan about whether there was any historical information on Musick's Ferry (New Halls Ferry and Douglas Roads at the Missouri River), we both began contacting historians and searching the internet. That resulted in an explosion of new information for us.

In September 2011, an Old Jamestown Association History Committee was formed and we gathered enough interesting material to present at the Association's general meeting in November 2011. Suggestions for writing a book flowed from that meeting but start of the book project was delayed by other time-consuming projects, both OJA and personal, until July 2013.

With fits and starts, the research continued and new discoveries continue to appear even as I write this. My longest profession was auditing and I've long been a wannabe journalist. Researching history is much like doing an audit or writing for a newspaper or magazine or blog – reviewing documents, interviewing knowledgeable individuals, and then attempting to prepare a report that makes it clear for others.

As the book progressed, I realized it would be more realistic to say that I was compiling a book instead of writing a book. I've quoted or adapted much of the text from material written by others. In the end notes, I provide the sources, most of which contain additional information.

My interest is in the stories and connections of people who lived in Old Jamestown over the years. This book is not intended to provide comprehensive genealogical or historic house information. I have provided many references so that those who are especially interested in those subjects can follow up and perhaps write their own book.

I could not have compiled the book without help from many, many sources. Hopefully I've included them all in the Acknowledgements and Bibliography sections in the back of the book.

I dedicate this book to my first loves and blessings:

    God, from whom every family in heaven and on earth is named (Ref. Eph. 3:14-21)

    My wonderful and supportive family:
    Ray -- Ken, Susan, Clayton and McKenna -- Kevin, Kelly, Brian and David

OLD JAMESTOWN ACROSS THE AGES

Note to Readers: "Old Jamestown" is used throughout this book when referring to activity at any time within the current Old Jamestown boundaries. "Musick's Ferry," at New Halls Ferry Road and Douglas Road next to the Missouri River, is still identified on maps and is used as a location when discussing any activity there. In an attempt to avoid distraction, the spelling of most location and family names has been standardized as much as possible.

Chapter 1 – Overview -- Old Jamestown Across the Ages

This chapter provides a quick snapshot of Old Jamestown. It touches briefly on just some of the themes covered in the book. See chapters referenced at the end of each topic for much more information.

In far north St. Louis County, Missouri, Old Jamestown is an area of rolling hills, beautiful river views and attractive subdivisions, many with lots over 3 acres. It is a unique, fascinating area that is mostly overlooked because its early identity was meshed with other areas in St. Ferdinand Township and its later identity was meshed with all areas of unincorporated St. Louis County.

St. Ferdinand Township, one of six townships in St. Louis County in the 1800s, included what are now Old Jamestown neighbors - Florissant, Black Jack, and Spanish Lake. Names applied to parts of Old Jamestown during the early years have been Coldwater, Patterson Settlement, The Sinks, and Jamestown. In 2010 Old Jamestown, bordered by the Missouri River, Coldwater Creek, New Halls Ferry Road, and MO-367/U.S. Hwy 67, became officially recognized as a CDP (Census Designated Place) and is now displayed on some maps.

[Map 1-1]

Much of the Old Jamestown neighborhood is a very low density, heavily wooded and sinkhole studded semi-rural environment, interspersed with still active farms. Situated along the bank of the Missouri River it is just a few miles upriver from the confluence of the Missouri and the Mississippi and has a rich history dating back to ancient times.

Old Jamestown's history includes an American Indian settlement associated with Cahokia Mounds, land grant holders of English and Scottish heritage who arrived in the late 1700s, German immigrant farmers who came during the 1800s, and prominent wealthy families who arrived in 1920-1940. Today it includes subdivisions and nonprofit organizations while retaining much of its rural ambiance.

With only two miles separating the Missouri and Mississippi Rivers just north of Old Jamestown, it provided desirable connections from St. Louis and Florissant to St. Charles County, which is home to Portage des Sioux, an early military outpost, and the City of St. Charles, Missouri's first state capitol (1821-1826). It was also connected through St. Charles County locations to Alton, Illinois.

Across the years, Old Jamestown residents have also been connected to national experiences – American Indian travels, Revolutionary War, Slavery, Civil War, Prohibition, World War I and World War II, etc.

Attraction of Old Jamestown

The most captivating description of Old Jamestown was written almost 200 years ago by Phinehas James when he advertised his development of 300 lots in a front page ad for "James' Town" in the Missouri Gazette, June 16, 1819:

> "JAMES' TOWN Is situated on a beautiful bluff, on the southern bank of the Missouri River, six miles above its confluence with the Mississippi. Being situated on a bluff, it has the advantage of a firm rock shore, along which there are a number of the safest harbors for boats that I presume any other town on these waters can boast of; also, several seats for mills that so large a water course can form. Near the public square, there is a cave through which passes a large body of cold, sweet lucid water which I think could, without much expense be raised and conveyed to every part of the town. The earth after removing the virgin soil is admirably calculated for brick, and the rock along the river, which can be easily procured, is of the best quality, either for building or manufacturing into lime; sand for making brick and mortar can be procured without much trouble or expense. Behind this desirable situation lays the rich and flourishing country of Florissant or St. Ferdinand and in front (beyond that majestic river that sweep[s] along its base) is to be seen that fertile bottom that intercepts the communication of those two splendid rivers (Mississippi and Missouri) which not only offers to the fancy a rich harvest of charms, but also to the town an abundant harvest of advantages. The situation of this town is so lofty and noble as never to offend by noxious fumes of putrid sickly air; and the eye has always presented to it, a beautiful and grand variety...."[1]

[Map 1-2] [Also Map 3-5 in Chapter 3]

See the full ad and more about the James Family and James' Town in Chapter 3.

Phinehas' dream of a large community on the bluff did not work out, perhaps due the collapse of land prices and recession about 1819, but the physical location of Old Jamestown area was attractive to many travelers and inhabitants both before and after his ad. Artifacts have been found that suggest many nomadic American Indian tribes passed through OJ area over thousands of years. In addition, it is very likely a large densely populated village associated with the Cahokia settlement in Illinois existed near the current Sioux Passage Park area from about 600 to 1200 A.D. In the late 1700s and early 1800s, explorers and settlers quickly recognized the value of the area. After Missouri was admitted to the United States as a slave state in 1821, many from the upper south, especially Kentucky and Tennessee, came to Missouri, many following Daniel Boone across the state. German farmers discovered it in the mid 1800s, and later prominent St. Louisans enjoyed its unique characteristics.

Old Jamestown bluffs are some of highest Missouri River bluffs in St. Louis County. The area avoids flooding because of the bluffs and because flood waters go to the flood plain between the Missouri and Mississippi Rivers just north of Old Jamestown.

> "Caves, springs, and sinkholes, were often revered in prehistoric times, for they were thought to represent portals to the Underworld."[2]

How did these wonderful geographic characteristics come to be?

As briefly described by Tim O'Neil in the ©St. Louis Post-Dispatch 2014:

> "Some time after the Beginning, much of what we call the Midwest was covered by a warm, shallow ocean. Millions of years of sediment and the remains of primordial creatures formed the limestone we rest upon. Achingly slow collisions of continents pushed the land out of the water. Volcanic bulges created granite heights such as the St. Francois Mountains (near Farmington, Mo.). Dinosaurs roamed, just as the children's books always say they did. The sea retreated south to the wide Delta flatland of the Bootheel. The geological evidence suggests all of that took about 2 billion years, give or take a few million.

> "A series of ice ages beginning about 2.5 million years ago ground up the land roughly as far south as St. Louis, gouging valleys for massive runoffs of melt that created major rivers — including the Missouri, Mississippi and Illinois, which merge into the fertile bottomland of the great confluence. The last glacial retreat, 12,000 or so years ago, left behind the meandering river courses framed by the high limestone bluffs we know today.

> "The strategic convenience of the confluence attracted humans...."[3]

See Appendices 2 and 3 for more on Old Jamestown area geography.

Major Themes

American Indians and Explorers

> "Grandfather God Great Spirit....
> Teach us to walk the soft earth as relatives to ALL that live"
> Sioux Prayer[4]

American Indians and then settlers long used the unique characteristics of the Old Jamestown area as preferred travel routes.

Lou Pondrom wrote: "The site of [Musick's] ferry landing at the end of Halls Ferry and Douglas Roads, was probably used as a crossing point by the Indians long before the French and Americans moved in. The Halls Ferry Road from the Mississippi at Cabaret Island at Baden, probably followed an Indian trail used as a cutoff across the north end of St. Louis County, the same as the 'Portage of the Sioux' was used to cross the tip of land in St. Charles to the Missouri River. Both were used to enter the Missouri to escape the treacherous currents at its entry into the Mississippi, especially during high water."[5]

From a 1919 ©St. Louis Post-Dispatch article: "It was at Portage des Sioux that Indians of the 'Upper Missouri' district made their headquarters for dealing in furs in pioneer days of Missouri. It was the custom, according to stories that have been told by the old residents of Florissant, that the Indians would cross the Missouri River from Portages des Sioux at a point near Musick's Ferry and carry their wares to Florissant, where they bartered with the early white settlers."[6]

"The spirit of Vouziers is one of people coming together."
Hal Kroeger.[7]

In 1992 Hal Kroeger, then owner of the former Desloge Vouziers estate at New Halls Ferry and Shackelford, talked about American Indians also using the area as a gathering place. "'The spirit of Vouziers is one of people coming together.' Indeed, historical evidence suggests that this has been a gathering place since ancient times. Archaeologists believe that at least 11,000 years ago, [American] Indian tribes came to this high point near the confluence of the Missouri, Mississippi and Illinois rivers each summer…to trade, to socialize, to compete at games, to arrange marriages."[8]

Sioux Passage Park is just one of the many areas in Old Jamestown where American Indian artifacts have been found. Well known and respected St. Louis Archaeologist Joe Harl gives this assessment of probable prehistoric activity in the Old Jamestown area: "We conducted a cultural resource survey of Sioux Passage Park in 2003. There are no mounds still standing within the park, but there are a number of significant prehistoric sites, including a large Mississippian site (A.D. 1050-1400); the same time as Cahokia Mounds. There are still mounds located nearby on private lands."[9]

See Chapter 2 for more on the American Indians.

Explorer Travel

Early explorers, Marquette (1670) and LaSalle (1682), noted the location and size of the Missouri River as they traveled down the Mississippi. They learned from American Indians about the Missouri's upper reaches. Later explorers passed Old Jamestown on their treks up the Missouri River to the unknown West. We all know about Lewis & Clark beginning their journey in 1804 from what was Wood River, Illinois, and two years later staying near Fort Belle Fontaine, just to the east of Old Jamestown, on their return trip. In his *Journal,* Zebulon Pike of Pike's Peak fame also mentions camping in an area near the location of Sioux Passage Park on his journey to explore the southern portion of the Louisiana Purchase.[10]

See Chapter 2 for more on the explorers.

Settlers

By the early 1800s, almost all of the land in Old Jamestown had been granted by the Spanish to the first settlers, most of whom were of British heritage. Earlier land grantees in nearby Florissant were French and Spanish.

Spain controlled the Louisiana territory on the west side of the Mississippi from 1763 to 1800 and then managed it during secret French ownership from 1800 to 1803. In 1796, Americans living in Kentucky and Tennessee were recruited to move to the "New Spain" and offered free land by the Spanish government. Others, including the Hodges family, came to Old Jamestown from Canada to receive the Spanish grants.

The appeal of land on or near the river was described in a book about Captain Edmund Hodges who, with four of his sons, held land grants along the Missouri River, "Captain Edmund Hodges and his sons settled on land adjacent to waterways [in Canada].... Lots near waterways were favored by settlers who relied on them to transport goods and supplies."[11]

John Patterson, Sr, arrived in the area with his family about 1797 and began to acquire land through grants and purchases. Before long the area that is now Old Jamestown was known as "The Patterson Settlement," which was about 10,000 acres (2000 were owned by the Patterson family). The Pattersons retained their Protestant faith through the services of a Methodist Minister known as "Father Clark, the first clergyman to hold a Protestant service west of the Mississippi. In the early 1800s, Clark was making regular visits to the settlements along Coldwater Creek and later established a church. Salem Baptist Church on Old Jamestown Road had its beginnings next to Cold Water Cemetery on Patterson land.

See Chapters 3, 4, and 5 for more on land grantees.

See Chapter 7 for more on Cold Water Cemetery and early churches.

Musick's Ferry

About 1800 Sarah James owned the land at the juncture of New Halls Ferry and Douglas Roads on the Missouri River and operated a ferry to St. Charles County. In 1817 Rufus Easton purchased the land from Sarah's son, Phineas. In 1848 the land and ferry were sold to Reuben Musick and his wife, Lydia Carrico Musick. Vincent Grey built Musick's Ferry Inn, which "thrived for many years as a center of commerce as well as entertainment, as not only farmers, halting there on their long and arduous trips to enjoy a good night's rest but also folks from both sides of the Missouri journeyed over the rough roads in wagons, buggies and on horseback to participate in the gaieties at the tavern and stay overnight for different shows on the showboats that would stop there."[12] Even after the inn was no longer used, Musick's Ferry continued to be a place of gathering and commerce.

See Chapter 6 for much more about Musick's Ferry.

Early Schools

Three very early schools were within the Old Jamestown boundaries. – Next to Cold Water Cemetery on Old Halls Ferry was the original Coldwater School, which was begun by the Patterson family in the early 1800s. The second Coldwater School was a one-room brick building built about 1860 on the west side of New Halls Ferry Road, it was closed in 1954. The one-room Brown School on Old Jamestown Road was built in 1860 of brick and was originally called James School, then changed names several times to Douglas and James and finally to Brown School. After Brown School was taken over by the new School District of Hazelwood in 1950, the building became a residence. Vossenkemper School was established near Hwy 67 and Robbins Mill Road in the mid-1800s. The last Vossenkemper graduation was held in 1954 after formation of the Hazelwood School District. The original Vossenkemper buildings are no longer standing.

See Chapter 7 for more stories about these schools.

Immigrants – Farming

Most of the original settlers came to Old Jamestown from other parts of the United States. However, in the mid 1800s most new families arrived directly from European countries.

Representative of many Germans, about 1840 the Rosenkoetter family boarded ships in Bremen, Germany, and took the two-month trip to New Orleans, then took steam boats for the two-week trip up the Mississippi to Missouri. Many left Germany because of the poor economic conditions at that time and some left to avoid serving in the Prussian military. Most Germans came to farm the land in Old Jamestown. The Rosekoetters also had stores/taverns at Cross Keys (Hwy 67 and New Halls Ferry) and Shoveltown (Hwy 67 and Old Halls Ferry).[13]

In 1903 a prominent member of the community was John H. C. Ruegg who was of Swiss/German descent. Ruegg and his partner established a branch of their mercantile business on the site of the Portland Cement Company's quarry at what is now MO-367/U.S. Hwy 67 and the Missouri River. The Ruegg Post Office was also established there. This 'company town' grew into a village of about nineteen houses and became a thriving settlement.[14]

Just a few of the other immigrant families were the Buengers, Meyers, Wehmers, and Gerlings.

See Chapter 8 for more on the Germans and other immigrants and on farming in Old Jamestown.

Civil War era

Missouri was admitted into the Confederate States of America in November 1861 but only the Confederate-sympathizing portion of the Missouri government seceded. The loyal Union portion of the state remained a part of the United States of America. Some Old Jamestown residents fought on the Union side, others for the Confederacy.

See Chapter 8 and Appendix 8 for more on the Civil War era related to Old Jamestown.

Wealthy Residents in mid 1900s

"[In] the 1920s, with the triumph of the automobile and the beginnings of highway improvement, 'Country living' really become a possibility. The foremost attraction of the north county was its spectacular views, and the most significant country villas are all perched on the bluffs of the Missouri."[15]

In 1919, Joseph Desloge, Sr., son of Firmin Desloge, bought a large tract of land near the intersection of what is now New Halls Ferry and Shackelford roads in North County and commissioned New Orleans architect Dennis McDonald to design a Louis XVI-style chateau.

In 1931, Shelby Curlee, owner of Curlee Clothing Company and a great-grandnephew of Daniel Boone, built a home overlooking the Car of Commerce Chute and the Missouri River. The large estate has since become Castlereagh Subdivision on Old Jamestown Road.

Also in the early 1930s, brothers John B.G. Mesker and Francis Mesker built large estates on Portage Road overlooking the Missouri River. They were sons of Frank Mesker, who with his brother Bernard Theodore Mesker, founded Mesker Brothers Iron Company in 1879. This is the site of the original "James' Town" promoted by Phinehas James in 1819.

Prominent Washington University physicians also discovered Old Jamestown. Evarts A. Graham, M.D., F.A.C.S. (1883-1957), a renowned researcher and physician, lived on Jamestown Acres in the 1940s and 1950s. His house was designed by Harris Armstrong, a well-known modern architect. Vilray P. Blair, M.D., a premier American pioneer in plastic surgery, lived on Portage Road. Alexis Hartmann, M.D., and later his son, Alexis Hartmann, Jr., M.D., prominent in pediatric medicine at Washington U. and Children's Hospital, had a summer home on Jamestown Acres.

William Scarlett, Bishop of the Missouri Episcopal Diocese from 1933 to 1952, moved to Jamestown Acres after his retirement.

See Chapter 9 for more about these prominent residents.

Unique Underground Features

Karst Geology

Karst geology is characterized by underground rivers, caves, springs, losing streams, voids, and fissures, which are the result of millions of years of water dissolving limestone formations that eventually result in surface collapse and visible sinkholes on the surface. The "Florissant karst," an area of four square miles within Old Jamestown is well known by geologists worldwide. All storm water runoff discharges directly into sinkholes and then to the network of underground water aquifers.

In the mid 1980s subdivision development moved further north in St. Louis County and many projects were proposed for the Old Jamestown area. In 1988, St. Louis County planned a study of the karst area but did not include any local residents on the study commission. Residents objected and re-activated the Old Jamestown Association, which had originally been incorporated in 1942. After completion of the study, the Association focused its efforts on working with St. Louis County to prevent residential or business development that would negatively impact sinkholes. After many years of supporting its concepts, in March 2009, St. Louis County enacted environmental legislation to preserve Old Jamestown's unique geological karst formations.

See Chapter 10 for more about the karst geology.

Laclede Gas storage facility

In the early 1950s, Laclede Gas Co. began looking for a place to store natural gas and chose a large property near Sinks and Old Jamestown Roads. Some gas companies had been using aquifers - sandstone formations that hold underground water - as safe and secure storage areas for gas since the early 20th century. Some landowners objected to losing their subsurface rights to Laclede, but the Missouri Supreme Court eventually cleared the company's right to take the aquifer. Today the gas company can store up to 5 billion cubic feet of gas in the underground aquifer by injecting it under pressure - between 300 and 630 pounds per square inch - into the sandstone.

See Chapter 10 for more about the Laclede Gas facility.

Across the Ages: The Tunstall-Douglass House

[Photo1-1]

Though we don't have specific information about American Indians who likely lived around the property at 15310 Old Halls Ferry Road, we do have specifics about the later history of the land and house, which is representative of the major transitions across Old Jamestown.

In the late 1700s, the ground on which the Tunstall-Douglass House stands was granted to David Brown by the Spanish. (Chapter 3) David died in 1803 and his representatives Daniel and Mary Brown sold it in 1819 to four of the five sons of another pioneer settler John Patterson, Sr. (Chapter 5). In 1853 a portion of the property was sold to Elizabeth B. Tunstall.

In 1858, the Tunstalls sold the property to Nicholas Blacklock Douglass and his wife, Margaret Patterson, daughter of John Patterson, Jr., and Jane Jamison (his step sister). The house was built by Douglass, constructed by slave labor with bricks kilned on the property. The Douglasses donated a portion of their property for use as Cold Water Cemetery and Church and School. Also, two of the Douglass' children, Mary and Virena, taught at Brown School on Old Jamestown. (Chapter 7) Mary and later Virena married Henri Chomeau who had also grown up in the area and later became a well known Clayton engineer and businessman. (Chapter 9)

In 1885 Herman C. Rosenkoetter, one of the many German farmers who had come to Old Jamestown in the mid-1800s, purchased the farm, which was then nearly 200 acres. In 1910, he farmed about 300 acres, specializing in growing fruit. (Chapter 8)

In 1940, Oscar Hammer and his wife Velma bought the house and the 100 acres surrounding it. During World War II, Hammer was vice president of materials with Curtiss Wright Aircraft Company and later held a similar position with McDonnell Douglas. In the 1950s, the Hammers also established the Old Halls Ferry Stables, raising and boarding thoroughbred horses. The property was then owned by Oscar and Velma Hammer's son and is known as Hammer's Farm, which until recently sold grass-fed beef and offered hayrides in the fall. (Chapter 9)

The back of the property is in the Karst area and abuts the Laclede Gas property on Sinks Road. (Chapter 10). The historic house was severely damaged by fire in 1992 and again in 2014 and is currently being dismantled. Any eventual development plans will have to consider restrictions of the Karst Protection District.

Expanded highlights of these and other stories of Old Jamestown history fill the rest of this book. Enjoy!

Chapter 1 Photos and Maps

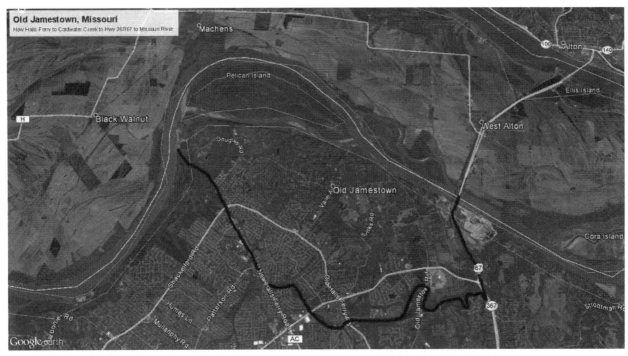

Map 1-1 Google Earth map of Old Jamestown, with boundaries marked.

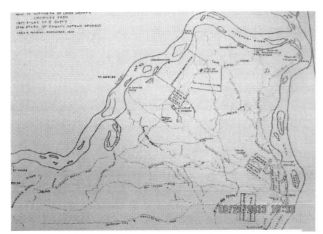

Map 1-2 Shows location of "Jamestown"
Compiled 1846 Atlas of Edward Hutawa and
1837 Atlas of E. Dupre
By Louis Pondrom, 1974

End Note: [16]

Photo 1-1 Tunstall-Douglass House in the mid 1900s
Photo from *The Past in our Presence*
St. Louis County Department of Parks and Recreation

End Note: [17]

Chapter 2 – American Indians and Explorers

Attraction of Old Jamestown

Sioux Passage Park is just one of the many areas in Old Jamestown where American Indian artifacts have been found. The park web page describes why that might be so: "The confluence of the Missouri River and Mill Creek was a favored campsite for Indians of the late Woodland and Mississippian periods. The area featured good hunting and fishing. A source of flint for the manufacture of tools and weapons was readily available. An easily accessible spring provided all-important drinking water. The area provided the needs of the early inhabitants. It is possible that Indians of the Middle Woodland period inhabited the area as early as 100 A.D...."[18]

Thousands of years before European explorers and settlers were in Old Jamestown, American Indians were at least traveling through the area. One thousand years ago they were very likely living in Old Jamestown in a large settlement connected to the Cahokia community in Illinois.

American Indians' arrival in America is described by Joe Harl and Robin Machiran of the Archaeological Research Center of St. Louis, Inc.: "....the first inhabitants of America appear to have come from Asia. Physically, American Indians are similar to people of Asia. They have a similar skeletal system, dentition, blood make-up, and DNA. Cultural similarities also are evidenced by the presence of tools in Alaska and other parts of America similar to ones used by the inhabitants of northeastern Siberia after 18,000 B.C. The first people likely came to America across a land bridge where the Bering Strait is now located. The natural bridge, known as Beringia, was exposed at various times during the [Pleistocene Epoch (Ice Age)], from 100,000 years ago until 14,000 years ago, when sea levels dropped as much as 330 feet, due to water being incorporated into glaciers. It is most likely that people crossed the land bridge the last time it was exposed between 23,000 and 14,000 years ago. A single migration, however, did not take place, but as suggested by DNA analysis, various waves of people came across this land bridge at different times."[19]

[Map 2-1]

Sioux Passage Park – Cahokia satellite community

Joe Harl gives this assessment of probable prehistoric activity in Old Jamestown:

> 'We conducted a cultural resource survey of Sioux Passage Park in 2003. There are no mounds still standing within the park, but there are a number of significant prehistoric sites, including a large Mississippian site (A.D. 1050-1400); the same time as Cahokia Mounds. There are still mounds located nearby on private lands.
>
> 'A number of mastodon bones have been identified along Coldwater Creek. This would be the perfect place to find a site of the earliest humans in this region. The rich soils of the area supported a number of large farming communities. One of these sites still contains a Mississippian platform mound and ridge shaped burial mound.

"The karst topography on the bluffs is further interesting. Caves, springs, and sinkholes, were often revered in prehistoric times, for they were thought to represent portals to the Underworld."[20]

According to Harl, the conditions in Old Jamestown were similar to the conditions in Wildwood, which he described for the City of Wildwood in 2013:

"Past people were able to engineer such elaborate societies because eastern Missouri contains a wealth of natural resources that could be exploited. This land was a virtual "Garden of Eden" with a wide range of plants and animals that could be acquired for food, fuel, medicines, construction, or art. American Indians had no problem in obtaining needed resources. In fact, these people generally worked far fewer hours and spent more time on leisure activities than we do today. The rivers…and tributary streams…offered a wealth of fish and migratory birds. These waters also drew various mammals, reptiles, and amphibians. The nearby river valleys were filled with lush oak-hickory forests that provided a wide range of plant and animal species such as various nuts, fruits, deer, turkey, squirrel, or bear. Portions of the uplands, especially to the north and northeast of Wildwood, contained tall grass prairies, which supported other types of plants and animals including various grasses, berries, prairie chickens, and elk. Residents of this region had a "smorgasbord" of foods from which to choose. Life was anything but hard, and it certainly was not a constant struggle to survive.

"In addition, this region offered an abundance of raw materials. Chief among these resources was Burlington chert present within the bedrock underlying most of Wildwood. This silica based stone could be easily worked into a wide variety of tools…. When first produced, these tools were sharper than any modern metal tool. This resource would have attracted the first humans to Wildwood. Burlington chert continued to be an important part of the local economy and at various times it was quarried and represented one of the earliest items traded to other regions."[21]

[Photos 2-1, 2-2, and 2-3]

Conditions specific to Old Jamestown are described in a 1974 St. Louis Globe-Democrat article, "Indians' suburbia found in Sioux Passage Park," in which Herman Blick, who led a group of amateur archaeologists conducting a salvage operation before proposed construction there, provides findings and speculation about the connection to Cahokia.

"Today it's only an unpretentious clearing in Sioux Passage County Park, but 1,000 years ago that small clearing was the site of a bustling Indian village. Quite probably it was a suburb of the huge Cahokia Indian mounds which lies 17 miles downriver via the Missouri and Mississippi[s] Rivers. No one yet knows for sure. ….

"Experts have long postulated satellite communities ringing Cahokia as a control area of Cahokia's trade routes, but the village along the Missouri River is the first indication that the trade network actually may have existed. ….

Just a short distance under the soil, Blick's party found occasional scraps of burnt bone and pottery, and at 13 inches they found a symmetrically shaped pit lined with small limestone rocks. They decided later that the pit was a roasting area. 'I IMMEDIATELY KNEW we had excavated a major village,' said Blick. 'You could tell from the amount of material we uncovered. Almost everywhere we found evidence of previous settlement.'

"Excavations on the Missouri floodplain and on an adjacent bluff
 gently rising 60 feet above showed that the area was continuously occupied between 600 and 1100 A.D. Blick said the village site represents a transition period between the Late Woodland period and the Mississippian period during which nearby Cahokia was to become the largest Indian settlement north of Mexico.

"Later, the excavators discovered the outlines of a 9 by 15 foot house structure which appears to parallel the shape of similar houses at Cahokia, leading experts to believe that the two sites likely are related. …. 'It looks like what we're seeing developing at Cahokia is developing simultaneously at Sioux Passage,' Blick said. … He thinks it more likely that [the park area] was a subordinate chattel village which perhaps screened visitors and trade heading for Cahokia or grew food for the mound city's population of perhaps 30,000 people. …"[22]

Speculation about the Cahokia connection seems to be confirmed in the 1970s Sioux Passage Park Application for the National Register for Historic Places. The full application is not available to any but archaeologists, but the Missouri Department of Natural Resources provided this summary statement of significance from the application.

"The Sioux Passage Park Archaeological Site is significant because it covers the transition from the Late Woodland through and including the Late Mississippian period and parallels the development stages at Cahokia. This village site…seems more Cahokian than anything* still in existence in Missouri and undoubtedly could shed some light on how the social grouping of this village compares with the Cahokia complex. From preliminary examinations of both lithic and ceramic material, it can be concluded that the site was densely populated and occupied from the Cahokia Patrick Phase (pre-A.D. 600) to and including the Cahokia Moorehead Phase (A.D. 1250).

"Due to the village location at the portage point used by the Indians in historic times between the Mississippi and Missouri rivers and of the large concentration of lithic and ceramic material found, it can be assumed that this village was used as some type of control area for the trade route built around Cahokia. Thus, the Sioux Passage Park Site is the first possible satellite community still remaining in the St. Louis area that is directly tied through an extensive trade network to the Cahokia Site and the destroyed St. Louis Mound City. "[23]

*Since this application was written, more St. Louis area connections to Cahokia have been discovered. A 2014 initiative promotes a national historic park or a national monument that would include Cahokia Mounds and similar sites.

[Maps 2-2 and 2-3]

Other American Indian presence near Old Jamestown

A location along the bluff of the Missouri River to the west of Old Jamestown evidences even earlier American Indian activity and suggests the inhabitants may have moved with the seasons between higher and lower ground. From the Charbonier Bluffs Application for National Register: "Archaeological studies show that Charbonier Bluff was an important camp/village site for American Indians dating from the Dalton (8000-7000 B.C.), Archaic (7000-1000 B.C.), Woodland (1-900 A.D.), and Emergent Mississippian/Mississippian (800-1400 A.D.) eras. Several sites would be considered special function camps, but two sites indicate villages occupied on a seasonal basis between the higher ground and the lower terrace on the east side of Charbonier Creek, at the confluence of the creek with the Missouri River. The Indians of the Middle-Late Woodland Period and the Emergent or Early Mississippian Periods occupied these sites, alternating between the blufftop area in the summer and the areas beside the river in the winter."[24]

American Indian Travel

Even if they didn't live there, through the ages other American Indians came through Old Jamestown. Those living along the Missouri River in Missouri were the Osages and the Missouris whose activities were described in a 2014 ©St. Louis Post-Dispatch Look Back 250 article by Tim O'Neil:

> "Long before Pierre Laclede showed up, the Osage tribe was the dominant force in present-day Missouri. Its hunting parties ranged for hundreds of miles from home villages on the Osage River.
>
> "Numbering perhaps 10,000 when St. Louis was established in 1764, the Osage people were strong enough to fend off Comanches to the west and the Sac and Fox from the Illinois country. Their warriors were tall, many well over 6 feet.
>
> "The tribe's main villages were in today's Vernon County, 75 miles south of Kansas City, with others along the Missouri River. The Osage wintered in large lodges, raised maize and beans, and hunted beaver, deer and bison for months each year.
>
> "Laclede encountered American Indians shortly after he established his town. About 600 members of the Missouria, a smaller area tribe, showed up and made themselves comfortable. Laclede wisely gave them presents and kind words and talked them into returning home up the river that bears their name.
>
> "St. Louis soon undertook a mutually profitable partnership with the Osage, who harvested pelts in return for guns, powder, kettles and baubles. Laclede descendants stayed for long periods in Osage villages, sometimes taking "country" wives and fathering children. Chiefs visited St. Louis for diplomatic meetings."[25]

In addition to their travels for food and social activities, American Indians traveled through Old Jamestown when they came to St. Louis from as far away as Canada during the 18th century to meet and trade with Spanish. At least twenty American Indian tribes received gifts at Spanish post in St. Louis in 1777 – Those from along the Missouri River in Central Missouri were the Little Osages, Big Osages, and Missouris. The Ottawas and Sauteurs lived as far away as 325 leagues (about 850 miles) in Canada. Closest were the Peorias and Kaskaskias located in Kaskaskia, 22 leagues away. Other tribes receiving gifts were: Kansas, Republic, Otoes, Pawnees, Mahas, Iowas, Sioux, Menominees, Renards (Foxes), Sac, Winnebagoes (Puans), Mascouten, Kickapoos, and Pottawatomies[26]

Kingshighway in St. Louis City is thought to originally have been an "American Indian trail from Jefferson County heading for a portage on the Missouri River."[27] American Indians who came ashore in Old Jamestown at the end of New Halls Ferry and near Portage Road would follow trails to Bellefontaine or Halls Ferry Roads and then south to City of St. Louis. They would also take Halls Ferry to Florissant to trade with the settlers there.

Old Jamestown was on many American Indian routes because it lies just across the Missouri River from Portage des Sioux in St. Charles County. Portage des Sioux is in a unique location between the Missouri and Mississippi Rivers. "It was at Portage des Sioux that Indians of the 'Upper Missouri' district made their headquarters for dealing in furs in pioneer days of Missouri. It was the custom, according to stories that have been told by the old residents of Florissant, that the Indians would cross the Missouri River from Portages des Sioux at a point near Musick Ferry and carry their wares to Florissant, where they bartered with the early white settlers."[28]

These excerpts from the 1940 WPA Guide to the "Show Me" State describe significant events at Portage des Sioux: [29]

> "The origin of the name Portage des Sioux is suggested by an Indian legend recorded in Alphonso Wetmore's Gazetteer of the State of Missouri (1837): 'The Sioux and a tribe of the Missouris being at war, a party of the former descended the Mississippi on a pillaging expedition. The Missouris…ambushed themselves at the mouth of the Missouri in considerable numbers, intending to take their enemies by surprise. The Sioux, being more cunning, instead of descending to the mouth of the Missouri, landed at the portage, took their canoes on their backs, and crossed over to the Missouri several miles above.'"

> "As the two-mile portage saved a river journey of some twenty-five miles, it acquired military and commercial importance. In 1799 the Spaniards erected a fort there against possible American expansion, and asked Francois Saucier, then living in St. Charles, to form a settlement. The War of 1812 brought prosperity to the village as the center of military operations against the Indians of Upper Louisiana. The treaty of peace with England, which required individual treaties with Britain's former Indian allies, increased Indian warfare on the Missouri frontier. During the summer of 1815, however, representatives of 19 Indian tribes came to the village to make treaties with the United States commissioners: Governor William Clark of Missouri Territory, Governor Ninian Edwards of Illinois, and Auguste Chouteau of St. Louis. These and similar treaties made at St. Louis the following year ended Indian depredations on the Missouri frontier."

Explorers on the Missouri River

In 1541, Hernando de Soto exploring from Florida claimed the Mississippi and all its tributaries for the Spanish crown. French exploration of the Mississippi River began during the reign of Louis XIV (1643-1715). Early French explorers Marquette (1670) and LaSalle (1682) noted the location and size of the Missouri River as they traveled down the Mississippi. They learned from American Indians about the Missouri's upper reaches.

Later explorers passed Old Jamestown as they traveled up the Missouri River. The Lewis & Clark Expedition began in 1804 from what was Wood River, Illinois -- they stopped near Old Jamestown twice on their way up and once on their return trip in 1806. Zebulon Pike of Pike's Peak fame camped in Old Jamestown as he began his journey.

[Map 2-4]

In 1904, Phil E. Chappell presented a paper on the History of the Missouri River, from which this is taken: "THERE is but little doubt that had the Missouri river been discovered before the Mississippi the name of the former would have been applied to both streams, the Missouri being considered the main stream and the upper Mississippi the tributary. From the mouth of the three forks of the Missouri, northwest of Yellowstone Park, to its mouth, as it meanders, is a distance of 2547 miles, and to the Gulf of Mexico the Missouri-Mississippi has a length of 3823 miles. The Missouri, including the Jefferson or Madison branches, is longer than the entire Mississippi, and more than twice as long as that part of the latter stream above their confluence. It drains a watershed of 580,000 square miles, and its mean total annual discharge is estimated to be twenty cubic miles, or at a mean rate of 94,000 cubic feet per second, which is more than twice the quantity of the water discharged by the upper Mississippi. It is by far the boldest, the most rapid and the most turbulent of the two streams, and its muddy water gives color to the lower Mississippi river to the Gulf of Mexico."[30]

While the length may be a bit different today, 112 years after Chappell's paper was read, if it was considered the main stream, the Missouri River would still be "the longest river in North America and the fourth longest river in the world. Its length….is exceeded only by the Nile, the Amazon, and perhaps the Yangtze River among the longest rivers in the world.[31]

More about what the early explorers learned about the Missouri in these excerpts from A History of the Missouri River by Chappell:

> "The Missouri River was the same ugly, muddy, tortuous, rapid stream when first seen by the early French explorers that it is to-day. When, about the 1st of July, 1673, the Jesuit explorers, Marquette and Joliet, (5) the first white men to descend the Mississippi, arrived at the mouth of the Missouri during the June rise, they were astonished to see flowing in from the west, a torrent of yellow, muddy water which rushed furiously athwart the clear blue current of the Mississippi, boiling and sweeping in its course logs, branches and uprooted trees.
>
> "Marquette was informed by the Indians that 'by ascending this river for five or six days one reaches a fine prairie, twenty or thirty leagues long. This must be crossed in a northwesterly direction, and it terminates at another small river, on which one may embark, for it is not very difficult to transport canoes through so fine a country as that prairie….'
>
> "The second expedition down the Mississippi was conducted by Robert Cavalier de La Salle in 1682. For several years La Salle, who had been an enterprising trader at Quebec, Canada, had contemplated completing the expedition of Marquette and Joliet by following the Mississippi to its entrance into the Gulf of Mexico and planting there the lilies of France. ….
>
> "La Salle's company consisted of thirty-one Indians and twenty-three Frenchman. Among the latter was Father Zenobius Membre, who has left an account of this famous expedition, from

which the following is taken: 'The ice which was floating down on the river [Mississippi] at [the mouth of the Illinois River] kept us there till the 13th of [February], when we set out, and six leagues lower down we found the river of the Ozages' coming from the West. It is full as large as the river [Mississippi], into which it empties, and which is so disturbed by it that from the mouth of this river the water is hardly drinkable. The Indians assured us that this river is formed by many others, and that they ascend it for ten or twelve days to a mountain where they have their source; and that beyond this mountain is the sea, where great ships are seen; that it is peopled by a great number of large villages, of several different nations; that there are lands and prairies, and great cattle and beaver hunting....'

"From [ ] testimony left us by the early explorers, which must be reliable, as it comes from so many different sources, it appears that the Osage Indians, at some time previous to 1682, dwelt near the mouth of the Osage river, either on the banks of that stream or on the Missouri. There is no question that about that time the lower Missouri tribes were attacked by the wild men from the East, the cruel and bloodthirsty Iroquois, who, as they were armed with British muskets, and the Missouri tribes had only the primitive bow and arrow, drove the Osages higher up their river, and the Missouris to the mouth of the Grand river. The beautiful country near the mouth of the Missouri was thus early abandoned by the red men."[32]

Just to the east of Old Jamestown is Fort Belle Fontaine. "The Fort's location near the confluence of the Missouri and Mississippi Rivers made it a launching point for a number of discovery expeditions to the American West. U.S. Army officer Zebulon Pike's explorations of the upper Mississippi in 1805 and of the Spanish southwest in 1806 began at Fort Belle Fontaine. Stephen Long's 1818 scientific expedition and Colonel Henry Atkinson's Yellowstone Expedition in 1819 also left from Fort Belle Fontaine."[33]

Lewis and Clark Expedition

[Map 2-5]

After the U.S. purchase of the Louisiana Territory in 1803, "Thomas Jefferson sent Meriwether Lewis and William Clark's Corps of Discovery to find a water route to the Pacific and explore the uncharted West. He believed woolly mammoths, erupting volcanoes, and a mountain of pure salt awaited them. What they found was no less mind-boggling: some 300 species unknown to science, nearly 50 Indian tribes, and the Rockies."[34]

When Napoleon secretly acquired Louisiana territory in 1800, Spain continued to administer it. In 1803 Spain refused Lewis and Clark permission to travel up the Missouri River since the transfer from France to the U.S. hadn't yet been made official. So they spent the winter in Camp Dubois near the Illinois side of the confluence of the Missouri and Mississippi Rivers. Their activities are described on the Camp Dubois web site: "In the spring, the camp became a beehive of activity as final preparations were made. On March 30, 1804, Lewis and Clark formally enlisted the soldiers and other men who would take part in the expedition. Volunteers who had been civilians were now in the U.S. military. On April 1 Clark issued Detachment Orders determining who would go all the way to the Pacific Ocean, the 'Expedition through the interior of the Continent of North America,' and others who would perform supportive roles.... The boats were altered to better fulfill the journey's needs. Gifts were packaged and organized in the order in which they were to be used based upon information obtained about American

Indian leaders they would encounter along the way. Food was prepared and packed, and included parched corn meal, deboned pork in brine, and sugar made from the sap of maple trees."[35]

On May 14, 1804, Clark started the expedition to St. Charles, Missouri, where Lewis joined them after making final arrangements in St. Louis.

Meriwether Lewis' notes referred to the expedition's point of departure as the "mouth of the River Dubois," which is Wood River, Illinois. However, because of flooding and the natural wandering of rivers, the mouth of the Dubois River has moved at least a mile east, as has the Mississippi itself. Lewis' point of departure is now located in West Alton, Missouri, which is just northeast of Old Jamestown, across the Missouri River. Clark's journal entry for May 14, the day of departure from Camp Dubois, says that their first overnight stop was on an island where they camped "opposite a creek on the South Side below a ledge of limestone rock called Colewater." Thus they were opposite the point where Fort Belle Fontaine would be built on Coldwater Creek, just east of Old Jamestown, in 1805.[36]

On May 20, 1804, William Clark and nearly four dozen other men met up with Meriwether Lewis in St. Charles. The Lewis and Clark expedition – "the Corps of Discovery" – began making its way up the Missouri aboard a 55-foot-long ... keelboat and two smaller pirogues. As they traveled, Clark spent most of his time on the keelboat, charting the course and making maps, while Lewis was often ashore, studying the rock formations, soil, animals, and plants along the way.[37]

On their return trip in 1806 the Corps spent the last night of their journey, September 22, at Fort Belle Fontaine before completing the Voyage of Discovery in St. Louis the next day.

Zebulon Pike Expedition

[Map 2-6]

The first Europeans to discover Pike's Peak in Colorado were the Spanish in the 1700s. The first American sighting is often credited to members of the Pike expedition, led by Zebulon Pike. Pike began his expedition to the American Southwest on July 15, 1806, from Fort Bellefontaine, just east of Old Jamestown. From accounts and maps, it is likely that they camped that night in Old Jamestown near the present Sioux Passage Park site and where the Mill Creek enters the Missouri River.

An account from that day is at http://zebulonpike.org/pike-in-missouri.htm: "Tuesday, July 15, 1806 – 'We sailed from the landing at Belle Fontaine about 3 o'clock p.m., in two boats. Our party consisted of two lieutenants, one surgeon, one sergeant, two corporals, 16 privates, and one interpreter. We had also under our charge chiefs of the Osage and Pawnees, who, with a number of women and children, had been to Washington. These Indians had been redeemed from captivity among the Potowatomies, and were now to be returned to their friends at the Osage towns. The whole number of Indians amounted to 51.'"[38]

On his way to the Southwest, Pike explored the Osage River through what is today Lake of the Ozarks and Truman Lake. As the boats made their way through the 180 degree loops in the river, the American Indians got off, took land routes that were much shorter, and re-joined the boats upstream.[39]

Even before the Louisiana Purchase and subsequent U.S. explorations, settlers had been moving to Old Jamestown, the first to arrive received land grants from Spain. As more Americans and Europeans arrived in the St. Louis area, American Indians were pushed out. Tim O'Neil writes in the ©St. Louis Post-Dispatch May 30, 2014:

> "…. The American notion of Indian relations largely consisted of removing tribes and taking over the fur business themselves.
>
> "William Clark, co-hero of the expedition to the Pacific Ocean, became federal Indian agent in St. Louis in 1807. He built a new installation, Fort Osage, on the Missouri River east of today's Kansas City, and instructed the chiefs to gather. Pierre Chouteau, sensing the changing winds, handled negotiations for Clark.
>
> "In November 1808, the Osage gave up claims to almost all of today's Missouri and northern Arkansas for $1,200 in cash and merchandise, a blacksmith shop and a $1,500 annual stipend. The Sac and Fox, who had decimated the Missouria in war, signed away nearly 15 million acres in a separate treaty.
>
> "The Sac and Fox had taken part in the British-led assault upon St. Louis in 1780. Bands of Osage periodically attacked isolated white settlements, but the tribe never made war against the town. In the end, it didn't matter whether a tribe was friend or foe. The Osage signed a second treaty in 1825 giving up what was left in the new state of Missouri. Within a decade, few American Indians of any tribe called Missouri home".[40]

Chapter 2 Photos and Maps

Photo 2-1 Axe of style that dates from 3000-1000 BC

Photo 2-2 Decorated piece of pottery from around AD 100-400

Photo 2-3 Pipe (most likely for tobacco) of style in AD 600-1200

Artifacts found at Musick's Ferry are curtesy of Professor Michael Fuller, St. Louis Community College[41]

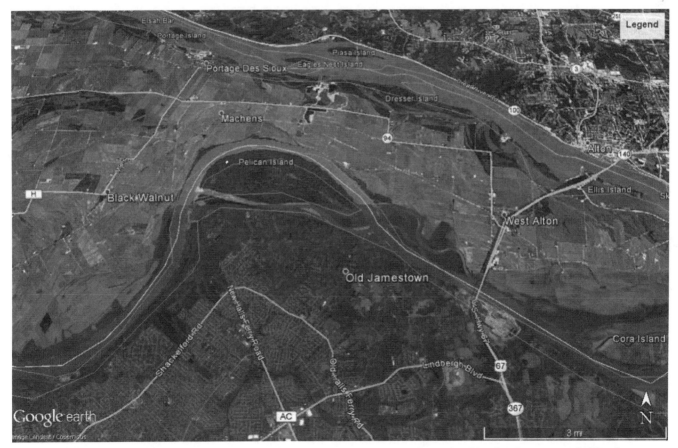

Map 2-1 Google Earth Map showing Old Jamestown across from St. Charles County and Illinois

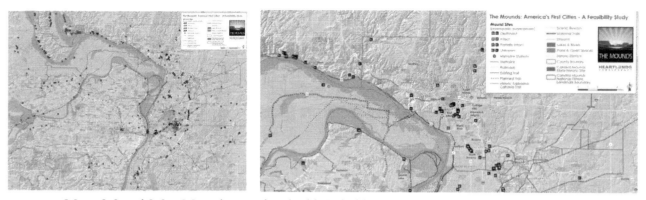

Maps 2-2 and 2-3 – Mounds associated with Cahokia Mounds.
Symbol near, but not in, Sioux Passage Park means the mound/s are intact.
The Mounds – America's First Cities – A Feasibility Study, Heartlands Conservancy

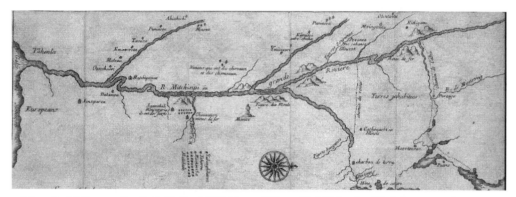

Map 2-4 Marquette & Joliet's 1673 Expedition, Published with Marquette's Journal 1681 – History of Saint Louis and County, 1883

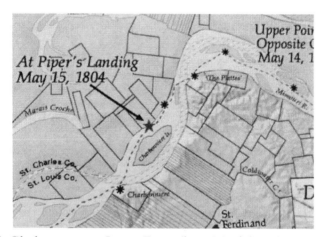

Map 2-5 Lewis & Clark route past James Ferry (later Musick's Ferry)
Larger stars denote campsites; smaller symbols denote waypoints and exploration sites
Atlas of Lewis & Clark in Missouri

End Notes for this page: Maps 2-2 and 2-3 [42]; Map 2-4 [43]; Map 2-5 [44]

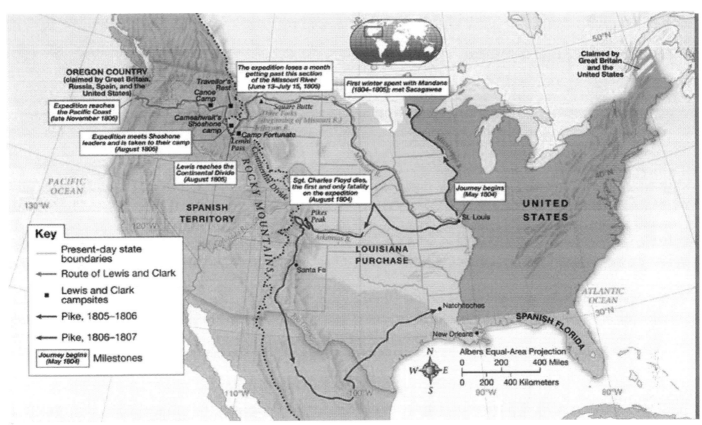

Map 2-6 The Expeditions of Lewis and Clark and Zebulon Pike – SlidePlayer

End Note[45]

Chapter 3 – Land Grants and Early Settlers (1)

Attraction of Old Jamestown

"During the 1790s, following the Revolutionary War, Upper Canada vied with Kentucky and the Ohio Valley in attracting settlers. Early settlements in Upper Canada included a mixture of both American patriots seeking to push westward and United Empire Loyalists escaping persecution for their loyalty to Britain during the Revolutionary War."[46]

Kentucky's appeal wore out quickly for those who had moved there because their land was fraudulently taken by speculators. In October 1796 letters were included in the Kentucky Gazette and other mid-South newspapers touting the [availability] of FREE land from the Spanish government, and a land which was "free from chicanery and lawyers." For the thousands of poor Kentuckians who had lost their claims to land speculators, these advertisements were a dream come true.[47]

Some of those who had moved to Canada and Kentucky moved again to Old Jamestown and obtained generous land grants from the Spanish for living in "New Spain." Most of these newcomers were of British heritage and settled north of Coldwater Creek. By the early 1800s, almost all of the land in far north St. Louis County had been granted to the first settlers. Earlier land grantees, French and Spanish residents of Florissant, were no longer able to hunt and forage north of Coldwater Creek.[48]

Between 1770 and 1803, Spanish lieutenant governors (sometimes called commandants) in St. Louis encouraged immigration and were quite generous in conceding large tracts of lands to the newcomers. The land grant situations were well described in these excerpts from the Arkansas Commissioner of State Lands web site…..

> "Land Grants represent some of the earliest land transactions and establishment of title. At different times from the late 1600s to 1803, the French and Spanish governments swapped control of the land that became the Louisiana Purchase. After the Louisiana Purchase in 1803, one of the major issues was whether the United States government would recognize those land titles from the earliest settlers that were obtained from the French and Spanish. In March 1805, Congress passed legislation establishing rules and procedures for these titles to be confirmed or unconfirmed by appointed land commissions.
>
> "This Act declared that persons who actually inhabited and cultivated said property and had a duly registered warrant obtained from the French or Spanish governments on or before October 1, 1800, were considered to have complete claims and were confirmed. Incomplete claims were not to be confirmed unless proof could be provided that the terms and conditions on which the completion of the original grant might depend were fulfilled. "Squatters who lived in the territory and didn't have grants from either government, but were head of the household and cultivated the property, could also make claims. All notice of claims had to be recorded before March 1, 1806, or they were considered void. All land grants or claims that were established after October 1, 1800, were not to be recognized. This legislation created a very contentious process and led to bitter land disputes that often took years to resolve."[49]

The "Louisiana" area west of the Mississippi had come under Spanish control in 1763. Napoleon Bonaparte returned Louisiana to France from Spain in 1800, under the Treaty of San Ildefonso....However, the treaty was kept secret, and Louisiana remained under Spanish control until a transfer of power to France on November 30, 1803, just three weeks before the cession to the United States.[50]

Spain was mostly a benign absentee landlord, administering Louisiana from Havana, Cuba, and contracting out governing to people from many nationalities as long as they swore allegiance to Spain....[51]

[Maps 3-1, 3-2, and 3-3]

Original Land Grant Owners in Old Jamestown – Survey Numbers are for the U.S. Confirmation of the Spanish land grants.[52] Along the river, west to east:

Survey No. 106 – Sarah James -- 340.28 ac – at the end of New Halls Ferry Road

Survey No. 1950 – Gilbert Hodges -- 340.28 ac -- married Sara James, daughter of Sarah James (106)

Survey No. 1898 – Samuel Hodges Jr – 204.16 ac – married Keziah Patterson, daughter of John Patterson (105)

Survey No. 2027 – Daniel Hodges Jr – 204.16 ac

Survey No. 474 – John N. Seeley – 680.56 ac

Survey No. 361 – Ebenezer Hodges – 425.35 ac – married Mary Seeley, sister of John Seeley (474)

Survey No. 934 -- Guy Seeley – 574.22 ac (incl. Sur. 784 and partial 791) -- married Rebecca James, daughter of Sarah James (106)

Survey No. 1960 – Charles Desjarlais – 255.21 ac (partially east of Old Jamestown) (sold to Morris James in 1805) -- married Julie Hodges

Other grants in Old Jamestown, most along Coldwater Creek

Survey No. 1968 – James James -- 403.23 ac – married Marie Seeley, daughter of John Seeley

Survey No. 405 – James Richardson – 850.70 ac

Survey No. 103 – Farquar McKensie – 340.28 ac

Survey No. 104 – John Brown – 510.42 ac

Survey No. 105 – John Patterson – 510.42 ac

Survey No. 107 – David Brown's Representatives – 340.28 ac

Survey No. 210 – William Patterson – 510.42 ac

Survey No. 338 – Daniel & Samuel Hodges under Edmund Hodges -- 557.20 ac (mostly west of Old Jamestown)

Survey No. 360 – Cumberland James – 340.28 ac – married Susan Seeley, daughter of Guy Seeley and Rebecca James

Survey No. 1907 – Morris James – 340.28 ac (also see Survey No. 1960) – married the widow of Ezekiel Lard whose land was adjacent to the east of Old Jamestown.

Survey No. 1012 – James B. Hart under Elisha Herrington – 640 ac (most south of Old Jamestown)

Survey No. 3023 – Benjamin Franklin James or his legal representatives – 804.89 ac (includes Sur. 798 and 805) – married Rachel Hodges, daughter of Edmund

Grants were awarded in arpens, which have been converted to acres. 400 arpens equals 340.28 acres.

Names of just a few early settlers are available from petitions signed by residents in 1805:

On June 18, 1805, a petition was filed by "inhabitants of Coldwater" requesting permission to open a road from "Sarah James Ferry to division line of settlements of St. Louis and Coldwater and thence to town of St. Louis." Not always easy to read, the signatures were from John Allen, Griffith Brown, John Brown, John Patterson, Wm Dunnet (sp), Morris James, William Jamison, Elisha Patterson, J Brown, J Jamison, Peter Ellis, William Patterson, Cumberland James, Geo Little, J James, J Jamison, Jacob Seeley, Solomon Griffith, Wm Davis, and John Ed. Allen.[53]

In 1805, most residents signed the "Wilkinson Memorial." The list of names was essentially a roster of men in the Missouri Territory in 1805. The Memorial was a collection of letters sent to President Jefferson in support of Governor Wilkinson. The president had planned to remove Wilkinson because of suspicions that he was part of Aaron Burr's conspiracy to set up an independent nation in the west.* Names with Old Jamestown connections: Charles Degerlais [probably Desjarlais], Daniel Hodges, Ebenezer Hodges, Gilbert Hodges, Durrett Hubbard, Daniel Hubbard, Benjamin James, C.Land [Cumberland] James, James James, Morris James, William Patterson, John Patterson, Elisha Patterson, John Brown, John N. Seeley, and Vincent Carrico. Other notables included Daniel Boone.[54]

*Jefferson's suspicions may have been partially caused by Wilkinson's advocacy in Kentucky: Until 1788 Kentucky was part of Virginia. One reason the people in Kentucky wanted to separate from Virginia was that Virginia refused to recognize the importance of trade along the Mississippi River to Kentucky's economy. It forbade trade with the Spanish colony of New Orleans, which controlled the mouth of the Mississippi, but this was important to Kentucky communities. During the 1780s, several constitutional conventions were held in Kentucky. During one, General James Wilkinson proposed

secession from both Virginia and the United States to become a ward of Spain, but the idea was defeated.[55]

James Richardson

Possibly the first English speaking resident of the Old Jamestown area, James Richardson received a large land grant in Old Jamestown in the early 1790s after already receiving grants in the Bridgeton area. Richardson was syndic (judge and jury) of Marais des Liards (cottonwood swamp) or Owen's Fort, which was later known as Bridgeton.

A St. Charles Cosmos newspaper article from the late 1800s tells a story of the activity and motivations of Richardson and other pioneers….

> "This Mr. James Richardson was a man of warm, generous impulses, and many were the poor immigrants that he befriended, helped and supported, not only those around him but to all passing through Owen's Fort, on their way to join Daniel Boone in his home in Northern Missouri. Richardson was a saddler by trade. Learning that the wife of the Spanish Alcalde was fond of equestrian exercise, but was denied the pleasure through want of a saddle, he made her one, gaining thereby not only her gratitude, but the old Alcalde's, who gave him 1000 arpens [850.7 acres] of land in the Florissant Valley, and which is known to this day as United States survey No. 405, including in its boundaries the present large farm of James, Stanton and George Hume, and the Tunstall and John Hyatt places.

> "…. Richardson was the chief man or captain at Owen's Fort [Bridgeton], and was, even in those days, a man of considerable property, which he used and generously shared with all deserving immigrants. It seemed to be the desire of Richardson to induce as many Americans as he could to move and settle here. Every Kentuckian that came here in those times wished to get as near to Daniel Boone as he could. The journey was long and dangerous, and generally on entering Missouri at St. Louis, they would start for Owen's Fort, where Richardson would rest them, supply them with what was most needed, and then forward them by guide to Pond's Fort, on the Boonville road in St. Charles County, and sometimes as far as Loutre's Fort, on Loutre Island, [Warren County] above St. Charles.

> "Every place in olden times that was settled by Americans was called a fort. Opposite Boonville are salt springs or "licks," and here was built Fort Cooper. These salt springs, or licks, were, for thirty or forty years, the only place from which salt could be procured. Said an old pioneer lady: 'In early days we had two things to trouble us—to get salt and pay taxes.' This same lady was married in August, and she quaintly remarked that the wedding guests ate a whole bullock, to keep it from being spoiled by the weather."[56]

On a trip back east James Richardson met John Patterson, Sr., in North Carolina. Richardson encouraged Patterson to pack up and go back with him to "Upper Louisiana." Patterson didn't follow immediately but John and his brother William did eventually receive land grants in Old Jamestown near Richardson.

According to the Cold Water Cemetery web site, in 1842 Judge Joseph L. Hyatt purchased a big tobacco barn that James Richardson had built on his property in Old Jamestown. Judge Hyatt converted the barn into a residence.[57]

See the whole Cosmos article in Appendix 3 and more information about the Patterson Family in Chapter 5.

Guy Seeley

[Photos 3-1, 3-2, and 3-3]

Another grantee, Guy Seeley, married Sarah James' daughter Rebecca in 1798. According to Seeley descendant Nancy Shattuck, his parents were Justus Azel Seeley and Sarah Stuart. Justus was a Loyalist and he died in Canada. There were seven brothers all born in Litchfield Co., Connecticut. Two stayed in Canada. The rest went to different areas in the US eventually. Guy was the only one who went west. Guy and Rebecca Seeley's daughter, Susan, married Cumberland James. Their son David James Seeley married Sophia Shattuck in Galena, Illinois. Another son, Anthony S. Seeley, married Laney Hodges in Greene Co., Illinois, and Americus G. Seeley married Keziah Hodges in Grant Co., Wisconsin. Many Seeleys moved to Greene County, Illinois, as did several of the Hodges family.[58]

Adapted from the Missouri Historical Research Record 1968: Lying directly across the Missouri River from Little's Island in St. Charles County, the Seeley tract [between the current Jamestown Farms and Portage Road area] was on the high ground of St. Louis County. The road was just an Indian trail at that time. Indians portaged across the Missouri River and followed the trail that connected with what was known as 'The Great Trail' (Bellefontaine Road), which ended at St. Louis. The log cabin that Seeley built was the site of many conferences with the natives. After the U.S. purchased the Louisiana Territory and took control, General Wilkinson came to the area to select a site for a military fort and trading post for the American Indians. He was a guest for nearly two weeks in the Seeley home. General Wilkinson selected his site and built Fort Bellefontaine which was east of Old Jamestown at the mouth of Coldwater Creek.[59]

In later years John Mullanphy, Missouri's first millionaire, bought the Guy Seeley property and deeded it to his youngest daughter, Eliza, who married James Clemens, Jr., on January 10, 1833. James W. Clemens was a successful businessman in St. Louis. He was born in 1791 in Danville, Kentucky and came to St. Louis in 1816. He was also second cousin to Mark Twain's father (who lived in Hannibal) and helped him out with a loan and other financial assistance.[60]

Seeley's log cabin still exists at the entrance to Jamestown Acres subdivision, but it is not recognizable because of additions to the house over the years.

John N. Seeley

John Nicholas Seeley came to Old Jamestown from Canada. His sister, Mary Seeley, had married Ebenezer Hodges in Canada and also came to Old Jamestown. They also were together in Alton where they moved before moving again to Greene County, Illinois.[61]   John N. Seeley's daughter, Marie, married James James, one of Sarah James' sons.

No direct connection between John N. Seeley and Guy Seeley has been found.

Carrico Family

Five members of the Carrico family settled in the Florissant, MO, area in the late 1700s and early 1800s. They were brothers Vincent, Walter, and Dennis, and sisters Theresa and Elizabeth.... They were all born in Charles County, Maryland, children of James Carrico and Elizabeth Clement [1745-1795][62]

The Carrico family did not have a land grant within Old Jamestown boundaries. However, Vincent Carrico (1764-1816) had a land grant just east of Old Jamestown and purchased John Brown's land grant. And several of his relatives (Walter, George and Silas) purchased land from Hodges family members who had received the grants. Vincent Carrico married his second wife, Susannah Quick, in Kentucky in 1796.

In addition several Carrico family members married others in Old Jamestown, including: Vincent's daughter Lydia Carrico (1805-1870) married Reuben Musick and they later owned the property and ferry at Musick's Ferry. She also inherited a portion of her father's plantation. (See more on Musick's Ferry in Chapter 6.) Dennis Carrico (177X-1852), married Amy Jamison James (1794-1865), daughter of James and Sally Hubbard Jamison and stepdaughter of John Patterson, Sr. Dennis Carrico was Amy Jamison's second husband. She had first been married to Phinehas James but evidently was divorced from him as both re-married.

Carrico documents are among many that confirm the existence of slavery as well as emancipation of a few selected slaves in Old Jamestown. In his 1816 will (recorded in 1831) Vincent said, "I give to my loving wife Susannah Carrico one Negro woman by the name of Ally, one Negro man by the name of Abraham...." And "I do will...say that in consideration of the faithful services of my Negro man Willis and have heretofore promised him that on the first day of January next I do emancipate and entirely free my said Negro man Willis from any demands that I myself, my heirs, executors or administrators may have on or against him and do expressly will that he shall from the first day of January next go forth free his own man in every sense of the word...."

In 1829, Vincent Carrico's Children issued an Order for the hire of slaves for one year at the widow Carrico's plantation. The slaves named Lewis and Loyd were sickly and weak, and were not hired at the auction; they were hired privately instead.[63]

Charles Desjarlais

Charles Desjarlais was born on March 26, 1775 in Quebec, Canada. He was the son of Jean Baptiste Desjarlais and of Angelique Renard. Charles Desjarlais settled in Missouri around 1799 and received a land grant on the Missouri River. The Bellefontaine Fort site chosen by General Wilkinson was on the portion of Desjarlais' property just east of Old Jamestown.

Julie/Lucie Hodges was born about 1777, probably in Hardwick, Worcester County, Massachusetts. Julie and Charles were married on February 27, 1800 at St. Ferdinand de Florissant, Missouri. See the marriage record for Ebenezer and Sara Hodges described in Chapter 4. The ceremonial questions and answers for Julie and Charles are similar except that Charles Desjarlais said he was Roman Catholic and Apostolic and Julie said she was Anabaptist. Julie Hodges Desjarlais was baptized into the Catholic Church as an adult immediately following their marriage. Julie Hodges died on July 11, 1817. Her death and burial were recorded in the register of the old Catholic cathedral of St. Louis.[64]

Brown Family

Little is known about the Brown family who received two land grants in Old Jamestown. John Brown's grant was on the same date as John Patterson's grant (Chapter 5) and was later sold to Vincent Carrico, holder of his own land grant just east of Old Jamestown. Half of this property was later inherited by Vincent's daughter, Lydia, who married Reuben Musick (Chapter 6). David Brown's grant property was sold by his heirs to four sons of John Patterson and is the site of the Tunstall-Douglass House (Chapter 1).

The name Brown appears in a few documents from the time but it is not known if or how they are related. For example, in 1805, a Griffith Brown and J. Brown signed a petition as residents of Coldwater requesting a road from Sarah James' ferry to St. Louis. In 1817, Jonathon Brown, Delilah Brown, and Oliver Brown are listed with Ebenezer and Mary Hodges as members of a new Methodist class formed in Upper Alton, which is where some of the Hodges family (Chapter 4) moved before moving further north to Greene County, Illinois.

Elisha Herrington/James B. Hart

Elisha Harrington received a land grant (Survey 1012) and built a flouring mill on Coldwater Creek before 1803. Harrington was a millwright and built several mills in the county. He came to the Coldwater District from his land in the Common Fields of St. Ferdinand with his wife and three children. In 1807, he sold the flouring mill along with the residence he had built to James Hart. Hart obtained U.S. confirmation of the land grant.[65]

Farquar McKensie

We have been unable to find any information on Farquar McKensie whose land grant was surrounded by the grants of James Richardson, John Patterson, David Brown, and Ebenezer Hodges. In 1806 a Farquar McKenzie was the plaintiff in a Court of Common Pleas lawsuit for "Trespass on the case" against Moses Croft. This is pure speculation but perhaps Farquar lived elsewhere and Croft started living on his land grant or using part of the property in his absence.

James Family

The James family received several land grants in Old Jamestown. In the 1790s, "Widow" Sarah Bishop James (widow of David James) came from North Carolina with her seven children, Benjamin, Cumberland, Morris, Rebecca, James, Sara, and Phinehas. Sarah obtained a grant on the river and four of her sons (Benjamin, Cumberland, Morris and James) obtained other grants in Old Jamestown. Daughter Sara married Ebenezer Hodges who had a grant on the river next to Sarah. Daughter Rebecca married Guy Seeley who also had a grant on the river.

Sarah James – Ferry

[Map 3-4]

Sarah James' land grant was along what is now New Halls Ferry and Douglas Roads at the Missouri River. In 1805 she had an opportunity to sell her land to the U.S. Government for the first American fort west of the Mississippi. Unfortunately for Sarah, she first said no and when she said yes it was too late. As adapted from a Missouri Historical Review article.[66]

> In the search for a site for the trading post and cantonment, Henry Dearborn, secretary of war, had written to General James Wilkinson as early as April 19, 1805, On the subject of Indian affairs you will please to ascertain, as early as practicable, the most suitable site for the Factory or Indian trading House about to be established in that country;—in doing which, it will be necessary to take into view, the accommodation of the Osages and other Missouri Indians, as well as those situate on the immediate waters of the Mississippi. I had contemplated a site on the portage across the neck of the peninsula, a few miles above the junction of the Missouri with the Mississippi.
>
> On the July 11, Colonel Return J. Meigs, Jr., who had been civil commandant of St. Charles under General William Henry Harrison, was, at the request of General Wilkinson, scouting for a favorable site in the neighborhood of St. Charles, and was supposed to have found one within four miles of the village.
>
> Sometime between Friday the 12th of July and Monday the 15th, Wilkinson and Meigs agreed upon the Widow James' farm near Florissant as a favorable site. On the 16th, [Lt. Colonel Jacob] Kingsbury ordered Lieutenant William Richardson with two non-commissioned officers and twenty-six privates to embark in two pirogues and two batteaux, descend the Mississippi to the mouth of the Missouri, and then ascend that river to the Widow James', where they were to halt and give immediate notice to Kingsbury of their arrival. Either on the 18th or 19th, Kingsbury...took up his station at the Widow James'.
>
> That lady, however, did not know her own mind. On the 19th, Kingsbury wrote to Wilkinson, The widow will not sell her land. I will meet you tomorrow morning at Florissant. By Sunday the 21st, Kingsbury reported, Mrs. James will sell her land, but probably she may be too late, as I am informed you have already purchased.
>
> On Tuesday, July 23, Wilkinson ordered Kingsbury from Widow James to Coldwater. "The Widow like many before her, has missed her Market…."
>
> On July 23rd Wilkinson decided on Coldwater as the site of his encampment. He wrote the Secretary of War on August 10, 1805, that he had encamped the troops at Coldwater, "on a high, dry, narrow bottom of the Missouri, near a fountain of pure water, competent to supply one thousand men daily." This was the beautiful spring which gave the name Bellefontaine to the cantonment.

As early as 1805, Sarah James had a ferry operation from her property to St. Charles County. The ferry was operated by Captain Hall starting about 1816 and by Reuben Musick starting in 1848. Also about

1818, Rufus Easton and Edward Bates extended the ferry service from St. Charles County to Alton, Illinois.

See Chapter 6 for much more on Musick's Ferry and activity in that area.

The ferry on Sarah James' land was referred to as James or Spring Ferry before becoming Halls Ferry and then Musick's Ferry. There was also a ferry crossing at what became Jamestown Landing on property first owned by Charles Desjarlais (Survey 1960) at the end of what is now Portage Road. Desjarlais obtained title from the Government, August 25, 1799, and sold the land to Morris James, December 30, 1805.[67] The road between the two ferries was called Accommodation Road until the 1930s.

Phinehas James – James' Town

The first historical reference to "Jamestown" was in June 1819 when Phinehas James advertised the sale of lots in what he called "James' Town." According to his plans, a sizeable community would be started on the limestone plateaus that border the Missouri River.[68] Some speculate Phinehas James had visions of this settlement someday rivaling the City of St. Louis.

[Photo 3-4]

A bit of speculation about the choice of the name "James' Town" for Phinehas' development: Phinehas' first wife was Amy Jamison. Amy's mother, Sally Hubbard Jamison Patterson, was the daughter of Eusebius Hubbard who was living near the family at the time of his death. Eusebius was from Virginia and his ancestors had lived near the original Jamestown colony in the 1600s. Seems like this would have been the topic of at least a few family conversations. Eusebius died in 1818 - Phinehas advertised the lots in June 1819. Perhaps he used "James' Town" as a deliberate connection to the Jamestown Colony?

Chapter 1 had the great description of the now Portage Road area from Phinehas' ad. Below is the full ad that appeared on the front page ad for "James' Town" in the Missouri Gazette, the St. Louis area's first newspaper, June 16, 1819:[69]

===

Notice

The subscriber informs the public that he has just completed laying off James' Town, and will offer the LOTS at public sale to the highest bidder on the fifteenth, sixteenth and seventeenth day of July next. The terms of said sale will be made known on the date of sale, at which a correct plat of the town can be seen.

JAMES' TOWN

Is situated on a beautiful bluff, on the southern bank of the Missouri River, six miles above its confluence with the Mississippi. Being situated on a bluff, it has the advantage of a firm rock shore, along which there are a number of the safest harbors for boats that I presume any other town on these waters can boast of; also, several seats for mills that so large a water course can form. Near the public square, there is a cave through which passes a large body of cold, sweet lucid water which I think could, without much expense, be raised and conveyed to every part of the town. The earth after removing the virgin soil is admirably calculated for brick, and the rock along the river, which can be easily procured, is of the best quality, either for building or manufacturing into lime; sand for making brick and mortar can be procured without much trouble or expense. Behind this desirable situation lays the rich and flourishing country of Florissant or St. Ferdinand and in front (beyond that majestic river that sweep[s] along its base) is to be seen that fertile bottom that intercepts the communication of those two splendid rivers (Mississippi and Missouri) which not only offers to the fancy a rich harvest of charms, but also to the town an abundant harvest of advantages. The situation of this town is so lofty and noble as never to offend by noxious fumes of putrid sickly air; and the eye has always presented to it, a beautiful and grand variety. In [conclusion], to give a more powerful and impressive idea of the value of the place, is but to observe that there are now about three hundred lots laid off, of which better than one sixth of that number are already disposed of, and most of the purchasers have promised to build on them immediately, which I consider as one strong, convincing proof of Jamestown having merit as an advantageous and desirable situation.

Phinehas James

June 14 - 4t - 39

N.B. The subscriber will also probably sell other property, consisting of Negroes, Oxen for the yoke, milch cows, Hogs, and a variety of Farming utensils.

P.N.

Notice

===

Phinehas James and his brother Morris, who bought the property from the land grant holder Charles Desjarlais in 1805, probably organized the town. By 1819 numerous lots had been sold. When Lot No. 2 was sold by Warren Hunt to Patrick Bill in that year, "the right of ferrying was reserved to Phinehas James".[70] The dream Mr. James held never materialized. The name "Jamestown" however was used on occasional maps and in naming roads.

Jamestown Road was first named in 1845 when Gilbert James (son of Cumberland James and Susan Seeley James) requested a road "commencing in Jamestown, running so as to intersect the road leading from Robbins Mill to Florissant (…Hwy 67 Blvd) at Gilbert James [farm], and thence southwestwardly until it intersects the road leading from Florissant to Mrs. Lords old place near Mr. Vanesco." (likely Parker Road).[71] The portion of the current Old Jamestown Road between Portage Road and Douglas was called Accommodation Road until the early 1930s when Jamestown to the river became the private Portage Road and home sites were sold to physicians and others.

Phinehas left the area about 1830 and led an adventuresome life – married 3 times, divorced twice. He fought in the Texas War for Independence and received a Land Bounty there of hundreds of acres. He became a promoter of land deals in Texas.[72]

[Maps 1-2 and 3-5]

These excerpts from Lou Pondrom describe some of the appearances of "Jamestown":[73]

> "The name Jamestown has survived through the years, if only barely as a specific site. Both Old Jamestown and New Jamestown Roads were named because of Jamestown.
>
> "On November 6, 1831, Phinehas James and his wife Rhoda sold to Francis Nash sixty arpens of land at a place called Jamestown, of which fifty arpens lay in the Jamestown tract, which Phinehas bought of Morris James, and the other ten arpens lay in the tract that Phinehas bought of Guy Seeley, excepting out of this sale such lots, squares, and streets of Jamestown lying within the said sixty arpens as have been heretofore sold and conveyed by said P. James to other persons. And the said Phinehas James does hereby grant to said Francis Nash all such rights and privileges of establishing and keeping a Ferry or Ferries across the Missouri at and from every part of the entire tract of land heretofore called Jamestown Tract.
>
> "Next to Charles Desjarlais grant upstream was that of Guy Seeley through which the "Little Coldwater" [probably Mill Creek] flowed and entered the Missouri just above Jamestown. The springs here are probably referred to in the testimony, and may be one of the "Dripping Springs" spoken of in this century. In 1831, in a deed between John F. Mudd and Phinehas James, "Cave Spring" is mentioned as being located in Jamestown.
>
> "In 1825, a Post Office was established at Jamestown, but no Postmaster is identified in the government records of Post Office appointments." [The Jamestown Post Office is shown as operating from 1820 to 1826 on the Missouri Postal History web site.[74]]

In an 1832 document, reference is made to the "ferry landing below where Phinehas James formerly lived in Jamestown."

"Jamestown" as a location was shown on an 1846 St. Louis County map and a Missouri map. "There were three and one-half blocks along the river, two full blocks and two half blocks in the second tier on the bluff, and two half blocks on the third tier, enough for about 30 homes."[75]

After about 1900, "Jamestown" no longer appeared on maps as a town. However, Jamestown Landing is still shown as a point of navigation on the Missouri River on the Corps of Engineers Map of navigation points. The St. Louis Daily Globe-Democrat in July 1876 reported that a meeting was held in St. Charles County to establish a steam ferry between Jamestown and the land of David Nicholson, who was then the owner of Little Island, across the Missouri River from Jamestown.[76]

Jamestown is also mentioned in the 1911 History of St. Louis County: "The situation at Black Jack was summarized, in 1877, in concise form as follows: "The village bearing the above name is… in St. Louis County, at the junction of the old Hall's Ferry road and the Parker road, about 3 ½ miles from Florissant, in the heart of a splendid farming country.... Cross Keys, Pulltight and Jamestown are neighboring villages, and it is said Black Jack proposes to put in a bid for the permanent county seat."[77]

Morris James

This story of Morris James who had a land grant (No. 1907) is adapted from an article in the Spring 2014 St. Louis Genealogical Society Quarterly:

> On September 10, 1797, Ezekiel Lard obtained a concession for 1,000 arpens of land along the Missouri River just east of Old Jamestown. Within a year he built both a grist mill and a saw mill on his property. Not long after his 1799 death, his widow, "Caty Sullivan Purcelle Lard," married Morris James whose land grant was next to Lard's plantation. Morris was also made guardian of her young children who were probably educated by Ebenezer Hodges and Benjamin Franklin James, a relative of Morris, both of whom were school teachers in the neighborhood.

> James's brother, Cumberland James, had a concession on Morris's western boundary. Morris James received a grant of 400 arpens from Lieutenant Governor Trudeau on September 1, 1797; bought another 300 arpent concession from Charles Desjarlais on June 3, 1803, and of course shared in land acquired by his wife, Lard's widow.

> Morris resided for a time on Cumberland's claim while his brother went down the Mississippi River. At the same time, he cut hay and sawed and hauled out logs from his own land. In July or August 1803, he built a corncrib on his own land and, the following winter, built a cabin where he then lived, improving his own claim with a garden and fields. He and Caty had a daughter, Sarah, born about 1810, and, perhaps, other children. Morris James became quite a prominent planter, miller and livestock raiser in the settlement. He died in August 1834.

> Morris and Caty James's only known child, Sarah "Sally" James, was married January 8, 1833, to John Blackburn of Spanish Pond. When Morris James died in August 1834, Blackburn was named executor of his estate. James's heirs were his grandchildren, children of Mrs. William McDowns and Mrs. Edith Neal; Blackburn's wife, Sarah, and Widow Caty James…. James, also, probably was buried on his home place. No death date or place of burial has been found for Catherine Sullivan "Caty" Lard-James, but she apparently was deceased before the 1850 Census was taken.[78]

Benjamin Franklin James

Benjamin Franklin James, son of David and Sarah James, was born in North Carolina and died in 1815 in Missouri. He received a land grant (No. 3023). He married Rachel Hodges October 12, 1801 in St. Ferdinand de Florissant, Missouri. Adapted from Hodges book:

> In testimony at the First Board of Land Commissioners in 1806, Ebenezer Hodges testified that Benjamin James "put up a cabin on said land in the spring of 1803, that in 1804 he kept a school, and has inhabited the land to this day." In 1834, "when this land was claimed by the heirs of Benjamin James, Catherine S. James (wife or widow of Morris James) swore…that in 1804 she saw a small field of corn growing and Benjamin James lived on his place until his death, which occurred in 1815. At the time of his death, he had several cabins and an orchard of apple and peach trees, and that he occasionally taught school in the neighborhood."

The probate file of Benjamin Franklin James contains various debt notes and receipts that indicate he was engaged in the business of ferrying passengers and goods across the Missouri River. Two receipts in the probate file seem to be the final settlement for the estate of Benjamin F. James payable to Hugh and Rachel Wells. In all probability then, the widow, Rachel (Hodges) James, had remarried to Hugh Wells by 1822.[79]

James James

James James was a son of Sarah James and received a land grant near Musick's Ferry and the Car of Commerce Chute. His children included "Uncle Billy" James who donated land for Brown School (See Chapter 7) and "Aunt Betsy" James Blackburn who ran the inn at Musick's Ferry (See Chapter 6).

Cumberland James

Cumberland James was also a son of Sarah James and held a land grant near his brother Morris' original grant. He married Susan Seeley, daughter of Guy Seeley and Rebecca James Seeley.

Note: Research has not uncovered any connection of the Old Jamestown James family to Frank and Jesse James or to members of a Catholic James family who were well known in the Florissant area, including Judge Samuel James and his uncle Thomas James who was a fur trader.

Chapter 3 Photos and Maps

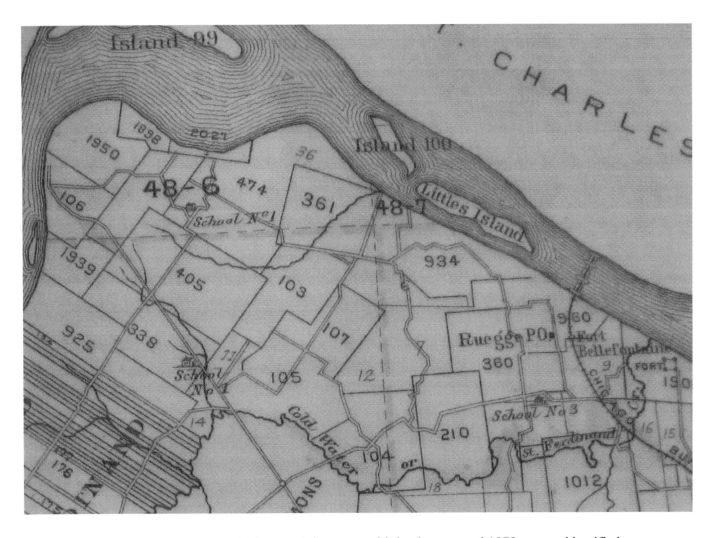

Maps 3-1, 3-2, and 3-3: 1878 Pitzman Atlas maps with land grants and 1878 owners identified.

Map 3-1, Old Jamestown with only the land grant survey numbers identified

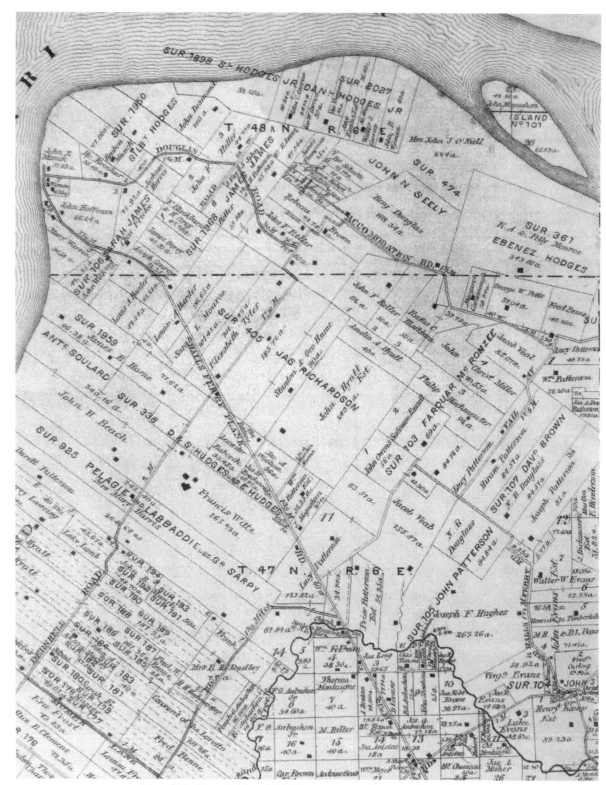

Map 3-2, West Side of Old Jamestown, See caption above

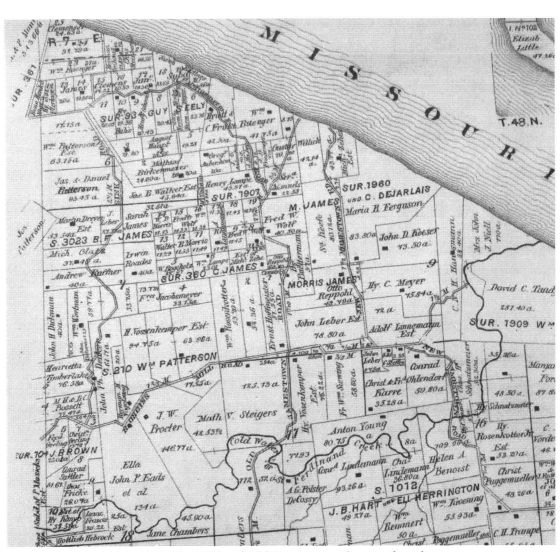

Map 3-3, East Side of Old Jamestown, See caption above

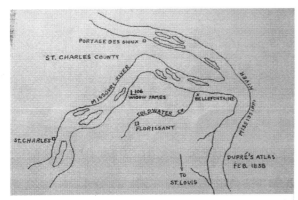

Map 3-4 "Widow James" property and Bellefontaine area (When Musick's Ferry area was being considered by military for the fort location) Dupre 1838 Atlas, State Historical Society of Missouri

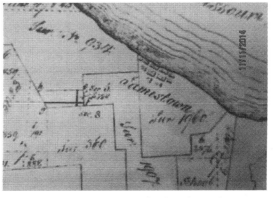

Map 3-5 Compiled 1846 Atlas of Edward Hutawa and 1837 Atlas of E. Dupre map showing location of "Jamestown" (Portage Road area) – Compiled by Louis Pondrom, 1974

Photos 3-1 and 3-2 Guy Seeley Cabin
Interior logs – Photo by Cindy Winkler
Current look after additions over the years -- Photo by Beverly Girardier

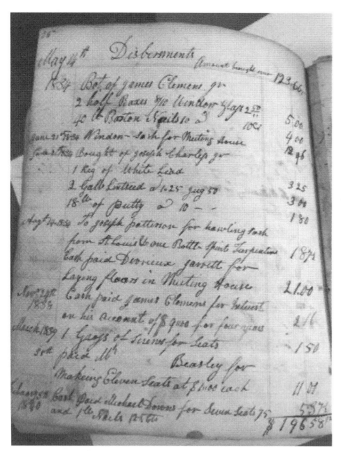

Photo 3-3 Cold Water Meeting House Notes show James Clemens, Jr., as being paid for building materials in 1834 and interest in 1838
Original Notes at Historic Florissant, Inc.

Photo 3-4 Memorial in Cold Water Cemetery, Eusebius Hubbard, grandfather of Amy Jamison James, first wife of Phineas James -- Photo by Peggy Kruse

Chapter 4 – Land Grants and Early Settlers (2) – Hodges Family

Hodges Family

[See Maps 3-1, 3-2, and 3-3 in Chapter 3.]

With permission, almost all of this chapter about the Hodges family is adapted from a comprehensive coverage of the family in the 2012 book, "Captain Edmund Hodges and His Descendants," by Kevin W. McKenney and Jeanne C. Hunter.[80]

Captain Edmund Hodges and four of his sons (Gilbert, Samuel, Daniel, and Ebenezer) obtained land grants in Old Jamestown for a total of 1731 acres. Daughter Rachel married Benjamin James who had a grant of 805 acres. Daughter Julie married Charles Desjarlais who had 255 acres. Ebenezer's wife Mary was probably the sister of John N. Seeley who had 681 acres. Six of these grants (2110 acres) were along the Missouri River or the Car of Commerce Chute. And Gilbert was married to Sara James (daughter of Sarah James who held an adjacent land grant of 340 acres).

Edmund and Rachel Godfrey Hodges were born and married in Massachusetts. Edmund was a direct descendant of Mayflower passengers Francis Cooke and Stephen and Elizabeth Fisher Hopkins. Rachel was a direct descendant of Mayflower passengers William Bradford, Thomas Rogers, John Alden, John's wife Priscilla Mullins, and William and Alice Mullins.

After the Revolutionary War, they moved to Vermont and then to Canada. From Canada they moved to Old Jamestown in 1797 with most of their children.

Edmund and Rachel's children were: (bolded names lived in Old Jamestown – their stories follow):

Margaret Hodges, born October 19, 1765, probably Norton, Bristol County, Massachusetts; married Seth Hodges, January 30, 1785, Pomfret, Windsor Couunty, Vermont; died November 13, 1856, Pomfret, Windsor County, Vermont.

Ebenezer Hodges, born about 1768, probably Norton, Bristol County, Massachusetts; **married Mary Seeley**, June 22, 1795, Niagara District, Upper Canada; died 1832, Greene County, Illinois.

Gilbert Hodges, born about 1774, probably Hardwick, Worcester County, Massachusetts; **married Sara James**, February 13, 1800, St. Ferdinand de Florissant, Missouri; married Elizabeth Anderson, about 1814; died about 1844, Franklin County, Missouri

Edmund Hodges, born about 1775, probably Hardwick, Worcester County, Massachusetts; died after 1829, probably Niagara District, Upper Canada.

Rachel Hodges, born about 1776, probably Hardwick, Worcester County, Massachusetts; **married Benjamin Franklin James**, October 12, 1801, St. Ferdinand de Florissant, Missouri

Julie Hodges, born about 1777, probably Hardwick, Worcester County, Massachusetts; **married Charles Desjarlais**, February 27, 1800, St. Ferdinand de Florissant, Missouri, died July 12, 1817, St. Louis, St. Louis County, Missouri Territory

Hannah Hodges, born about 1779, probably Barnard, Windsor County, Vermont; married Joseph Dockstader, about 1795, Ontario, Canada; died June 6, 1841, Ontario, Canada

Daniel D. Hodges, born about 1783, probably Pomfret, Windsor County, Vermont; married **Alletha (Hodges)**, about 1804; married Mary W. Tharp, on August 7, 1848, Boone County, Missouri; died April 17, 1861, White Hall, Greene County, Illinois

Samuel Hodges, born about 1784, probably Pomfret, Windsor County, Vermont; **married Keziah Patterson**, married Susan Tincher, September 2, 1823, Boone County, Missouri; died December 1826, White Hall, Greene County, Illinois.

Captain Edmund Hodges

Edmund and his family moved from Massachusetts in 1777. The American Revolutionary War was certainly the catalyst for Edmund's decision to move. The sale of his land in Hardwick in the spring of 1777 immediately followed his commission as Captain on March 18, 1777. Edmund's experience during the Revolutionary War (and the preceding French and Indian War) made him a clear fit for the role of Captain.

Late in 1777 (or early in 1778), he was persuaded (along with many others from Hardwick) to move his family to Barnard, Vermont. There, in March 1778, Captain Edmund Hodges represented Barnard during the first session of the Vermont legislature.

Edmund Hodges' land claims all over Vermont indicate the likelihood that he was engaged in land speculation to some extent like his second-cousin, Seth Hodges Senior of Pomfret, who "bought and sold land with quick returns and profit." Edmund was delinquent in paying taxes on many of his land claims in Vermont (at various times) probably due to the fact that he had limited contact with the townships where his disparate land claims were located….

From Barnard, Captain Edmund and Rachel moved to Pomfret, Vermont, where Edmund was elected to various town offices from 1780 to 1785.

Sometime between 1787 and 1792, Captain Edmund Hodges moved to the Niagara District of Upper Canada which is now part of the Province of Ontario, Canada. During the 1790s, following the Revolutionary War, Upper Canada vied with Kentucky and the Ohio Valley in attracting settlers. Early settlements in Upper Canada included a mixture of both American patriots seeking to push westward and United Empire Loyalists escaping persecution for their loyalty to Britain during the Revolutionary War. Captain Edmund Hodges and his sons received land grants and settled on land adjacent to waterways including the Chappawa Creek …. Lots near waterways were favored by settlers who relied on them to transport goods and supplies.

When he came to Old Jamestown, about 1797, Edmund's previous experience with land claims in Vermont and Upper Canada probably inspired him to insist that each of his sons obtain separate surveys for their own land claims in Missouri.

Prior to 1803, Old Jamestown was still part of the Louisiana Territory under the control of Spain, although owned by France. Edmund Hodges was appointed a "syndic" (judge and jury) and commandant near the settlement of St. Ferdinand north of St. Louis.

As described in "A History of Missouri" by Louis Houck: "….Cases arising in the several settlements and falling within the jurisdiction of the local commandants were quickly tried and adjusted [check] by them or by the Syndics appointed and acting under them. The Syndics resided usually in the remoter settlements, and in the dependencies of the several posts. This position was filled for a time by…..Edmund Hodges, north of St. Louis in the neighborhood of Spanish Pond…..These Syndics received no salary….."[81]:

One of Hodges' cases involved horse thievery[82]:

> In the year 1801, the northeast portion of this county, north of the present village of Baden, was under the charge of one Edmund Hodges, an uneducated but efficient man, as supervisor for Gov. Delassus of that portion of this district.
>
> A young man named Samuel Fallis, whose parents lived across the Missouri in St. Charles County, spent much of his time in this district. For some time back a number of horses had been missing from the pastures of some of the inhabitants, which at first were supposed to be stolen by roving Indians from both sides of the Mississippi, but from certain circumstances that subsequently transpired, Fallis was strongly suspected of being a party to their disappearance; thereupon he was apprehended by Hodges assisted by others and brought to St. Louis, where after an examination by Gov. Delassus, he was committed to prison August 20th, 1801, to await his trial, pending which the following petition was prepared and presented to the governor: --
>
> "To Don Chas. Dehault Delassus, Lieutenant Governor of Upper Louisiana:
>
> SIR. – ISAAC Fallis and Susan Fallis petitioners, have the honor to represent to you, with all the respect which is your due, that the detention of their son Samuel, causes them great injury, seeing that he is the one of their children who is their greatest help in their old age.
>
> Your petitioners are far from excusing their child, he is no doubt guilty since the law has punished him severely; but Sir, will you not allow yourself to be softened by the tears of a whole virtuous family, afflicted by the misdeed of one of its members, who all his life had been brought up in correct principles, with which they are themselves penetrated. Cannot the rigors of the law be softened on behalf of a son who was always correct up to the moment when, perhaps misled and encouraged by evil advice, he wandered from the straight path of duty, and brought grief to the bosom of his family, your heart is compassionate Sir, allow mercy to act in behalf of a father and mother, be pleased as judge to ameliorate the law which condemns our son, deign to grant pardon to Samuel

Fallis, not alone to his parents but also to the honest inhabitants who join with us to obtain it from your clemency; Samuel Fallis raised in the principles of an honest man, will easily recover from the correction you inflicted on him, the punishment from which he will escape but by an especial favor is almost a certain guarantee that he will in the future conduct himself as he should, his parents may venture to be responsible to you on that score, and cheerfully pledge themselves to pay all the costs, which their son may have occasioned by his misconduct.

St. Louis Sept. 20th, 1801

This petition was also signed by other residents in the area.

The confidence of his parents in the future good conduct of their son was verified, as we find him a few years later purchasing from Adam Brown a farm of 140 acres near Owen's Station [Bridgeton] at $4 per acre, $560. A brother, Geo. Fallis had a large farm in the St. Ferdinand prairie.

At least three Hodges marriages took place at St. Ferdinand de Florissant. Edmund's son, Gilbert, married Sara James on February 13, 1800. Daughter Lucie/Julie married Charles Desjarlais on February 17, 1800. And daughter Rachel married Benjamin Franklin James on October 12, 1801.

Accounts of the weddings shed light on how the Catholic Spanish regime, which allowed no Protestant religious services, handled weddings.

For example: Though Gilbert Hodges and Sara James (daughter of David* and Sarah Bishop James) were married at St. Ferdinand, their marriage was recorded in the Register of Marriages of Protestants 1798-1808 of St. Charles Borromeo Catholic Church in St. Charles, Missouri, which was established in 1791. The St. Charles Borromeo priest also served the St. Ferdinand Parish. The record can be translated (in part) from the original French as follows [spelling of some names corrected for readability]:

> The 13th of February, 1800, presented before us, Brother Leandre Lusson, Religious Recollect Priest, cure of St. Charles of Missouri and servant of the Saint Ferdinand Parish, Gilbert Hodges, majority age and legitimate son of Edmund Hodges and of Rachel, his father and mother, residents of this parish, on the one hand, and Sara James, her father* and mother also residents of this said parish of St. Ferdinand. They have declared that their intention was to give to each other mutually the faith of marriage, after having received their oath on the Holy Bible to respond with truth to all of the questions which I could ask them; they consented and responded to them.
>
> I asked what religion they profess. The said Gilbert Hodges responded that he professes the Presbyterian religion and the said Sara James responded that she professes the Anabaptist religion.
>
> I asked if they had ever already married other persons or if they had promised to marry them, they responded no.

I asked if they promised to bring to the church closest to their residence the children who could come from their union and to send them to Instruction. They responded yes.

I asked them if they are relatives in any degree or following their religion that they could not contract a marriage. They responded no.

I asked what country they were from. They both responded that they reside here at their parents' house, residents of this parish.

I asked if their father and mother or relatives on whom they depend consent to their mutual promise of marriage. Their fathers* and mothers here present responded that they consent to it.

I asked if they were constrained by authority, threats, or by violence to give each other mutually to the faith of marriage. They responded no.

After the above said information, the said Gilbert Hodges took in our presence the said Sara James for his wife and legitimate spouse and to promise her faith of marriage, similarly the said Sara James took the said Gilbert Hodges for her husband and legitimate spouse and promised him the faith of marriage and in the presence of Sirs William Griffin, John Chitwood, Morris James, William Griffin Jr. and several others, all relatives and friends who have signed with us the said day and year above.

Signatures – Gilbert Hodges, Edmund Hodges, William Griffin, William Griffin, Jr., Sally James, Sarah James, Jon Chitwood, Morris James, signature F.L. Lusson, ptre Rec. Cure' de St. Charles.

[*While reference is made to Sara James' father David, there is no signature from David. It's possible the priest thought Morris James or someone else was the father. David's wife, Sarah Bishop James, was reportedly a widow when she moved to Old Jamestown so David would not have been with the family.]

Ebenezer Hodges

Ebenezer Hodges, a silversmith, went to the Niagara District of Upper Canada with his father in 1792. There, he married Polly/Mary Seeley on June 22, 1795. Ebenezer moved with his father, Edmund, and his brothers to Missouri about 1797 and was granted land adjacent to his brothers.

In 1801, Ebenezer purchased a water mill in St. Ferdinand from William Musick. Ebenezer's residence at that time was said to be "at the portage of the Sioux" (which is today Sioux Passage Park), an area along the Missouri River where Indians frequently camped. This makes it likely that Ebenezer was engaged in trade with both local settlers and Indians of the area. The deed for the property includes payment – part in 'animals on demand of said vendor,' and the 'remaining six hundred dollars one half in deerskins and the other three hundred dollars payable in wheat and rye.'

In 1837 the administrator of Morris James' estate advertised James' interest in a tract of land as "300 acres on the headwaters of Hodges Mill Creek," which possibly explains the naming of the "Mill Creek" running through Briscoe Park and Sioux Passage Park.

[Photo 4-1]

Commerce during the early 1800s can be glimpsed in some of the many law suits filed for and against Hodges family members. In March 1806, Ebenezer Hodges sued Christy Romine in the St. Louis Circuit Court of Common Pleas for one hundred dollars for failing to deliver "seventeen bushels of good merchantable salt" that was due on October 1, 1805. In 1807, Robert Young sued Samuel Adams (for the use of Ebenezer Hodges) over a dispute for the payment of eleven cows and calves.

Ebenezer and Mary Hodges sold their land in Old Jamestown in several parcels over several years. In 1813 they sold land to William Jamison and in 1817 they sold land to Samuel Hodges, to Mary's brother John N. Seeley, and to John Jamison (the Jamisons were descendants of Jane Hubbard Jamison Patterson].

During this period, Ebenezer and Mary moved ten miles east across the Missouri and Mississippi Rivers to Madison County, Illinois. There, they were early settlers in Upper Alton. [Members of the Hodges family had sold parts of their Old Jamestown land grants in 1810 and 1815 to Rufus Easton who developed Alton.]

The Gazetteer of Madison County records the following: "In 1817, the first class of Methodists was organized [at Upper Alton], composed of Ebenezer Hodges, Mary Hodges, Jonathan Brown, Delila Brown, Oliver Brown and John Seeley. The first services were held in the cabin of father E. Hodges...."[83]

Ebenezer Hodges died in 1832 in Greene County, Illinois. There were several outbreaks of Cholera in Madison and Greene County, Illinois in the early 1830s. It is possible that Ebenezer was a victim of such an outbreak although no specific record indicates a cause of death. Mary Seeley Hodges died sometime after 1850, likely in Wisconsin where she was then living with her daughter and near her son.

Gilbert Hodges

Gilbert moved with his father, Edmund, and his brothers to Missouri about 1797 where he was granted land adjacent to his brothers. His wife Sara James, daughter of David and Sarah (Bishop) James was born in North Carolina and died before 1814 when Gilbert married his second wife, Elizabeth Anderson.

In 1813, Gilbert Hodges sold land on the Missouri River (reserving the 400 arpens of land on which he "lately resided") to William Russell.....

In 1815, Gilbert Hodges and his wife, Elizabeth, sold 150 arpens of land to Rufus Easton who was a land speculator in addition to many other pursuits. (Chapter 6)

In 1816, Gilbert Hodges and his wife, Elizabeth, sold 400 arpens of land on the Missouri River to Jacob Seeley....

Sometime before 1819, Gilbert Hodges settled in Franklin County, Missouri and remained there until his death.

Rachel Hodges (m. Benjamin Franklin James)

See Benjamin Franklin James in Chapter 3.

Julie Hodges (m. Charles Desjarlais)

See Charles Desjarlais in Chapter 3.

Daniel Hodges

Daniel Hodges moved with his father, Edmund, and his brothers to Missouri about 1797 and was granted land near his family. His survey was recorded in 1802. Daniel sold his land to William Davis in 1808. In 1802, William Davis built a distillery. In 1813, Daniel and Samuel Hodges filed a lawsuit against the estate of William Davis to recover an unpaid debt of two hundred gallons of 'merchantable whiskey.'

Daniel and Alletha A. Hodges sold their homestead land in St. Ferdinand, Missouri to Greenberry Baxter in 1813….After leaving St. Ferdinand, Daniel and his brother Samuel Hodges settled in Boone County, Missouri. Sometime before 1830, Daniel Hodges and his family relocated again to Greene County, Illinois. Following the death of his first wife, Alletha, in 1845 Daniel married Mary Tharp.

Daniel Hodges died on April 17, 1861 at the age of 78 in Greene County, Illinois.

Samuel Hodges

Samuel Hodges moved with his father, Edmund, and his brothers to Old Jamestown about 1797 and was granted land adjacent to his brothers. He was involved in several land transactions for his and his father's land.

On January 23, 1805, Captain Edmund Hodges sold the remainder of his land to his two youngest sons, Daniel and Samuel…. Daniel and Samuel Hodges sold a portion of the land that was transferred to them by their father to Charles Davis in 1813…. Samuel Hodges sold the remainder of his land in St. Ferdinand Township in 1823 to Alexander Stuart…. After leaving St. Ferdinand, Samuel and his brother, Daniel, settled in Boone County, Missouri…. From Boone County, Missouri, Samuel Hodges moved to Greene County, Illinois where his brothers, Daniel and Ebenezer had settled.

The same day [1810] that the Board of Land Commissioners recorded their opinion that the land once belonging to William Davis should not be confirmed to Samuel Hodges, brothers Daniel and Samuel Hodges sold their right and title to the land to Rufus Easton for the small sum of five dollars with the condition that they would not be responsible if the land was not obtained by them.

Samuel Hodges and Keziah Patterson, daughter of John and Keziah Patterson, were married sometime before 1810. Keziah Patterson died about 1823 in Boone County, Missouri. Samuel Hodges and Susan Tincher were married on September 2, 1823 in Boone County, Missouri.

Captain Edmund Hodges died on June 1, 1805 in the *District of Coldwater* near St. Ferdinand, where he had spent the last years of his life as syndic and commandant. He was only 60 years old when he died; and he left no will indicating perhaps that his death came unexpectedly. His estate was probated on July 15, 1805 in St. Louis with his oldest son, Ebenezer, acting as administrator. Edmund died owing debts to various individuals. As a result, his possessions were sold at public auction.

Edmund Hodges' grave has never been found and no record or tradition exists concerning his final resting place. It is possible that he was buried on or near his homestead which today is near the intersection of New Halls Ferry Road and Shackelford Road.

Economic conditions and land values had deteriorated in Missouri and across the United States about 1818 and 1819 and may be the reason that by the 1820s Edmund's wife, Rachel and all his sons had moved from Old Jamestown. They went to Boone and Franklin Counties in Missouri and Greene County in Illinois.

If they had stayed a bit longer, perhaps there would be a Hodgestown or Hodges Road in north St. Louis County.

For many, many legal documents related to the Hodges family, see the comprehensive "Captain Edmund Hodges and His Descendants," written by Kevin W. McKenney and Jeanne C. Hunter, 2012.

Chapter 4 Photos and Maps

See Maps 3-1, 3-2, and 3-3 in Chapter 3.

Photo 4-1 Waterfall on Mill Creek in Briscoe Park
Photo by Julie Burgess

Chapter 5 – Land Grants and Early Settlers (3) – Patterson Family

Patterson Family

[See Chapter 3 Maps -- 3-1, 3-2, and 3-3]

The Patterson family was among a small but important group of families who relocated from Pennsylvania, Virginia, and the Carolinas into the St. Louis area prior to the Louisiana Purchase. They were among the first settlers of English origin and one of the first Protestant families in St. Louis County.... The...family was Scotch Irish and came to America in the early 1700s arriving in the Port of Philadelphia. Like many others, the family came to Penn's Colony to escape persecutions at home and to find a better life in the New World.

The family of John Patterson, Sr., came from Bucks County, Pennsylvania, and moved to Orange County in North Carolina before the Revolution. Two of his sons, John Jr. (later Sr.) and William, later moved to Old Jamestown with their families and obtained land grants of 510 acres each on Coldwater Creek

> The Patterson family was one of the first Protestant families and among the first settlers of English origin in predominantly French Catholic St. Louis County. Because of their unique needs, they had to establish institutions consistent with their culture and beliefs. From a very early date, the Pattersons helped finance and build a church and a school for the use of their family and neighbors. These institutions formed an important ensemble, establishing the Patterson Settlement as a self-contained small community.[84]

The "Patterson Settlement," encompassing almost all of what is now Old Jamestown, was 10,000 acres. About 2000 acres, acquired through land grants to John Jr. and William and later family purchases were actually owned by members of the Patterson family. Patterson Road still runs from Florissant to the former Patterson property.

John Patterson, Jr.

John Patterson, Jr., a Revolutionary War veteran, came to Old Jamestown about 1797. A late 1800s St. Charles Cosmos article, adapted here, provides some facts and spins a fanciful tale of his motivations and travel.[85]

> About the year 1780, there resided in the western part of North Carolina, a Mr. John Patterson. The soil of that part of the State being thin, and distance from market too serious an obstacle to the transportation of farm products, the worldly condition of Mr. John Patterson was far from opulent. A large family of sons was growing up around him, and, if a desire to better his condition rose within him, the knowledge of the way to do so was unrevealed and unknown to him.

> One evening two travelers rode up to the Patterson homestead, asked for a night's lodging and were kindly bidden to stay. The next morning one of the travelers mounted his horse and rode off, leaving his companion still domiciled at the house. Acquaintance, fellowship and friendship soon sprung up between the guest, Mr. James Richardson, and Mr. John Patterson. Richardson told Patterson that he and his friend were from Missouri, then called Upper Louisiana; that it was the country for poor men like Patterson, and that the Spanish Alcalde gave large tracts of land to actual settlers; and ended by advising his new friend to pack up and go back with him to Upper Louisiana, promising him all the assistance in his power.

The year after Richardson's visit to North Carolina, John Patterson started to move to Missouri. The whole wealth of the family was packed on the backs of four horses. There were no roads, no bridges and no ferries, so that it was impossible to travel by wagons. With plenty of powder and balls, a few axes, a small amount of clothing, and a gun for every one capable of handling the same, even to the mother, they began their journey of over 1,200 miles.

That was a memorable migration. Arriving on the banks of a stream, search was made up and down its banks for a ford, and should none be discovered, constructing a rude raft and floating thereon the mother and children. At night they lay down without fire, for fear of lurking [Indians], whilst by turns they stood guard over the sleepers. Their food was the wild game that came in their way, cooked and eaten without salt or bread. Sometimes a few wild herbs, a scant supply of berries or some forest fruit provided them with a change of diet.

Thus they journeyed through Kentucky and Illinois, until they arrived at Kaskaskia, where they were warned to stop and take shelter in the fort, as the Indians were on the war-path, and even threatened that stronghold. For eighteen months they rested here, starved here, fought the Indians and tried to raise corn, but always had it destroyed by the [American Indians] before maturity.

This is known to all the Pattersons as the "starving time," and to this day, Mrs. Acena Patterson, now very old, declares she dislikes to see even the smallest bit of bread wasted.

Again taking up the westward march, John Patterson and his family entered the Territory of Upper Louisiana.... The country was under Spanish rule, Zenon Trudeau being the Alcalde or Governor. St. Louis had but ten or twelve dwellings, besides a fort. To Owen's Fort [Bridgeton] went John Patterson and family, where they were graciously received by their old friend Richardson.

The Spanish Alcalde refused them a grant of land, but lion-hearted and generous Richardson soon found a farm for sale suited to them, and with his assistance they were soon settled in their Western home. There was a log cabin, fifteen by twenty, on the farm; a few acres were already cleared and broke, and, with nothing but an ax, Mr. Patterson set to work to make himself furniture, plows and farm utensils.

[In 1798 John Patterson did receive a land grant.]

Notwithstanding John Patterson was born and raised in a slave State, he was, undoubtedly, the first Free Soiler in the West. He was bitterly opposed to slavery; believed it a sin and demoralizing in its effects on both slave and master. When it came to the question of freedom or slavery on the admission of the State of Missouri in the Union, he boldly spoke and used all his influence in favor of freedom. None of his children have ever owned slaves by purchase; some, it is true, came in their possession by inheritance, but they were so humanely treated that today they are employed by their former unwilling owners.

Another portion of the article is included in James Richardson's story in Chapter 3 and the whole article, which includes stories of life in their new land, is in Appendix 3.

John Patterson and his first wife, Keziah Hornaday Patterson, had 12 children. After her death in 1809, he married the widow of Joseph Jamison, Sally/Sarah Jamison, who had 12 children of her own. Together they had one additional child, David.

Sally, born in Henry County Virginia in 1766, was a daughter of Eusebius Hubbard (1744-1818), also a Revolutionary War veteran, and Amy Durrett Hubbard. John Patterson was again widowed when Sally died on July 7, 1832. John died in 1839. Eusebius, John, Sally, and Keziah are all buried in Cold Water Cemetery.

William Patterson

John's brother William also was a Revolutionary War veteran and also received a land grant in Old Jamestown. He had married Hannah before arriving in Old Jamestown and separated from her in 1818 after they had moved to Pike County, Missouri. William had about nine children with Hannah and possibly two or more children with his slave, Fanny.

Pike County Genealogical Society reports that "John and James Patterson, sons of the Revolutionary soldier, William Patterson, came to Pike county Missouri in 1817, and that year erected a small grist mill near Rock Ford.... In 1818 their father sold his land holdings in St. Louis County, and with his remaining family and slaves moved to Pike County where he staked a claim for property."[86]

The Pike County Genealogical Society web site tells us: "The first to weave cloth was Hannah Patterson, who as early as the year 1818 had supplied her own family and some of her neighbors with the product of the loom.... In 1842 Hannah Patterson hung herself with a skein of yarn in an old shop situated on the farm."

In 1845 85-year-old William Patterson applied for a military pension and stated that he enlisted in the United States Army in 1777, was discharged 1778, enlisted again in 1779, and did not get clear of the army until August 1781.

Nine children are named in William's will. "As for my children who are John Patterson, James Patterson and William Patterson, Nancy Bolden, Sarah Walker and Mary Walker, Elizabeth Crowder, Azenethe Price and Ann Harpool all and each of whom I have heretofore given about an equal portion of land, money, and personal property in advancement, I therefore do not desire to bequeath either or any of them or their heirs anything more at my death."

William's will also freed all his slaves at his death, "to wit, my Negro man named Major slave for life aged about twenty three years - my Negro woman slave for life named Fanny aged about fifty years - my negro woman slave for life named Nancy aged about twenty-one years - my Negro boy slave for life named Madison aged about 6 months. All of which said slaves I do hereby will decree and set free to be perfectly free at my death from the claim or claims of any person whosoever. I further give and bequeath provisions to be given to them at my death together with the bedding and kitchen furniture which said Negroes now use."

William Patterson died 1 Sept. 1847 and was buried on his farm in Calumet Township in Pike County.[87]

Elisha and Lucy Patterson

This information about Elisha and Lucy Hubbard Patterson is adapted from the National Register of Historic Places application for the Elisha and Lucy Patterson Farmstead. [ADDRESS][88]

Elisha Patterson was the second son of John Patterson and a significant presence in Old Jamestown. He was born in 1784 in Orange County, North Carolina and moved to St. Louis County with his parents in the late 1790s. Elisha served in the War of 1812 as a sergeant in Captain James Musick's Militia Company.

Elisha married Lucy Hubbard in January 1806. Her father was Durrett Hubbard, born in 1765 to Eusebius and Amy Durrett Hubbard. Durrett was the brother of Sally Hubbard Jamison, John Patterson's second wife.

Elisha and Lucy Patterson established their home in 1806. Elisha's initial residence must have been on his father's original land grant property. John Patterson sub-divided his property and provided farmsteads for each of his children. Elisha's title to his portion of his father's property was made official in 1818 when Elisha was thirty-four years old. Elisha received two parcels from the original farm….

Elisha Patterson bought and sold property throughout his life, even holding a half-block in the Village of Florissant for a time. Following his father's precedent, Elisha ensured his family's success by providing property and houses for each of his children. This arrangement was understood and is the reason why neither Elisha nor Lucy had Wills at the time of their deaths. The 1878 atlas, which coincides with Lucy Patterson's death, clearly shows that there were enough houses provided on the various family properties to accommodate all of the children.

Elisha Patterson later provided sites on his property at New Halls Ferry and Patterson Roads, which had been purchased in 1823, for a school and the new family church. In 1851, the new Coldwater Church was erected. It was called an "Orthodox Protestant Church" in Elisha's deed of the parcel to the church's trustees. The deed also states that Elisha had previously built a school on this part of his property. The church trustees were obligated to build another school on the site to replace the earlier building.

The 1850 Agricultural Census indicates that Elisha Patterson's farm was a very profitable venture. At that time he was raising wheat, Indian corn, and Irish potatoes. The farm comprised fifteen horses, six 'milch' cows, two working oxen, twelve other cattle, fifty sheep and sixty swine. Elisha had 460 acres of farmland, 35% of which was improved for agricultural production. The average St. Louis County farm in 1850 was only 148 acres. The Patterson Farm had a cash value of $12,000. This compares to a County average of only $4,600. Similarly, the value of the farm's livestock, animals slaughtered, and farm implements all were more than twice the county average.

Elisha Patterson died in 1854 and Lucy died in 1876. Lucy's life was summed up in the obituary published in the St. Louis Christian Advocate on November 15, 1876:

Lucy Hubbard was born in the State of Virginia, March 13, 1790; moved with her family when a child, stopping for a short time in Kentucky, and arriving in Missouri in 1800. Her father settled in the charming valley of Florissant, about 15 miles from the then French village of St. Louis, where she spent the remainder of a rather extraordinary life. On January 9, 1806, she was married to Elisha Patterson, with whom she happily spent more than 50 years of married life. She became the mother of 15 children, fourteen of whom lived to be heads of families, her first born dying at five years of age. Her entire progeny before death numbered 15 sons and daughters, 93 grandchildren and 75 great-grandchildren.... Sister Patterson, with her husband, was received into the Methodist Church by Rev. John Clark, in 1806.[89]

Elisha Patterson's commitment to his faith, and to Reverend Clark, who was a very early Protestant minister in Old Jamestown (See Chapter 8), had continued throughout his life. Clark died November 15, 1833 in the home of Elisha and Lucy Hubbard Patterson whom he had married twenty-seven years before.

Elisha, Lucy and Reverend Clark are all buried in Cold Water Cemetery where many Pattersons and their descendants are buried.

[Photos 5-1, 5-2, and 5-3]

See more on Cold Water Cemetery and early churches and schools in Chapter 7.

Hume Family

The Hume family's journey to Old Jamestown was similar to that of the land grant holders but they arrived about 20 years later. John Hume (1769-1842) was born in Madison County, Virginia, and married Anna Crigler (1771-1841), also of Madison County, Virginia, in 1792. They moved to Madison County in Kentucky about 1802. In 1817 they moved to St. Louis County in Missouri. This was the beginning of a large family of Humes who later married into the Patterson and Hyatt families.

Following are only a few of the Hume family connections to notable others in Old Jamestown. To prevent completely glazing over readers' eyes, we haven't attempted to trace the myriad of possible interconnections. For a comprehensive genealogy report for the Patterson and Hume families, see www.billputman.com from which this is adapted.90

John and Anna Hume's daughter Moriah (1794-1839) married Judge Frederick Hyatt of Florissant. After she died, Fred had four more wives, and most were Humes or Breckenridges. He was obviously a good friend of the family. There were six children in the marriage, including John Hyatt (1815-1907) who married Pamelia Clark Musick in 1840, Amelia Hyatt (1817-1892) who married Franklin Utz (Hazelwood history), and James Hyatt (1829-1879) who married Sarah Patterson.

Another of John and Anna Hume's daughters, Martha Hume, was the second wife of Judge Frederick Hyatt after her sister died. She later died and the good Judge married three more times. The other wives of Frederick Hyatt were all widows. Wife three was Ann G. Whistler widow of General Whistler. Four was Mildred (Mellon) Latimer and finally Elizabeth Breckenridge, the widow of Thomas Ferguson.

John and Anna Hume's son, Stanton Hume, Sr., (1799-1850) married Sarah Ann Breckenridge in 1822. Sarah had come from Kentucky with her parents in 1820. Their children were Elizabeth, Talitha, Lewis, James, John, Minerva, Maria, Stanton, Sarah, Julia Henly, George, and Mary Thomas.

[Photo: 5-4]

Stanton Hume, son of Stanton and Sarah, was born in 1836, and according to The History of St. Louis County Missouri, written in 1911, was a "...highly esteemed resident and successful agriculturist of St. Ferdinand Township, the owner of a fine farm of one hundred and eighty acres. Stanton Hume obtained his early education in the old-time subscription schools and in 1854 spent six months as a student at Rev. John N. Gilbreath's Institute. During the period of the Civil War he served in the Confederate army, being connected with Slack's Division, which was under command of Colonel Hill of Carrollton, Missouri. General agricultural pursuits have claimed his attention throughout his entire business career and his life has been that of an intelligent, industrious and prosperous farmer. He is a lover of livestock, especially horses, and is a close observer of plant and animal life. The farm on which he has resided since 1839 comprises one hundred and eighty acres of rich and productive land and is a part of the old Patterson settlement, on the Hall's ferry road, a mile and a half from Musick's ferry and two and a half miles from Cross Keys. Mr. and Mrs. Hume occupy a comfortable and attractive two-story frame residence, which is surrounded by a neatly arranged garden and well tilled fields. There are also barns and outbuildings for the shelter of grain and stock, and the neat and thrifty appearance of the place gives evidence of the supervision of a practical and progressive owner."[91]

Stanton Hume married Virginia Ferguson in 1857 and the couple had two children, "one of whom died in infancy. The other is Robert Hume, now a resident of Slater, Saline county, Missouri, who married Miss Ann E. Hyatt, a daughter of Judge Joseph L. Hyatt. They have two children: Virginia E., who gave her hand in marriage to Silas Thompson [son of James Thompson, Chapter 8]; and Joe H. Hume, an agriculturist by occupation. Stanton Hume is a Baptist in religious faith and is an exemplary member of the Coldwater Church. Travel has afforded him both recreation and pleasure and he has visited many parts of the country, from the eastern and Canadian cities to the Rocky Mountains."[92]

And we learn about a later Hume family member's Old Jamestown connections from the Salem Baptist Church Lamplighter July 1977 newsletter once posted on the Cold Water Cemetery web site:[93]

> Edward Charles Hume (1898-1977), son of Elisha Patterson Hume and Mary Lindemann Hume, was born in a log house on the bluff of the Missouri River near the corner of Shackelford and New Halls Ferry Roads. There were ten children in the family. The father was a farmer and the family lived in several homes in the Hume and Patterson settlements. Ed attended the one room Coldwater School (Chapter 7). In 1921, Ed Hume married Margaret Marie Patterson in a garden rainbow wedding at the home of her parents, John and Margaret Patterson. Dr. S. E. Ewing, executive secretary of the St. Louis Baptist Mission Board performed the ceremony. Through the years the Humes lived within a few miles of the birthplace of both. These houses included at least three log houses covered with siding. Their son James was born in the old Patterson homestead on Sinks Road. The other three children were born in the old brick Coldwater Church on New Halls Ferry Road at Patterson Road, which Ed's father owned at the time.
>
> A very hard working man, Ed farmed, worked for Fischer's Ice and Coal Co., Shelby Curlee Possum Hollow Farm (Chapter 9), and Florissant Valley Elevator Cooperative, drove school buses for Hazelwood School District and Custom Coach, was a custodian for Salem Church, gardener for Welch's and caretaker of Cold Water Cemetery. He loved God's great outdoors. He loved horses, had several and rode quite well. He also raised collie dogs.
>
> Ed attended the Coldwater-Salem Church all his life. In 1916 he walked several miles through the snow to be baptized in the little white frame Salem Baptist Church (Chapter 7) where he was

a faithful member for 61 years. His three sons are deacons and all family members are active. He and his wife boarded school teachers as well as the men who were putting in the dikes on the Missouri River (Chapter 6). He and his wife shared their home and their meals with many, many people through the years. Ed's smile, twinkling eye and witty replies as well as his helping hand will be greatly missed by all who knew and loved him.

According to the Cold Water Cemetery web site, in 1842 Judge Joseph L. Hyatt, son of Judge Frederick and Anna Hume Hyatt purchased a big tobacco barn that James Richardson had built on his property in Old Jamestown (Survey 405, Chapter 3). Judge Hyatt converted the barn into a residence on Old Halls Ferry.[94]

Later residents on Patterson land grants

These later owners of the Patterson and Hume/Hyatt homes are just a sampling of the many people who have lived in Old Jamestown over the years. Their history is adapted from Historic Inventory Forms prepared by Esley Hamilton, St. Louis County.

14501 Old Halls Ferry Road is on land granted to John Patterson by the Spanish in 1798 and confirmed by the U.S. in 1822. He died in 1838, and in 1842 his sons Elisha and David sold this property to John Crowbarger. In that deed the tract is described as "the one on which John Patterson, Sr., resided at the time of his death and was called in his will the Home Place." However, the architecture of the current house suggests it was built in 1860 or even later. The property changed ownership again in 1851, when it was sold to Thomas G. Breckenridge; in 1859 when John H. Shackelford (for whom Shackelford Road is named) bought it; and in 1864, when it was acquired by James Ferguson. Ferguson lived in Howard County, Missouri, and he intended this property for his daughter Mary and her husband Joseph F. Hughes, who lived on it. Ferguson died in 1878, leaving this farm to Mary, and in 1882 she and her husband sold it to William Krueger. He died there in 1905.[95]

[Photo 5-5]

The Amanda Krueger House at 15205 Old Halls Ferry Road was constructed about 1913 and was part of the larger farm of John Patterson, which had been acquired by her father, William Krueger. The main farmhouse stands at 14501 Old Halls Ferry Road. After William's wife Caroline's death in 1909, their four daughters went to court to subdivide the land. Each girl got 70.96 acres in the July 1911 settlement. Dora got Lot 1 with the big house, and Amalie got Lot 4 with a smaller house and barn. Augusta got Lot 2 and Amanda got Lot 3. Dora married Charles H. Oetker the very next month. Amalie had already been married since 1908 to Fred W. Rosenkoetter, the eldest son of Herman Rosenkoetter, who lived in the old Douglass farm across the street (now #15310). Amalie bought 12.33 acres of Amanda's tract to enlarge hers. Eventually, however, she and Fred moved to Pittsburg, Texas. Amanda married one of Fred's younger brothers, John H. Rosenkoetter, in December of 1913. Four months before that, she borrowed $4500 against this property, and she probably used that money to build this house. She and John lived here less than three years, however, selling in 1916 to George B. Schuler for $4242 plus the outstanding mortgage. Neither John nor any children are listed among his father's heirs in 1933, so presumably he died before that time.[96]

15505 New Halls Ferry Road was constructed about 1860 in the Elisha and Lucy Patterson Farmstead Historic District. From 1823 until 1998 all ownership transfers of the District were made either among members of the family or their nearby north St. Louis County neighbors.[97] In 1881, Ernst Hoffmeister, a native of Prussia, apparently bought this farm for his 38 year old son, Fred Hoffmeister, and his wife, Fredericka. The Agriculture Census in 1880 shows that Fred Hoffmeister was renting 101 acres of farmland. He was growing corn, oats, wheat, and potatoes, and he had four mules, two 'milch' cows, one beef cow, five sheep, 10 swine, and 36 chickens.

In 1888, after the death of his wife, Ernst sold this property to Frederick Fischer, another German immigrant who already owned property in the area. It became known as Fred Fischer's Farm, although in later years Charles Fischer, one of the ten children, leased the farm from his father for $250 per year. Fred Fischer was a director of the Coldwater School in 1904....Fred Fischer died in 1910 and the family had to go to court to settle the estate.

> The court commissioners sold the property in 1911 to Henry Birkemeier who paid $230 per acre, for a total cost of $10.698.45. The Birkemeiers were Catholic and worshipped in Florissant at the Sacred Heart Church. Henry's widowed mother, Elise or Elisabeth Birkemeier, who was born about 1833 in Prussia, lived directly across the street on the other side of New Halls Ferry Road. Elise's land had been part of Elisha Patterson's farm; she had purchased the property at the time of the Patterson partition. Elise Birkemeier died in 1908 and Henry in 1916. He left a widow, Gertrude, a son, Joseph, and six daughters.

> Ultimately the homestead was inherited by daughter Mary who married Herman J. Meyer. The property was later inherited by Herman and Mary's daughter, Celeste Meyer. During the 1950s, much of the property was sold for the development of Wedgewood Subdivision. Celeste Meyer sold the house and remaining property in 1998 to Russell and Barbara Marty who sold it in 2009 to David and Lisa Goodwin.

"Koester's Mystery Hill Farm" at 14511 Sinks Road was on land once owned by members of the Hume and Hyatt families. The house was built in 1927, but the farm itself goes back to the late 1850s. The ground, originally totaling 90 acres, was acquired before 1837 by Lewis Hume and his son-in-law Frederick Hyatt. William Wortmann, a German from Bielefeld, came here after operating a vinegar factory in Philadelphia for a short time. He is said to have come to this region because his sister was already here. He bought a half interest in 40 acres of this property from Hume's executors December 12, 1857, and the other half from Hyatt on February 6, 1858, then added another thirty four acres in 1867 and 1868. He died in 1877 leaving a widow Mary and five children, ranging in age from 21 to 9. At that time the farmhouse was described as a log dwelling of 3 rooms and garret, measuring 18 x 32 feet. One of the children, Louisa Eliza (later Elise, 1861-1938) married Barney Koester, and about 1904 acquired full title to the property from her siblings. In 1988, the owner was their daughter, Aldine M. Koester, who planned to sell the property.[98] The property was sold to a developer who had a dream of starting a winery and subdivision on the beautiful property. Like Phineas James' dream of "James Town" it hasn't come to fruition. Lots on Old Jamestown Winery Road are still undeveloped, a few are listed for sale. The karst topography (Chapter 10) likely interferes with plans to build homes on some of them.

Chapter 5 Photos

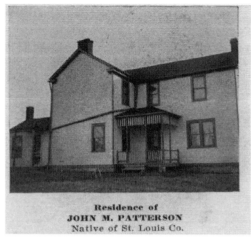

Photo 5-1 Sinks Road Home of John McAllister Patterson, great grandson of John and Keziah Patterson, grandson of Elisha and Lucy Hubbard Patterson -- 1909 Plat Book, Scan by Missouri History Museum of St. Louis

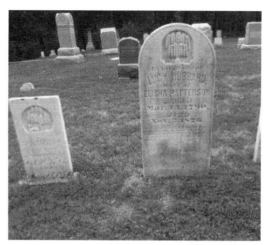

Photo 5-2 Gravestones of Elisha and Lucy Hubbard Patterson in Cold Water Cemetery – Photo by Bev Girardier

This is to certify to all whom it may concern, that I, John Clark, minister of the gospel of the order called the Baptized Church of Christ, Friends to Humanity, have on the 5th day of November 1831, joined together in holy matrimony Joseph Patterson, and Mary James, both of the county of St Louis and State of Missouri. at the house of Mr William Patterson's Settlement in the State & county aforesaid. Given under my hand this 7th day of said month and in said year. John Clark

Recorded 7 December 1832 minister and Pastor of Cold water Church of the above faith & order, and in the said County and State.

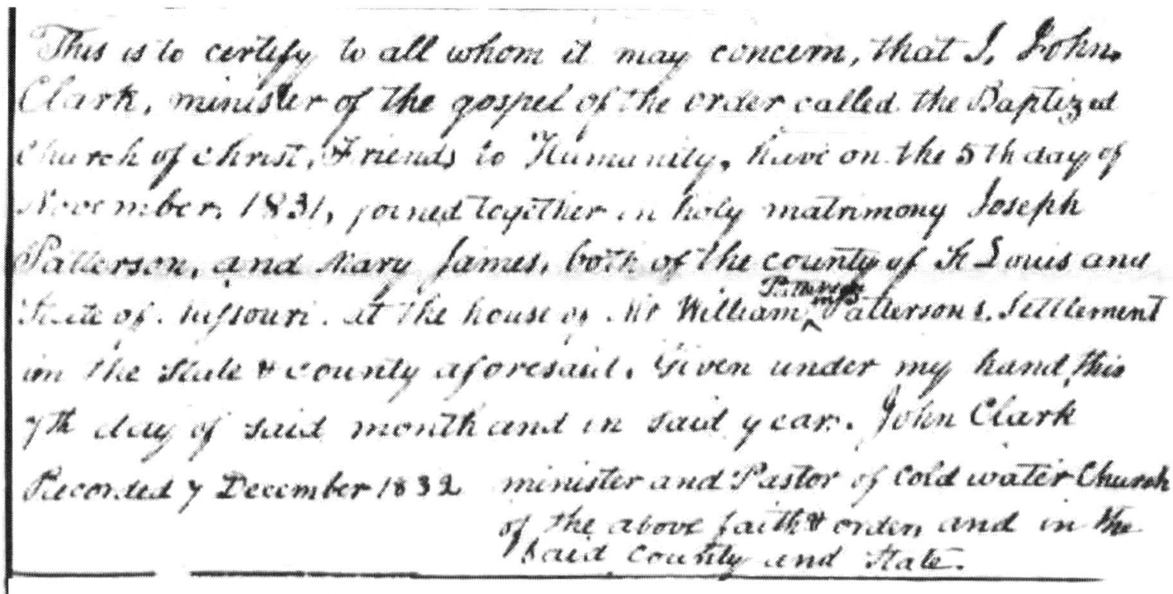

Photo 5-3 Rev. John Clark's certification of the marriage of Elisha and Lucy Hubbard Patterson

Photo 5-4 Stanton Hume, 1909 Plat Book, Scan by Missouri History Museum of St. Louis

Photo 5-5 Residence of Amanda Krueger – 1909 Plat Book, Scan by Missouri History Museum of St. Louis

Chapter 6 – Musick's Ferry Area

Attraction of Old Jamestown

The Musick's Ferry area on the Missouri River was long recognized as a great location for connecting St. Louis and Florissant with St. Charles County and Illinois and it became a focal point for much of the activity in Old Jamestown.

[Maps 6-1 and 6-2]

Still appearing on many maps is Musick's Ferry, where New Halls Ferry and Douglas Roads meet the Missouri River, just to the west of Pelican Island. The area is very quiet now but for many years Musick's Ferry was a place of gathering and commerce. In addition to the ferry operation, there has been a store, a tavern, a grist mill, a quarry and a saw mill. Next to the shore were showboats and a government dike building operation. And for a long time there was an imposing stone 19-room inn. As late as 1924, a ferry operation was re-started.

About 1797, Sarah James received a 340 acre land grant for this property and as early as 1805[99] operated a ferry that brought travelers across the Missouri River to and from St. Charles County. In 1813, her son Phinehas James purchased the land from Sarah for $1000. In 1816, after "Hall's Ferry Road" was surveyed, Phinehas sold the land to Rufus Easton for $3000.[100] (See more on Sarah and Phinehas James in Chapter 3.)

Easton had previously purchased nearby land from the Hodges family. (See Chapter 4.) In addition to being a land speculator, Easton (1774-1834) was a well known attorney, politician, and postmaster. He served as a non-voting delegate to the United States House of Representatives from the Missouri Territory prior to statehood. After statehood he became Missouri's second Attorney General. Rufus Easton was also the founder of Alton, Illinois, and father of Mary Easton Sibley who with her husband founded Lindenwood College in St. Charles. In addition to his duties as judge, Easton was asked by President Jefferson to keep an eye on the Territorial Governor, General James Wilkinson, because Wilkinson was suspected of collaborating with Aaron Burr to support secession of the western part of the United States.

Rufus Easton was also a friend and mentor of Edward Bates whose family later lived in or near Musick's Ferry. Bates studied law with Easton and boarded with his family. After being admitted to the bar, Bates worked as Easton's partner. Edward Bates (1793-1869) was a U.S. lawyer and statesman. He was the first attorney general of Missouri and the United States Attorney General under President Abraham Lincoln. Bates was the younger brother of Frederick Bates, second governor of Missouri. Edward moved to St. Louis in 1814 with his older brother James, who started working as an attorney. Frederick was already in St. Louis by that time, where he had served as Secretary of the Louisiana Territory and Secretary of the Missouri Territory.

Bates died in 1869 and was buried in the Edward Bates' family cemetery that was just west of Old Jamestown on the southwest corner of Shackelford and Weithaupt[101]. As reported in a 1919 ©St. Louis Post-Dispatch article: "for a sidewalk George Warren, whose family lived and worked in Musick's Ferry since the mid 1850s, has the slabs of stone that formed the [top of] the wall of the private cemetery of Gen. Edward Bates which was located on the Bates farm nearby and abandoned some years ago....

Three large slabs that lay over the graves of Caroline, Matilda, Sarah and Edward Bates form the door stoop. His body was reinterred in 1906 in Bellefontaine Cemetery in St. Louis."[102]

In 1817, Easton and Bates organized a ferry that ran to Alton, Illinois.[103]

According to Louis Pondrom's history, in 1830 Thomas Blair was granted a license "to keep a ferry across the Missouri at his stand commonly called Spring Ferry." [104] This could be the second ferry location off New Halls Ferry just to the southwest of James Ferry, but we have found no other information on Thomas Blair's stand or ferry.

In 1848, the land and ferry was sold to Reuben Musick and his wife, Lydia Carrico Musick and the name Musick was associated with the ferry. Lydia died in 1870 and Reuben in 1871. In 1875 the Musicks' lands and Bates Farm properties were divided into lots and sold at auction but the identification of the area as Musick's Ferry continues.[105]

Musick's Ferry and Inn

> "In the summer months, besides ferries and river traffic, a variety of showboats anchored at Musick's Landing. It became fashionable for residents of towns in west St. Louis County to drive out to Hall's Ferry Road, dine at Musick's Tavern, and see a showboat performance. Many rented a room and remained for additional shows, which were changed every night. Matinees were given Saturday and Sunday afternoons. Business prospered, and the tavern was enlarged several times...." The Helmholz Papers via Musick Family Association of America.[106]

[Photo 6-1]

What started as the James Ferry in the early 1800s and later Hall's Ferry became Musick's Ferry after being purchased by Reuben Musick in 1848. Musick's Ferry Inn was built in the 1850s for those who used the ferry to cross the river with their crops or furs but had to wait for transportation to St. Louis, which was about 17 miles[107] away.

A 1931 newspaper article in the St. Louis County Watchman Advocate provided many fascinating details about the operation of the ferry and inn.[108]

> "One day, some years before the outbreak of the Civil War, the problem of overnight accommodations for transient farmers and furriers who hauled their products from the St. Charles and northern Missouri district, via Musick's Ferry, to St. Louis, was taken up by the few business men of Musick's Ferry.... [Musick's Ferry was] a little settlement at the end of Hall's Ferry road, which figured prominently in the early development of St. Louis County.... [The building] still stands as though in majestic pride of the distinction it bears as being the first hotel building in this county.
>
> "Work on the old building was started in the early [eighteen] fifties and its nineteen rooms are encased in a stone hulk, the walls of which measure nearly two feet in thickness. The stones, huge blocks with their outer surface smoothly finished, were quarried and dressed right in the neighborhood by native artisans, who were evidently experts and used to good advantage the few

tools available to stone mason workers in this early period, as is evidenced by the finish on some of the blocks.

"Vincent Grey was the builder and he erected the building for his mother-in-law, Mrs. Blackburn, known in the neighborhood as 'Aunt Betsy,' a daughter of James James, and a great aunt of James Brown, who now has a Chevrolet agency at Halls Ferry and Chambers roads.

"The tavern was named Musick's Ferry Inn and presided over by Aunt Betsy. According to residents of that neighborhood, it thrived for many years as a great center of commerce as well as entertainment, as not only farmers, halting here on their long and arduous trips to enjoy a good night's rest and partake of Aunt Betsy's wholesome meals took advantage of its accommodations, but…pioneer folk from both sides of the old Missouri journeyed over the rough roads in wagons, buggies and on horseback to participate in the gaieties at the tavern.

"According to Patterson Hume, now nearing the three-quarter century mark, a descendant of Lewis Hume, Sr., who [arrived in the area] in 1797, Reuben Musick, the pioneer 'land King' of St. Louis County, in those days was the central business figure of the community. He ran the ferry boat, which was operated by horse-power, between the St. Louis County side and Walnut Landing in St. Charles County, and he owned the grist mill, a quarry and a sawmill. It was at this saw mill, 'that many of the boards, sawed from the ruff timber, were used in planking Halls Ferry road,' one of the first and best improved roads of the county.

"'The old ferry, a roofless, flat boat arrangement, was propelled at first by a horse-power tread-mill, the horses, you see just kept on walking but got nowhere, as the old tread-platform moved instead, turning a shaft which kept the wheel in motion to push the boat across the river. Later on a new contrivance for…power was used. The horses were hitched to a pole and instead of being put through a forward movement they walked around a circle. While this arrangement took up more room I believe it proved more practical.

"'Of course the old Missouri in those days was not as wide as it is today, and the crossing was accomplished, as I have been told in pretty good time.' Although the country to the north was pretty well developed and populated, travel was not so heavy, and then too, there was another ferry at St. Charles, and this cared for a good bit of business. But, nevertheless the old Inn did a thriving business for a while, some nights accommodating as high as 15 and 20 farmers, who after crossing the stream would stop there for the night before continuing their journey the next morning to St. Louis, and likewise, those returning from St. Louis, arriving at the river too late to be ferried across would put up there for the night.

"Just how long the old rock building was operated as an inn is not known to any of the residents of that district, but Mr. Hume said, that to the best of his recollection, in time it passed into the hands of a man by the name of Joseph Conroy, who had charge of the quarry in that neighborhood, and that he used the building as quarters for his workmen. John Heins, who has been living in the building for the past 30 years, said it had been vacant for many years before he took possession and that all the old furnishings had been removed.

"'The old building,' said Heins, 'is beyond repair, and I am figuring on tearing it down during the spring or summer. I have managed to keep the lower rooms which I occupy in repair but the upper floors are in bad condition.'"

Musick's Ferry Inn was torn down in June 1938.[109]

A 1919 ©St. Louis Post-Dispatch article about a road trip to Musick's Ferry provides a glimpse of the area about that time. "There is a now a stand at Musick's Ferry where refreshments and a light lunch may be purchased. Motorists who would care to bring their lunch in a basket will find numerous points along the river that are ideal for a family spread. The cars will have to be parked at Musick's Ferry, as the roadway is poor from there on, narrowing to a path." And "10 or 15 summer cottages have been leased by St. Louisans."[110]

As reported in the St. Charles Cosmos-Monitor in August 1924, after no ferry activity for 20 years, a ferry between Musick's Ferry and Black Walnut (St. Charles County) was put in operation by the Halls Ferry and Transfer Company. Fifty-two sacks of onions were sent across the river on the first few trips of the boat. The roads are good, the drive is pleasant but the charges for crossing the river are not very attractive. The charge for a small car is 50 cents then five cents for each passenger, while the same car could cross the St. Charles highway bridge for 30 cents. The steamboat that is used is the Perryville, with a capacity of twenty automobiles and capable of ferrying trucks of the largest sizes. It is of the "Bootjack" shape, which makes it possible to drive a vehicle on and off without "backing and filling." It also has a cabin for passengers. The Perryville formerly operated as the Sidney street ferry across the Mississippi River at the foot of Sidney Street in St. Louis before the Municipal Free Bridge was opened and spoiled the ferry business there.[111]

[Photos 6-2 and 6-3]

Over the years showboats docked at Musick's Ferry, including one called Golden Rod. The Hollywood Showboat visited Musick's Ferry in 1932.

The Encyclopedia of Louisville, Kentucky, describes showboat activity during the early 1900s and the history of the Hollywood. -- One popular and pervasive form of riverfront entertainment was Showboats, barges fitted up as Theaters and propelled by small steamboats that stopped for riverside engagements in the towns and cities along its banks. Most of the showboats of the late nineteenth and early twentieth century tended to bypass the river's largest cities, where citizens were already amply entertained at local theaters, music halls, and opera houses. The Hollywood had 3 names in her fast paced history. She was built as the America in 1911 for Walter Needham in Cincinnati, OH. She was sold to the Thompson brothers in 1916, sold to Ralph Emerson in 1917, later the same year sold to E.A Price who renamed her Columbia. His son Steve Price operated her until 1928 when she was sold to the Menke Brothers and renamed Hollywood. She was in winter quarters in the Clark River above Paducah when she was crushed by ice in 1941.[112]

From a 1932 ©St. Louis Post-Dispatch article about the Hollywood at Musick's Ferry -- Business on the Boom at Oldtime Showboat – 600-Seat Theater on Missouri River Filled Nearly Every Night:[113]

> "Attracted by old-time melodramas aboard a showboat…more than 26,000 persons have attended performances at the 'Hollywood' since August 2, when it tied up on the Missouri River at the end of Hall's Ferry road, about 20 miles from the heart of the city. Capt 'Bill' Menke,

skipper of the craft and one of the owners of the 'Golden Rod,' an even bigger showboat, now playing at Pittsburgh, announced today he intended to remain near St. Louis 'as long as business is good.'...

"The boat is sold out now for two weeks in advance. It is presenting 'St. Elmo' next week and already has staged such 'tried and true' dramas of the gay nineties as 'Tempest and Sunshine,' 'Lena Rivers' and 'The Sweetest Girl in Dixie.' 'Lots of folks get a big kick out of [cheering] the hero and hissing the villain,' Menke observed, 'while others go out just to hear the wise cracks from the audience. But most of them get serious before the show's over. There's something about the tried and true sentiments -- home and mother and all the rest -- that tugs at folks' heartstrings.....'"

Musick Family

Reuben Musick was the son of Abraham Musick and Rachel Fugate who were born in Virginia and came to St. Louis County with their children. Abraham and Rachel had property in Columbia Bottoms. In 1844, before purchasing the land that is now Musick's Ferry, Reuben Musick and five others gave notice that they intended to apply for a license to establish a horse ferry to run from the Illinois River at Madison landing to a place opposite on the Missouri shore and also to Chouteau's Island. This likely would have been on or near property owned by the Musick family in Columbia Bottoms.

Before their marriage, Reuben's wife, Lydia, inherited part of land grant Survey No. 104 from her father, Vincent Carrico, who had purchased it from John Brown, the grantee. Vincent also had his own land grant east of Old Jamestown. Lydia was also a sister of Walter Carrico who owned land near the ferry property. (See more about the Carrico family in Chapter 3.)

Reuben Musick and Lydia Carrico were married about 1825 in St. Louis, Missouri. According to the Musick Family Papers, "Reuben and Lydia didn't have children of their own, they just raised everybody elses." In a deposition about their estate, Lydia's sister, Malena Fugate, stated that Reuben's own children died at birth. They always had a house full. For example, when Reuben's nephew, also named Reuben, died in 1859, his widow and children went to live with Reuben and Lydia.[114]

Warren Family

[Photos 6-4, 6-5, and 6-6]

Another early resident at Musick's Ferry was John B. Warren who rented, then owned land there. Warren also operated the stone quarry on his property and his son George A. Warren took some wonderful photos of the area, some of which are included in this book. George had many occupations, most of which were centered on the river that flowed by his house. Their stories follow.

Information about John B. Warren was adapted from The 1911 History of St. Louis County Volume II:[115]

John B. (Jean Baptiste) Warren was born in France on July 4, 1847, a son of Michael J. and Mary B. (Collett) Warren. His father died in France and his mother immigrated to the United States with her only child in 1854 to join her Collett relatives who had been in Florissant since the early 1700s. John's school days began before leaving France, and after they became settled here his mother sent him to the common schools near them. Being unable to speak English, this was a somewhat trying ordeal for the lad, who to evade the difficulty ran away and as a result obtained very little schooling. When the call came for troops in the early days of the [Civil War], 14-year-old John responded, enlisting as a drummer boy in 1861. Soon thereafter he was placed in the ranks. He left military service in 1865, immediately returning home, where soon after he became ill. Although not strong, the following summer he was able to do a little work, finding employment as a driver, which he continued doing for four years.

In 1869, Warren married Mary J. Egan, a daughter of William H. and Ann (Coffey) Egan, the father a native of Port Royal, Virginia, and the mother of Tipperary County, Ireland. Mary Egan Warren's mother came to St. Louis as a young woman. Her father had passed away with cholera in 1849 when Mrs. Warren, an only child, was still in her infancy. Her mother died in 1896.

After his marriage Warren rented some land at Musick's Ferry, continuing to farm as a renter until 1879 when he purchased forty-two acres, all but possibly ten acres of which was claimed by the Missouri river. Later he bought seventy-six acres of land and later added another tract of sixty-six acres, a total of one hundred and forty-two acres. In connection with the cultivation of his fields, Mr. Warren has for many years engaged in the operation of a fine stone quarry which is on his property. During the thirty years [1881-1911] he has been working this he has taken out many thousand perches of stone, this having proven to be quite a lucrative venture.

John and Mary had ten children, only two of whom were surviving in 1911: Julius W., a stationary engineer at the Portland Cement Works; and George A., who is operating the home farm. Family members are communicants of the Roman Catholic Church, and Warren served for twelve years as a member of the school board.

This information about John Warren's son George comes from George's granddaughter, Barbara Lindemann.[116]

George Adrian Warren's family came to Florissant from Nancy, France. Their original name was St. Vrain, the name was later changed to Warren. He was from a family of quarry owners, farmers, a piano teacher, land surveyors, a town-cryer, and map makers. George was a professional photographer, farmer, wild-craft winemaker, and constable. He leased his land to the Corps of Engineers for construction of river dikes and operated his limestone quarry. He was a lamplighter for river navigation, and his home also served as a land-line house for the riverboats

One of George's daughters, Betty Jane Warren Lindemann (1922-2015), was born at home at Musick's Ferry and attended old Brown School. In 1922, the Betty Jane Creek that spills into the Missouri River was named for her. Betty served on the School Board of the old Hyatt School District from the late 1940s to early 1950s.

The Missouri History Museum reports that George Warren took photos for the U.S. Army Corps of Engineers from 1907 to 1918, including many photos of the Musick's Ferry area and other areas in north St. Louis County. The Missouri History Museum has copies of over 80 of his photographs.

[Photos 6-7, 6-8, 6-9, and 6-10]

Desloge Estate

The Desloge "Vouziers" Mansion on New Halls Ferry at Shackelford was built by Joseph Desloge, Sr., who owned hundreds of acres in and near Old Jamestown. Desloge descendants still own some property in the Musick's Ferry area. In 1919 Joseph commissioned New Orleans architect Dennis McDonald to design a Louis XVI-style chateau, which Desloge named Vouziers. By 1926, the 10-bedroom, four-story manor had been completed. (See Chapter 9 and Appendix 10 for much more about Joseph Desloge, his home and family.)

A very old log cabin still exists on Desloge property on the west side of New Halls Ferry north of the current Boeing property. We don't know the origins of the house, but it was lived in by renters Henry and Mary Schlueter from the l880s until about 1915 when they moved to a farm on Vaile Avenue. The Schlueters were farmers who rented their homes. A later resident in the home was Ethel Riddle, M.D., who was a friend of the Desloges. The last renter was Mark Heil.

[Photo 6-11]

Boeing Leadership Center

The impressive Boeing Leadership Center complex is part of the Musick's Ferry property. Despite not being very noticeable from the road, it is a significant presence in the neighborhood. (See Chapter 11 for information about the Boeing Leadership Center.)

[Photo 6-12]

Stories from Musick's Ferry

Newspaper articles and other documents provided many stories about activity in the Musick's Ferry area.

Possible Underground Railroad from Musick's Ferry to Alton

A Robert Swanson article on Halls Ferry Road in the Florissant Valley Reporter said that Captain Hall was a friend of Alton abolitionist Elijah Lovejoy and that he helped hundreds of escaping southern slaves flee to freedom…. "By day, the negroes were concealed in a cave in the limestone bluffs that walled the river. The river was not as wide then and at night, Captain Hall rowed them in a skiff to a secret rendezvous with other members from an Underground Station on the St. Charles side of the river." From there the Negroes crossed the Mississippi river, escaping into Illinois and beyond.[117]

Robert Swanson's stories need to be taken with a large grain of salt but according to the Alton Museum web site, Alton was an important Underground Railroad location. Within a seven-block radius in Upper Alton, there are five documentable Underground Railroad stations; most are private homes. The

Ursuline Sisters, the AME churches, and some of the American Baptist churches are among the groups involved in assisting escaping slaves. In the 1830s, escaping slaves were being absorbed by the free Black communities around Alton.[118]

Rufus Easton and Edward Bates, operators of a ferry from Musick's Ferry to Alton may have been connected to Elijah Lovejoy.

Congressional Testimony – Election Judge at Musick's Ferry

As early as 1876, Musick's Ferry was the site of a polling place (District 50, Yaeger's Store). Voting there was also the subject of this testimony before a U.S. Congressional hearing in 1882. Congress was investigating possible irregularities during a recent election, whether some voters were incorrectly denied the right to vote and whether nonresidents were allowed to vote. This is just a brief excerpt of a Musick's Ferry election judge's testimony.[119] (See Appendix 4 for the longer transcript.)

Question. What is your full name? – Answer. Gustavus Wittich.

Q. Where do you live? – A. Saint Ferdinand Township

Q. You were a judge at the election up there on that day? – A. Yes, sir.

Q. What is the number of your precinct of which you were a judge, sir? – A. Number 11, on Musick's Ferry.

….

Q. How many votes were cast at your poll for Frost and how many for Sessinghaus? – A. Well, it was close to 75 for Frost and 25 for Sessinghaus.

Q. You are giving your best recollection of the returns, are you? – A. I am giving my best recollection; yes, sir. It was close on 100; and it was three-fourth for Frost and one-fourth for Sessinghaus.

Q. Are there any colored men in that polling district? – A. Not very many, so far as I can recollect – six or seven.

Q. Do you know whether they live in the vicinity of Musick's Ferry? -- A. Yes, sir.

Q. Farm hands there? – A. Well, some farm hands.

Q. Do you know whether any came from Illinois to vote at that poll? – A. No, sir; not one; the vote was honest and fair.

Q. How far is Black Jack from Musick's Ferry? – A. About six miles.

Q. You were not down at Black Jack that day? – A. No, sir; I was not down there.

Q. Do you know of colored men being brought over from Illinois to vote at Black Jack? – A. No, I guess I never heard of it.

Q. How long have you lived, Mr. Wittich, in Saint Ferdinand Township? – A. I have lived there for about twenty-five years.

Q. Have you ever been at the poll at Black Jack? – A. I was there a good many times.

Q. Do you know whether it is a habit of Republican managers to bring negroes from Illinois to vote them on every election? – A. I never heard of this.

Prohibition at Musick's Ferry and on Pelican Island

This Day in St. Louis History, January 16, 1920 – Missouri History Museum Facebook Page: "On January 17, 1920, America officially ran dry with the enactment of Prohibition. St. Louis, with a massive brewing industry, would be one of the hardest hit cities in the country, but also one of the cities where the law was most openly disobeyed! Houses around St. Louis would have false basements for giant liquor mash storage tubs, illegal speakeasies would appear around the city, and homebrewed beer would become a staple of dinners among friends. Gangs, like the Egan's Rats and rival Hogan Gang, would take over illegal distribution and turf war shoot outs and murders were frequent. St. Louis had 20 breweries in operation when Prohibition was enacted, and their closing meant the loss of thousands of jobs, particularly in German communities." Prohibition was repealed by the 21st Amendment in 1933.[120]

Situated in a remote area that was connected via the rivers and railroad to another county, state, and beyond, Musick's Ferry was a great location for illegal distilleries and distribution.

According to Don Gerling who lived in the Musick's Ferry area and heard stories from his uncle, there were many stills on farms along New Halls Ferry and Douglas Roads and on Pelican Island. He said moonshine was taken by boat to West Alton (St. Charles County) to be distributed in Illinois. It was also taken by boat to the MKT railroad (St. Charles County) and sold in other areas of the country. Police knew about the illegal booze and normally collected on Sundays their share of booze or money to keep quiet.

Roads End Tavern was at the end of New Halls Ferry and served as a speakeasy during Prohibition. The tavern was shut down in the 1960s by Joe Desloge, Sr., who bought it and turned it into a rental residence because he was not happy with the type of people it was attracting.

Showboats, including the Hollywood Showboat in 1932, also visited Musick's Ferry and could very well have served as speakeasies.

While all of the above was hearsay, this 1927 Daily St. Charles Cosmos-Monitor newspaper story of a raid on Pelican Island confirms that there were stills in the area.[121]

"Another Raid made by Chief Prohibition Officer on Pelican Island near Alton, Ill.:

"Chief Federal Agent James Dillon's two-day prohibition attack upon the still-infected islands near the juncture of the Missouri and Mississippi rivers ended yesterday with the dynamiting of a huge whisky and beer making plant, capable of turning out 300 gallons of whiskey a day, and representing an investment of approximately $40,000 in buildings and equipment.

"The still and brewery, the prize after which Dillon had set out, was discovered early yesterday afternoon on Pelican Island, in the Missouri River, approximately two miles northeast of Musick's ferry. Only the telltale smokestack showed through the thick willow banks when Dillon approached. It had been carefully camouflaged, and even the bare spot in the shore used to land boats and barges had been covered with willows to make the landing invisible. When Dillon and his men took to their boat again the buildings were a mass of flames.

"This was the most successful of Dillon's four raids and as many searches during the two days – successful at least according to Dillon's prohibition philosophy of: "Blow 'em up and ther' done for." The plant was composed of two houses, the larger, approximately 50 feet square and two stories high, housing the illicit liquor plant, while a smaller bunk house contained beds for six and [ample] food supply on hand. In ten huge wooden vats were 60,000 gallons of whiskey mash and another 60,000 gallons of beer mash with machinery, pumps, boilers, compressors, stills and hoists to give the place appearance of a pre-prohibition distillery.

"Outside was dumped a carload of coke and soft coal with more than 1000 2-gallon tin liquor containers, wagons and an ample gasoline supply for the pumps. A lone hound stood on guard when Dillon arrived, but was soon on friendly terms when the agents started to feed him his master's eggs, several dozen being found in the bunkhouse."

1888 Fight across from Musick's Ferry

This edited May 30, 1888, St. Louis Post-Dispatch article[122] about a dramatic and unusual gunfight provides a glimpse into conditions and connections in the late 1800s. A summary of the story also appeared in the May 31, 1888, New York Times.

Fight across from Musick's Ferry -- Sheriff R. C. Allen and Deputies Fired on by Fishermen.

> Mayor Charles Costello of Florissant came into the city this morning with news of a bloody encounter. He reported that Deputy Sheriff Charles C. Garrett had arrived in Florissant from Musick's Ferry. He had been shot in the forehead and in the left arm. Garrett told the mayor that he had gone with Sheriff Allen and Constable Ahlfeldt to Musick's Ferry to serve a warrant for the arrest of three fishermen – two brothers by the name of Kunz and one Hellman -- for stealing a horse-power ferry boat used at the ferry and owned by Capt. Smith. The ferry was taken to the place last winter by Smith and put in service, but he had not been using it long when it was stolen and taken over to the St. Charles County side by the brothers Kunz and Hellman, who are vagabond fishermen. Smith recovered his boat and worked it until three or four weeks ago, when it was again stolen. He had applied for a warrant for the arrest of the men and it was issued by the mayor.
>
> Garrett said that at Musick's Ferry they left their team and employed a boatman, John Monahan, to row them across to the St. Charles County side, where the ferry was lying. As they approached the boat they were cautious fearing there would be some shooting but Hellman appeared on the bank and motioned for them to come on shore. They landed, and, feeling perfectly safe, walked up the shore to where Hellman was standing. There were four men standing back of Hellman at some distance. They did not appear unfriendly. Garrett, when he got close to Hellman, drew his pistol and at the same time said: "You are my prisoner." At that Hellman fell upon his knees and shouted "fire!" The four fishermen back of him, -- two of

whom are thought to be the Kunz brothers – blazed away at Garrett and his companions. Garrett returned the fire and they fired another volley. The Deputy Sheriff fired three shots at them and does not think he hit them.

Garrett ran away after he saw his companions were hurt. He ran up the shore to where the fishermen lived and got one of their women to row him across the river. There he got Sheriff Allen's rig and drove to Florissant to have his wounds dressed.

Later it was learned in Florissant that boatman Henry Beckman was shot. Boatman Monahan rowed Beckman to Musick's Ferry and there obtained a wagon in which to carry the wounded man to St. Louis. When he was placed in the wagon it was learned he could not stand the journey over the rough road to the city, and a messenger was dispatched to Florissant for a physician. Dr. Tandy drove down to the ferry in response to the call.

Nothing was known at the ferry of Ahlfeldt's fate and it was believed there that he was killed. The reporter could not reach Garrett in Florissant because he had gone home to Clayton where his wife was "dangerously sick." Beckman died the next day.

At the end of the article is another paragraph about the gunfight, which had been sent by telegraph from St. Charles to the St. Louis Post-Dispatch. It included information that Sheriff Allen came to St. Charles for assistance and had also placed the matter before County Attorney Mudd, who sent the St. Charles County Sheriff to arrest John and Jacob Kuhn, Henry Goerken and Louis Hunn.

Subsequent St. Louis Post-Dispatch articles provided more information about the incident. On May 31, the defendants went to Justice Valentine of Portage who assisted them when they turned themselves in. They said the shooting was a great mistake and that they did not know Sheriff Allen and his deputies – they said they mistook them to be the owner of the ferry and his friends from whom they had been expecting an attack. They also claimed that they recovered the ferry when it broke loose after river ice had broken up in January. On July 2, Justice Thro, who presided at the preliminary trial, released John and Jacob Kuhn without bail and remanded Louis Hunn and Henry Goerken to jail without bail.

Deputy Sheriff Charles C. Garrett was a brother of Sidney Garrett, a Florissant postmaster and mayor. Sidney's great grandson, Robert Garrett, has served on the Florissant City Council.

Steamboats

Steamboat schedules published in old newspapers list steamboat stops at Musick's Ferry. Given fires and explosions, many steamboats did not last long – they had average lives of 5 to 10 years. The Car of Commerce Chute around Pelican Island is named for an early steamboat that sank there in 1832. (Pelican Island, Chapter 10)

Steamboats not only carried passengers, but served as workboats carrying equipment and pushing barges and showboats on the river. Many of these were seen at Musick's Ferry. The progression of steamboats on the Missouri River was described in 1904 by Phil Chappell, who did comprehensive research on the river and steamboats:[123]

The first steamboat to ascend the Missouri river was a boat called the Independence. She came up as high as the mouth of the Chariton River in the spring of 1819, and thus demonstrated that the river was navigable by steamboats. There were few steamboats, however, on the river previous to 1840, owing to the sparsely settled condition of the country and the limited demands of commerce. Those that were built for the trade during this early period were small, lubberly craft, exceedingly slow and of heavy draft. They were single-engine, one-boiler side-wheelers, without the modern cabin, and had no conveniences for the comfort and safety of the passengers. With the rapid increase of population along the lower river, in the decade from 1830 to 1840 came an increased demand for additional transportation facilities; larger boats were built; the modern cabin was adopted; and additional improvements were made, both in the hull, so as to lessen the draft, and in the machinery, to increase the speed. These improvements kept pace with the trade as it increased until the '50's, when the boats built for the lower river during the decade from 1850 to 1860 were veritable floating palaces, and were unsurpassed in speed, splendor and luxurious furnishings by any inland water craft in the world.

It was during this period (1859), when the Missouri river steamboat had reached its perfection, and the business its highest degree of prosperity (there being not less than 100 boats on the river), that the railroads invaded…and sounded the death-knell of steam boating. The contest which ensued between the two rival methods of transportation was short and decisive, and it soon became apparent to the steamboat-owner that he could not compete successfully with this modern competitor for the commerce of the West.

And steamboat activity was described on a Kansas City public radio station web site[124]:

Freight took priority over lower-level passengers, the people who only paid $3 or $4 for a ticket west. "Most steamboat captains loaded cargo and animals first and then passengers took up whatever place they could on the deck. The deck passengers were just regular people who had to bring their own food, they took their chances with the elements; they basically lived outside."

Meanwhile on the upper decks, the cabin passengers paid double what the deck passengers did, but had their own private room and a very different experience. They ate in stately dining rooms, were served cuisine on par with the finest hotels. They drank in bars with gambling tables, or lounged on the deck and watched the river.

But regardless of whether you were rich or poor, the river was dangerous. If the river and the boat didn't get you, the other passengers might. "Most people had to worry about getting their stuff stolen or taken from them." With gambling and booze on board, riverboats developed a reputation. Even the captains weren't necessarily trustworthy. Some captains hired professional gamblers to take money from their passengers.

Halls Ferry Road

[Photo 6-13]

Hall's Ferry Road (St. Louis County Road No. 1) was surveyed in 1815 from St. Louis to the Missouri River, where it was connected by Hall's Ferry with a road in St. Charles County running to Portage des Sioux. Old records at Clayton Court House include the original petition for the construction of the road…. In the petition it was set out, "that the only road which leads from the Ferry to St. Louis, was laid out by the United States soldiers more for the purpose of the express from Portage des Sioux to headquarters and that, it was difficult to use it even on horseback."[125] This first route was along Old Halls Ferry Road and Douglas Road to the river.

Like most roads, Halls Ferry Road was first paved with wooden planks. One court order recording the contract for a section of the road sets out that, "the boards now at Bremen…are to be laid as far as they will go at $15 a mile and the agreed price per lineal foot."[126]

In 1857, Gustavus Waagner created a topographical map of St. Louis City and County, which shows what is now New Halls Ferry Road as "Musick Ferry Plank Road" and Old Halls Ferry/Douglas Road to the Missouri River as "Old County Road." ("Jamestown" is shown on the map with 20 houses in a grid.)

Chapter 6 Photos and Maps

Map 6-1 Google Earth Map of Musick's Ferry area

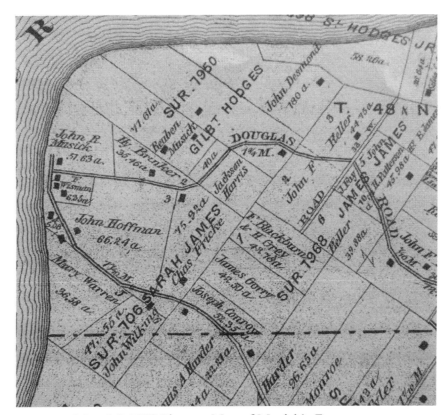

Map 6-2 1878 Pitzman Map of Musick's Ferry area

Photo 6-1 Musick's Ferry Inn about 1910
George A. Warren Collection, Missouri History Museum of St. Louis

Photo 6-2 Hollywood Showboat docked at Musick's Ferry summer of 1932
Postcard shared by Lois Hoffman

Photo 6-3 A Goldenrod Showboat at Musick's Ferry, about 1910
George A. Warren Collection, Missouri History Museum of St. Louis

Photo 6-4 -- 1909 Plat Book, Scan by Missouri History Museum of St. Louis

Photos 6-5 and 6-6 Existing Warren Family Barn and Small Shed – Photos by Peggy Kruse

Photos 6-7 (Building Dike), 6-8 (Couple at light house),
6-9 (Quarry), and 6-10 (Postal Delivery), all at Musick's Ferry area about 1910 --
George A. Warren Collection, Missouri History Museum of St. Louis

Photo 6-11 House built over log cabin, on Desloge property, north of Boeing Leadership Center. 1980s Photo by Bernice Keeven-Schlueter

Photo 6-12 Boeing Leadership Center from St. Charles County across from Musick's Ferry -- Photo by Cindy Winkler

Photo 6-13 Paving New Halls Ferry about 1910 – George A. Warren Collection, Missouri History Museum

Chapter 7 – Very Early Schools, Churches, Cemeteries

Cemeteries

Cold Water Cemetery

[Map 7-1]

[Photos: 7-1, 7-2, and 7-3]

The Cold Water Cemetery web site has much on its history, from which this is adapted: [127]

> Cold Water Cemetery on Old Halls Ferry Road is considered to be the oldest Protestant cemetery, still in use, west of the Mississippi River. It is probably the oldest existing burial ground of the American settlers who came west of the Mississippi River, when those lands were still under the rule of Spain. It was first the Patterson family burial ground, then the Patterson-Piggott, then the Patterson-Hume burial ground, and as it then served the neighborhood, it finally became Cold Water Cemetery.
>
> The cemetery is located on the original David Brown land grant property. Elisha Patterson and his three oldest brothers purchased the land from Brown's representatives in 1818. They then divided the estate into four equal parcels, one for each of their families. The plot containing Cold Water Cemetery was deeded to the oldest brother, William. Later, William deeded the property to his eldest son, Joseph. In the 1850s, the land was deeded to the cemetery and church by Nicholas and Margaret Patterson Douglass.
>
> Three known Revolutionary War Soldiers are buried there, John Patterson, Sr., in 1839, Rev. John Clark in 1833, and Eusebius Hubbard in 1818, as well as soldiers who fought in the War of 1812, the Seminole War, the War Between the States, the Mexican War, World Wars I and II, the Korean War, and the Vietnam War. Also buried in Cold Water Cemetery is Rev. John Clark, first Protestant minister to preach west of the Mississippi. Several churches got their start on the cemetery grounds.
>
> The name "Coldwater" comes from the little spring fed creek that meanders through the neighborhood. It was called Coldwater by both the French and Spanish explorers. The creek gave its name to the community, to the churches, both Baptist and Methodist, to the school and to the burial ground.
>
> Although records indicate that the first burial may have been John Patterson's first wife in 1809, the first well-documented burial at the cemetery was that of Revolutionary War patriot Eusebius Hubbard, who was born in 1744 and died in 1818.

And this description is adapted from National Register of Historic Places Application for Cold Water Cemetery[128]:

> In many ways Cold Water Cemetery is typical of the family cemeteries in St. Louis County. Most of the early interments in family cemeteries were settlers who arrived from the southern states. The burials are located on a quiet hilltop surrounded by

trees. The tombstones are usually simple stone markers and some historic plantings, including three cedar trees, remain. Cold Water is unique in that it was later developed into a cemetery serving a Protestant church and continues to be an actively used cemetery.

While maintaining its character as an early family graveyard, it also shows influence of later burial practices, notably those identified in the county's Protestant churchyard cemeteries. Cold Water has a circular drive to provide access to all burial plots. It contains simple grave markers with low relief carvings such as weeping willows and hands pointing toward heaven.

The history of the cemetery in the late 1800s and early 1900s is somewhat sketchy. Sometime after 1870, the congregation moved to a new location. Around 1929 a group of descendants and those interested in preserving the cemetery organized the Cold Water Cemetery Association. Maintenance of the cemetery was an overwhelming task and the cemetery continued to deteriorate. The group apparently reorganized in 1950 and restarted their effort to maintain and restore the graveyard. In 1963, the Missouri Society Daughters of the American Revolution received the cemetery as a gift.

The cemetery is still the property of the Missouri State Society Daughters of the American Revolution who maintain it and have a traditional Memorial Day ceremony that includes the SAR, CAR and special memorial services for the deceased DAR members and for the many veterans buried there.

The cemetery was cleaned up and enclosed in 1870 as a cemetery and the old Cold Water Church building was later removed.

New Coldwater Burying Ground Memorial Park Cemetery

[Photo 7-4]

Adapted from *Reviving a dead cemetery*, North County Journal, June 18, 1995:[129]

> On the border of Old Jamestown, at 13711 Old Halls Ferry Road, just south of Coldwater Creek, is the 1/2-acre New Coldwater Burying Ground Cemetery, which was used as a cemetery from 1886 until it became mostly inactive in 1949 [Frazier Vincent burial in 1963]. It was one of the few graveyards in Missouri both owned by African Americans and reserved for African Americans during that time. The land was next to another half acre, which had been purchased for $1.00 in 1868 and was being used for a church and school.
>
> According to the deed executed September 27, 1886, Henry Vincent, Louis Gassaway, William Cooper, Mike Francis and William Brooks as trustees, purchased a half acre of land to be used as a cemetery. The cemetery was bought to provide a burying ground to the area's African American population. Henry Vincent collected $50.00 from the local African Americans, their contributions ranging from $.25 to $3.00. Mr. Vincent, who was an ex-slave, kept a written record of the monies he collected.

The last known person to be buried in the cemetery was Frazier Vincent (1882-1963), son of Henry Vincent. Frazier Vincent and his family had once lived in Old Jamestown and worked as farmers and for the Desloge family.

After 1949, the cemetery became inactive and maintenance was erratic after 1963 when Frazier Vincent died. In 1993, the City of Black Jack took over responsibility for maintenance of the cemetery and held a rededication ceremony in 1995.

A 1959 Florissant Valley Reporter article[130] provides Frazier Vincent's stories about his family and the cemetery: (See Appendix 5 for the full article.)

> The sole trustee today of the New Coldwater Burial Ground is Frazier Vincent, Sr., who looks 20 years younger than his 77 years. Both of his parents were slaves. Both are buried in the little cemetery. Frazier's father died in 1900. His mother, Delia (Hayes) Vincent died in 1909.
>
> His mother had been sold at the age of 16 for $800. "She was a fine looking woman," he said. His father, he said, was a slave in Bridgeton. He thought his parents had met at a church function. Speaking of his parents' slavehood, Mr. Vincent said that "Some had good homes and some had bad homes," but his parents had "good homes."
>
> Later the family lived for 14 years on New Halls Ferry Road near Shackelford on property which they rented to farm. Delia and Henry Vincent had five children, some of whom are buried in the little cemetery.
>
> Mr. Vincent said the site for the cemetery was chosen near land already occupied by the African American Church and school. "We had a preacher, mostly every Sunday," told Mr. Vincent. And then with his eyes dancing, he began to tell about the good old days when, right after church, good ol' basket dinners would be spread out under the shade of some big trees which once were nearby the church.
>
> Mr. Vincent figured that a couple hundred persons must have been interred in the small cemetery over the years without charge. "Some are strangers. Not plum strangers but were not known to all the family," related Mr. Vincent. In the deed it states that permission must come from the trustees for burial there and the order in which they will be buried.
>
> "I've done something of everything" said Mr. Vincent of his former jobs. Primarily he was a farmer, now retired. He spoke with pride of his son James who was in the Navy during WW II and of his son Frazier who was in the Army and stationed in Germany in WW II.

Churches begun on Cold Water Cemetery ground

The early churches in Old Jamestown were Protestant (Methodist, Baptist, and Presbyterian) and had their beginning on the Cold Water Cemetery grounds. Even before Protestant services were legal, they were being led by Reverend John Clark in Old Jamestown homes. About 1797, John Patterson, Sr., arrived in the Coldwater Creek area from the Carolinas. The area was under Catholic Spanish Rule at the time and the Spanish did not allow Protestant services. The Pattersons retained their Protestant faith through the services of a Methodist, later Baptist, minister known as "Father Clark."

Rev. John Clark – Protestant in Spanish Catholic Times

[Photo 7-5]

The story of Reverend Clark is adapted from the Cold Water Cemetery web site:[131]

> Reverend John Clark, buried in Cold Water Cemetery, was an early Protestant minister in the area, ministering to John Patterson and members of his family. The Reverend Clark's background was checkered and adventurous but he was by every measure a gentleman, one with genteel manners and speech, neat in appearance and dress. Perhaps it was this bearing which made him a welcome guest across the continent and particularly at the Coldwater settlement.
>
> Of Scottish extraction, Clark had many adventures, starting when he was 20 years old and became a crewman on a British transport ship ferrying supplies to the Royal Army in America during the Revolutionary War and including 19 months spent in Cuba as a Spanish prisoner of war.
>
> In 1786, he became a school teacher in Georgia where he came in contact with the Methodists and under the fervor of their evangelistic preaching he progressed from conviction to the work of leading a Methodist class and preaching. Two years later in 1788 he returned to the British Isles for a visit with his family. Stopping in London on the return trip, he visited the famed Foundry Meeting House, a pioneer Methodist Church. There he attended a class meeting and heard the venerable John Wesley preach, an experience that was to remain with him all of his life.
>
> In 1796, he set out for Illinois, traveling on foot, spending a term teaching in Kentucky, then coming to the New Design Community in Monroe County, IL in 1797. He resumed his contacts with Methodist people and was soon preaching again in the informal services of that day.
>
> According to an often-told story, Clark began preaching to a group of American settlers in the Louisiana Territory who had gathered at Bates' Rock near the mouth of Joachim Creek at Herculaneum in Jefferson County, Missouri. It is said that Zenon Trudeau, the Spanish Commandant in St. Louis, had a friendship for Clark but publicly warned him of the stern penalties for disobedience to the law. The story goes that Trudeau never sent officers to arrest Clark until he was certain that the Methodist preacher was safely back in Illinois. He would give him three days to get out of Spanish Territory which would allow him enough time to finish preaching and return home in Illinois. In any event, Clark was probably the first Protestant minister to preach on the west side of the river and, at the turn of the century, was making regular visits to the settlements along Coldwater Creek. The first marriage in this community was that of Elisha Patterson, the son of John Patterson, Sr. and Lucy Hubbard on January 9, 1806, with the Reverend Clark, hearing the vows.
>
> In May 1805, after the U.S. purchased the Louisiana Territory and Protestant services were no longer banned, a Methodist class was formed in the Spanish Pond area of Coldwater Creek. At about the same time another class was formed in the home of Elisha and Lucy Hubbard Patterson.

About 1810, Clark became closely associated with a Baptist group called the "Friends to Humanity". He was probably attracted to them because of their abolitionist stance and because he favored Baptist polity over the Methodist appointive system. In 1811, Clark affiliated with the Baptists and continued in that denominational ministry until his death twenty-two years later. See Appendix 8 for more information on the Baptist Friends to Humanity.

On November 15, 1833, he died at the age of seventy-five in the home of Elisha and Lucy Hubbard Patterson. His grave in Cold Water Cemetery is probably unusual in that both the Baptists and the Methodists have marked it.

Coldwater Church

[Photo 7-6]

This history of the Coldwater Church is adapted from Section 8 of the National Register of Historic Places Application for the Elisha and Lucy Patterson Farm[132]

> When first organized, Coldwater Church services were held in members' homes. A log church was built at the Cold Water Cemetery in 1832. The Journal of the Coldwater Church / Union Meeting House shows that the church on the Cold Water Cemetery site remained in continuous use into the 1870s. Elisha Patterson was extremely active in this church and served as commissioner and treasurer for many years.[133]
>
> In 1809 Coldwater Church separated from the organized Methodist Church and continued as an independent Protestant church. The church became affiliated with the "Friends to Humanity," a Baptist denomination that abhorred slavery. Members of the congregation were encouraged to work for emancipation, including purchasing slaves in order to give those slaves freedom.
>
> A new "Orthodox Protestant Church" was built in 1851 on a corner of the Elisha and Lucy Patterson Farm. This church was built three years before Elisha's death. The reasons for the second Patterson family church are unknown. It is clear, however, that by deeding part of his property to the church Elisha Patterson was instrumental in providing this church to serve his family's nearby farms. The "Coldwater Church" appellation was transferred to this building. Although much altered, this structure still exists. It is currently owned by the Fraternal Order of Eagles Lodge #3638.

Salem Baptist Church

Salem Baptist Church, 19715 Old Jamestown Road, Florissant, held special activities on May 30 and 31, 2009, as it celebrated its 200th Anniversary. The church was founded in 1809 at the site of Cold Water Cemetery and is the second oldest protestant church west of the Mississippi River.

"In 1839, six years after Rev. Clark's death, the Baptized Church of Christ Friends to Humanity, which had been organized on Cold Water the year after his death, ceased to exist. On September 23, 1841, Salem Baptist was organized by members "from the old extinct churches of Union and Cold Water," and came from many of the families whose markers are still visible in Cold Water cemetery: Assenath Piggott Patterson (wife of William Patterson), Cumberland James, Gilbert James, Keziah Patterson James, Elizabeth Blackburn, Edward Hall, Solomon Russel, Ann E. Henley, Sarah Hume, Eveline James, Ellender A. Russel, and Frances Monroe."[134]

Salem Baptist was across the street from the original Brown School (below). When the Hazelwood School District was organized in 1950, the school building was sold to the church as a parsonage. Among many other notable Old Jamestown residents, the Wehmer (Chapter 8) and Hammer (Chapter 9) families were longtime members of the congregation.

African American Church and School on New Coldwater Burying Ground

The New Coldwater Burying Ground, described above, was annexed to a ½-acre tract located southeast of the cemetery. The earlier tract was purchased in 1868 for $1.00 from William and May Hammersen by Irvin Rhodes and Louis Gassaway, trustees, to be used as an African American church and school. The church and school no longer exist, but the cemetery and some of the people buried there have historical significance dating back to the Civil War Era.

As reported in a 1959 Florissant Valley Reporter Article on New Coldwater Burying Ground, Frazier "Vincent said he went to school in the little combination school and church which he estimated burned about 30 years ago [1929]." "He estimated that he went to school off and on, quitting to help on the farm with what was a fourth grade education. He also told of going to another school in the area called 'Sink' which was held in a two-room home, in one room of which was carried on a basket weaving trade, and the other the school."[135] (See Appendix 6 for the full article.)

Schools

[See Map 3-1 in Chapter 3]

In addition to their religious education, the Patterson Family (Chapter 5) provided for their children's formal education. Before about 1845, there were no public schools. Schools were a matter of private contract between a teacher and a few heads of families. Benjamin James (Chapter 3) was one of the early settlers who taught school near his home. When public school districts began in the mid 1800s, three of them were in Old Jamestown – Brown, Coldwater and Vossenkemper. After the following brief history of these schools are memories from a few Old Jamestown residents who attended them.

Brown School

[Photos 7-7, 7-8, 7-9, and 7-10]

Original Brown School on Old Jamestown

Old Brown School, 19719 Old Jamestown Road, was constructed about 1860. The school was called the James School until the 1890s, then Douglas School, and later Brown School. The school served until 1950, when the district was merged with the new Hazelwood School District. The building was then used by Salem Baptist Church for a parsonage and is now a private residence.

John N. Seely had received a land grant that included the property in 1800. In 1834, he deeded much of his land to his grandson William "Uncle Billy" James. (John N. Seely's daughter, Marie, was married to William's father, James James, holder of a nearby land grant. (See more on the Seely and James families in Chapter 3.) Adapted from Franzwa's History of Hazelwood School District:

> In the 1840s the settlers were anything but crowded, but the little log school near the Cold Water cemetery - the only one for miles around - was bursting at the seams. The children on Shackelford, New Halls Ferry and Old Jamestown roads had a long way to walk to school in the biting winters of the mid-century.
>
> Uncle Billy James did something about it. On December 9, 1859, he deeded 3/4-acre of ground to the three directors on the board of education - Peter Temple, Benjamin Douglas and Lewis Patterson. On this ground a tiny, one-room school was built of brick, probably hand-fired in the neighborhood. There is some speculation that slaves might have built the building, and this is entirely possible. [136]
>
> In 1949 Elm Grove School District on Hwy 67 reorganized as a six-director district and became Hazelwood School District, which in 1950 annexed Brown School. And soon the building changed from a school building to a parsonage for Salem Baptist Church.
>
> A sample of the annual teacher salaries at Brown: 1911- $855; 1923 - $900; 1932 - $1,035; 1933 - dropped to $765 as the depression deepened; 1941- $1,000; 1949 - $1,620. [137]

Two early teachers at the James/Douglas/Brown School were nieces of Benjamin Douglas. Mary and then Virena Douglas, who lived in the Tunstall-Douglass House on Old Halls Ferry taught there in the late 1800s. Mary was there first. Virena became the teacher when Mary married Henri Chomeau. Virena then married Henri Chomeau after Mary died in childbirth. (See more on the Douglass/Chomeau family in Chapter 9.)

Coldwater School

[Photos 7-11 and 7-12]

In the early 1800s, school was held in the Coldwater Church/Union Meeting House in Cold Water Cemetery. Members objected to this location because they felt that it was inhumane to require their children to attend school in a cemetery.

In response to the concerns of location and overcrowding, Elisha Patterson built a school building in the southeast corner of his own property (New Halls Ferry and Patterson). This school was used until after the Coldwater Church moved to the same lot. In 1859, shortly after Elisha's death, members of his family built a new school approximately one-fourth mile north. The historic building, 15875 New Halls Ferry Road, sits in front of Hazelwood Central High School, and is currently owned and maintained by the Hazelwood School District.

The 1-1/2 acres for this school was purchased for $150 from Thomas and Mary Tunstall on August 5, 1859. The building was probably erected the same year. The belfrey was added in 1898 or 1899, the cloakroom about 1900, and the vestibule about 1906. The school district was annexed by the new Hazelwood R-1 School District in 1950 and this building was closed in 1954. After Hazelwood High School opened immediately behind this school in 1965, the old building was saved by the Heritage Foundation organized for the purpose of preserving the building.[138]

Vossenkemper School

Henry Vossenkemper, for whom Vossenkemper School was named, was a native of Germany and married Henrietta Hoffmeister, a native of St. Louis County. He was a prosperous farmer who left his son, also named Henry, a farm of one hundred and eight acres.

Adapted from History of Hazelwood School District:[139]

> The early history of the Vossenkemper School still is much a mystery. The old timers heard that the one-room brick school, torn down in 1927, stood exactly 60 years, and that there was an earlier log or frame building on the site.
>
> On July 28, 1852, Jacob and Lydia Veale had deeded a quarter-acre of land "or more, if absolutely necessary," for school purposes. There was a restriction on the gift, which stated that the land must house a school within two years or the land would revert to the donors. It also specified that if a school was erected but wasn't used as such for a period of more than two years, the title would revert back to the Veales. On December 30, 1867, Henry Vossenkemper and his wife conveyed this same tract to the school district. This suggests the land reverted back to the Veales and they transferred it when they sold the rest of their ground to Vossenkemper. This deed was unrestricted and carried a price tag of $175 - the fair rate for an acre in that year.
>
> On August 20, 1874, the ground was deeded from the Coldwater trustees to Vossenkemper, then a member of the Vossenkemper board, and two other board members, John Leber and Andrew Ruffner, and their successors.
>
> The second Vossenkemper School was at 6200 North Hwy 67, a big two-roomer on the southwest corner of the highway and Robbins Mill Road. That building was sold to the developers of the adjacent Jamestown Mall and razed in 1975.
>
> On May 22, 1951, Vossenkemper voted itself into the School District of Hazelwood No. R-1, and held its last graduation in June 1954.

Ray Rosenkoetter, who was a Vossenkemper board member from 1942-1951, shared some memories of his time with maintenance of Vossenkemper with Gregory Franzwa who included them in his History of the Hazelwood School District.[140]

> Back in those days the board wasn't exactly frivolous with its money. They got rid of the janitor because they thought he used too much coal. They hired me at 50¢ a day to come in and carry out the ashes and fire up the furnace in the morning, and bank the fire every night. I guess that's when I became interested in school business. After I went on the board, we found ourselves with a little surplus money. Two of us wanted to give the two teachers a $25 bonus at Christmas

time. They were only getting $90 a month then. You know we actually had to overrule the third member!

When we got our new furnace in 1944 the contractor wouldn't take a school voucher. I had to write out my personal check and wait until the next board meeting for my money. And then when the board of health condemned our water supply we had to buy tank trucks of water, hauled in from West End Fuel Company on Natural Bridge, and they wouldn't take a check of any kind. So I had to give them four dollars of my own money every time they made a trip. "

Tight as they were, those early board members had the loyalty of their teachers. Christian Nolte, a really great schoolmaster, taught for 27 years in the old building. He died in 1935. Before him there was Elizabeth Mills, who stayed for 25 years.

Student Memories from the Early Schools

Aurelia Thompson Wehmer

Aurelia "Rill" Thompson Wehmer attended the James [Brown] School from 1893 to 1901.

Rill was born in 1887, daughter of James Thompson, a farmer and threshing machine operator from Glasgow, Scotland, and Margaret Carrico, daughter of Walter Carrico who had land adjacent to Thompson's. (See more on the Carricos in Chapter 3 and more on James Thompson in Chapter 8.)

Her memories were shared with Gregory Franzwa who recorded them in his book, History of the Hazelwood School District, which is adapted here.[141]

> In 1893 Rill Thompson started at the then James [Brown] School and finished up in 1901. Not wanting to take the arduous examination from the County Superintendent, she went to live with her brother in St. Louis, attending the Clay school on 20th Street. After she received her diploma she attended Central and Yateman high schools, then came home to marry and raise a family.
>
> Rill remembers: "We had a well in front with two wooden buckets on a chain. My, how those boys would delight in dousing me with water when I walked by. There was a chimney at each end and a pot belly stove on one end only. I'd burn up on one side and freeze on the other. I can remember the boys throwing wood in that stove like it was yesterday. There were blackboards at each end of the room and double seats - two children for each desk. We had no cloakroom - hooks on the wall did the job. The windowsills held our sack lunches."
>
> Rill had fond memories of her cousin, Clarence Carrico. "My, he was slick. He could chew a plug of tobacco an hour and the teacher knew darned well he was doing it but do you think she could catch him at it? No sir she couldn't. Clarence went on to be a famous osteopathic doctor."

Ralph Wehmer

One of Rill's sons, Ralph, told this story about his time at Brown School in the 1920s.[142] (See Appendix

9 for more of Ralph's stories about living in Old Jamestown.)

"One foggy morning, around 8:30, while outside, at school, we heard a noise that caught our attention. That was Brown School, which is now a residence right down the road here, near Carrico Road, across from the church. We saw a plane coming down low in front of our school. The plane was really low, probably 50 feet in the air. The plane would come down low and go back up again. As the plane came down low, he cut the engine and hollered, 'Where's the nearest airport?' We pointed in the direction of the airport, which was then Anglum, Missouri [now Robertson]. We kids made a 'human arrow'. The oldest kid, Bill Brinker, organized us. He circled back around and yelled down, 'Thank you!' The person in the plane happened to be Charles Lindbergh! [At the time, there were spotlights every 10 miles from Alton, over Vaile to Florissant and on to the airport for pilots to find their way. It was so foggy that morning, that he couldn't see them.]

"….I graduated from the eighth grade at the age of 13. One afternoon, in August, my mother took me to Ferguson (and I drove the car) to enroll in high school. I asked, 'How am going to get to school?' She said, 'Son, you are going to drive to school.' Even though I was only 13, I drove myself to school every day."

Alice Dale Wehmer

Alice Dale (Mrs. Henry W.) Wehmer was one of the foremost authorities on the lore of the old Coldwater School building. She was a long-time teacher of the Hazelwood School District, who on July 1, 1961, became the first teacher to retire from the system.

Adapted from History of Hazelwood School District.[143]

Alice attended Coldwater School from 1897 until 1905, when she became the first Coldwater alumnus to actually get a diploma. Her mother, Anna Belle Smiley Dale, attended the old Brown school in the early 1870s. The family lived on New Halls Ferry near the river and then moved almost opposite the Coldwater School. Alice was the oldest of the eight Dale children.

"The one person who had the most influence on my life was my teacher at Coldwater - a pretty wisp of an 18-year-old girl named Rose Brier," she said. "She was a quiet girl - very tidy. She customarily wore a shirtwaist and skirt - and always a white apron - always. Her home was in Ferguson but she boarded at the Herman Kamp farm. Her father, a German immigrant who taught at Normandy, also was the county superintendent at one time."

Just prior to the end of the school year Alice's aunt took her to Clayton, the county seat, for the graduation examination. They walked to Florissant, took the street car to Suburban Park in Wellston, and then transferred to a Clayton car. The exams, administered by J. Will Andrae, the county superintendent, covered nine subjects and took all day to complete.

The one room building was small, about 24 feet by 30 feet, but large enough to accommodate 50 or 55 students seated in double desks placed in four rows with aisles between and one on each side. As time went by, seating arrangements were changed as class attendance diminished. In the early days, a pot-bellied stove stood near the center of the front part of the building, surrounded by a metal jacket which acted as a circulator and protected those who sat nearest the stove. At closing time in winter, ink bottles were frequently placed near the stove to keep them from freezing during the night when the fire died down. A large coal box was placed at the right side of the stove. This was filled each evening and held enough coal to replenish the fire during the coming day. Coal, always in generous supply, was kept in a shed at the rear of the school building.

The teacher's desk was on a raised platform or rostrum in the back part of the room. There were few discipline problems - spit balls, pig-tails dipped in ink wells, and most serious, snowballing as pupils dashed along the hard beaten paths to the two important little houses on the opposite corners of the school yard. Some very old timers say that boys and girls were not restricted from attending school because of age - some boys coming with full-grown mustaches, and children at a very early age. They were mostly farm children, and attendance swelled when they were not needed on the farm. This worked a hardship on the teachers but they were patient, gentle and understanding and they were most all loved and respected.

The earliest texts were McGuffy readers, Websters Blue Back spellers, and Ray's arithmetic. Later these were replaced by such texts as agriculture, physiology, Franklin's readers, English grammar, U .S. history, civil government (later known as political science), geography, New Spelling Copy books, and some years the German language was taught. An eighth grade graduate was required to pass an examination in each of the above subjects, except German, which was optional. Much of the work was oral, often by rote, or repetition, and by the time one reached the eighth grade he knew most of the answers. This accounts for the excellent foundation and ability to retain fundamental facts.

After graduation Mrs. Wehmer attended the old Ferguson High School on Wesley Avenue. "Dad paid the $50 tuition. I would walk past the store and post office at Cross Keys and on into Florissant every morning. Then I took the street car to Ferguson. During the dead of winter I would board there."

Mary Lange Stellhorn

In 2016, Mary Lange Stellhorn shared her experiences at both Coldwater and Vossenkemper Schools in the 1940s.[144] (See Chapter 8 for more stories about Mary's family.)

I began attending the one-room Coldwater School in September 1943 as a first grader. No kindergartens back then. There were 37 students in the eight grades that year. In nice weather, I and my neighboring friends walked to school – a 2-1/2 mile hike along Vaile Ave and New Halls Ferry Road.

Christmas and graduation programs were held at Coldwater Hall, now the Eagles' Lodge, at New Halls Ferry Road and Coldwater Creek. The whole school would walk to the hall for rehearsals. In one of the programs, I was Mary as in "Mary had a little lamb." I carried a cloth lamb, probably made by my mother, and my staff was a cane borrowed from a relative. At the graduation ceremonies, two hymns that were always sung were "Come, Thou Almighty King" and "Holy, Holy, Holy", and whenever I sing those in church today, my thoughts always go back to that wonderful old Coldwater School.

Originally, heat came from a pot-bellied stove in the front of the room. But when I attended, there was a furnace in the basement. Our drinking water came from a bucket on a bench in front of the room and everyone used the same dipper to drink from. Restroom facilities were two "outhouses" behind the school – one for the boys and one for the girls.

Recesses were great – swings, see-saws and a wonderful, huge merry-go-round. Roots that extended out from huge trees made dividers for "rooms" for us girls to play house in. In winter, we played "Mother, may I?" in the back of the room.

We entered the school building through an "anteroom" where we hung our coats on hooks along the wall and placed our lunch boxes on shelves. In good weather, we ate our lunch outdoors. A huge bell hung in the bell tower, and it called us into the building at the beginning of school each day and at the end of recesses. At the back of the school building, a room had been added to the original one-room – a library, filled with bookshelves stacked with wonderful books to read.

At the end of the school year, the school board had a picnic for students and their families with such goodies as ice cream, candy, and soda, which were real treats as many of us didn't have those treats available to us at home.

When I was in fifth grade, our family moved to a different farm located on Sinks Road, just across the school boundary line that divided Coldwater from Vossenkemper. So I had to leave dear little Coldwater and my dear friends, some of whom I am still friends with today, and begin attending the big, two-room Vossenkemper School.

At Vossenkemper that year, there were 18 students in the "big room", grades 5-8. My sister and brother were in the "little room," grades 1-4. A number of the students were from families whose fathers worked for the Portland Cement Co. In my graduation class of five, two were Portland boys.

The basement of the building had two big rooms for indoor play, one for the girls and one for the boys. There were indoor plumbing facilities. And I had my own telescoping drinking cup.

Graduations and picnics were combined and held at the Black Jack Hall on Parker Road in Black Jack. Following the afternoon graduation ceremony, there were games of all kinds for adults and kids, and lots of food. In the evening, there was a dance and the community was always welcome.

A pdf file with the 1977 Gregory Franzwa book, "History of the Hazelwood School District," can be accessed on the Hazelwood School District web site. http://www.hazelwoodschools.org/Domain/360

Chapter 7 Photos and Maps

Map 7-1 Google Map SE of Old Halls Ferry and Vaile. Cold Water Cemetery is in clearing in center of tree cover.

Photos 7-1 and 7-2 Cold Water Cemetery -- Drone photos taken by Chan Mahanta

Photo 7-3 Cold Water Cemetery in 2011 -- Photo by Peggy Kruse

Photo 7-4 New Coldwater Burying Ground Memorial Park Cemetery, June 1995. North County Journal

End Note[145]

Photo 7-5 Memorial for Rev. John Clark in Cold Water Cemetery in 2011 -- Photo by Peggy Kruse

Photo 7-6 1834 page in Minutes of Union Meeting House with pledges for furnishing seats. – original at Historic Florissant, Inc.

Photos 7-7 and 7-8 Brown School about 1900 and 1969 -- History of Hazelwood School District,

End Note: [146]

Photo 7-9 Brown School building, now a residence, 2015 Google Map

Photo 7-10 Virena Douglas Chomeau and Anna Belle Smiley Dale – History of Hazelwood School District

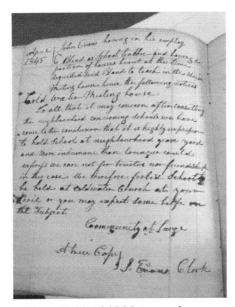
Photo 7-11 1845 Notes and Minutes from Coldwater Church (Union Meeting House), denying use of Coldwater Church for school – original at Historic Florissant, Inc.

Photo 7-12 Coldwater School in 1969 – History of Hazelwood School District

End Note for 7-10 and 7-12[147]

Chapter 8 – Farmers, Immigrants

This chapter has background information about farming in the Old Jamestown area and stories about many individual farmers who came directly from Germany and other countries. At the end is a section on the divided loyalties of Old Jamestown residents during the Civil War.

Attraction of Old Jamestown

The influx of Germans, attracted by the fertile farmland, beginning in the 1840s was funneled into this area through Baden. Many of them came from Bielefeld, a town in the region of Westphalia. So numerous were they that the crossroads community of Black Jack was originally called New Bielefeld. Salem Lutheran Church was a unifying force in the community. … Many Old Jamestown families continue their association with the church, which was officially organized in 1849 as Salem Evangelical Church of New Bielefeld. The German dominance of the region was almost complete by the 1870s.[148]

An early German family was the Rosenkoetters who also had stores/taverns at Cross Keys (Hwy 67 and New Halls Ferry) and Shoveltown (Hwy 67 and Old Halls Ferry). Like many Germans immigrants, about 1840 Rosenkoetter family members boarded ships in Bremen, Germany, and took the two-month trip to New Orleans, then took steam boats for the two-week trip up the Mississippi to Missouri. Many left Germany because of the poor economic conditions at that time and some left to avoid serving in the Prussian military.[149] More on the Rosenkoetters later in this chapter.

Farming in Old Jamestown area

Prices for the same land increased fivefold between 1853 and 1876. Nevertheless many German settlers were able to buy their own – sometimes fairly large – farms.[150]

Descriptions of the Elisha and Lucy Patterson Farmstead in the Application for National Register of Historic Places provide insight into the main means of livelihood that once dominated St. Louis County and the rest of the Midwest.[151]

> The continuous use of the property as a farm by successive generations of the Elisha and Lucy Patterson family demonstrates a typical tradition of settlement; the family provided property and a livelihood for their descendants. Property acquisition and division was a common pattern for ensuring the well-being of family members through successive generations.
>
> The farm's later families, Hoffmeister, Fischer, and Birkemeier, were part of the wave of German settlement that gradually transformed the County in the second half of the nineteenth century. Like the Pattersons, the Birkemeiers owned the property through several generations.
>
> The Patterson Farmstead represents a period when the farm had become fully established. The period of self-sufficient settlement farming had been replaced by cash crop farming. Although the farm had been substantially reduced in size during the period before Fred Fischer bought the property in 1888, the new farming techniques and technologies still provided a profitable livelihood for the owners. Less than fifty acres of land provided over sixty years of income for the Fischer and Birkemeier families.

See more on Elisha and Lucy Patterson in Chapter 5.

The 10 children of Joseph Herman Kohnen (son of Herman and Mary Birkemier Kohnen) and Gertrude Stroer Kohnen (daughter of John W. and Teresa Gettemier Stroer) didn't grow up in Old Jamestown but in nearby Florissant. However, one daughter, Margie Kohnen Hepperman, currently lives with her husband on Sinks Road in the house where they raised their own five children. And one son, John Kohnen, now lives in Parc Argonne. His memories of growing up on a truck farm are probably similar to those of many who lived in Old Jamestown in the 1930s.[152]

> "Growing up on what was known as a truck farm, nearly all of our needs were met by crops and essentials raised on the farm. Other than flour, sugar, salt, yeast, and coffee, nearly everything else was home grown.
>
> "Cash crops included potatoes, sweet potatoes, corn, sweet corn, wheat, alfalfa, tomatoes, turnips, and horseradish. Garden crops included onions, beets, carrots, peas, butter beans, string beans, okra, pickles, strawberries, and grapes. Fruit trees included peach, apple, and cherry. A cow provided milk, hogs were raised for meat, chickens provided eggs and meat. Mules were the draft animals that provided the only assistance other than human labor required to accomplish whatever was needed to be done. We loved all of the animals but the mules were always special, at least they were the only animals to be given names, other than the dogs.
>
> "Everything that was raised on the farm was either sold, fed to the animals, eaten, canned or preserved and stored for the winter. By the fall of the year, the shelves in the basement were lined with mason jars filled with everything that a bountiful harvest provided. Many a day was spent stirring the old copper kettle over an open fire while the apple butter or ketchup cooked to perfection.
>
> "Butchering days in the winter were almost a holiday as the neighbors got together during the day doing the necessary chores and the men played pinochle and drank port wine in the evening. Nearly all of the farmers made their own wine and during Prohibition most made their own beer...." [Making wine for your household was legal during Prohibition; making beer was not.]

Rosenkoetter Family

The Rosenkoetters were a prominent and extensive farm family in north St. Louis County, some of whom lived in Old Jamestown. We learn much about the family's background and activities from the book "From Westphalia Into the World, A Farmer's Family from Westphalia in Search of a Better Future in the U.S.A."[153], from which much of the following is adapted.

> Between 1841 and 1853, the Rosenkoetters traveled from Germany to New Orleans and up the Mississippi river to Black Jack/Spanish Lake north of St. Louis. The voyage from East Westphalia to America was long, troublesome and hard. The closest port was Bremen and emigrants traveled there by small riverboats or with carts and wagons. In Bremen the emigrants had to wait – sometimes for weeks – for the next departure of a ship. The average travel time on a sailing ship from Germany to New Orleans was 59 days. The trip from New Orleans to St. Louis on a steamboat took two weeks.

Johann Heinrich Adolph "Henry" Rosenkoetter and his wife Anne Marie Catherine Fredericke Lindemann were the first Rosenkoetters who immigrated to America. They arrived in New Orleans on June 19, 1841, and eventually lived near Salem Lutheran Church in Black Jack. Many Rosenkoetters who followed Henry also ended up in Black Jack or Spanish Lake. But some bought and farmed land in Old Jamestown.

One Old Jamestown resident was Herman C. (Hermann Karl Gustav) Rosenkoetter, grandson of "Henry's" cousin Herman and Louisa, who arrived with their family in 1843. Herman C. was five years old when his father was killed by the Confederate Army (See Civil War at end of this chapter.) and eleven when he lost his mother. He had two older sisters, but he was the eldest boy in the family and thus responsible for the farm. In 1876 he moved with his step-father William Meyer to Memphis, Tennessee, where Meyer died of yellow fever in 1878. The following year Herman C. returned to St. Louis County, where he worked in a mill for two years and then engaged in the saloon business in Black Jack [Krueger's saloon], ...for four years.

In 1882 he married Miss Eliza Schnitker, a native of Illinois and a daughter of Fred Schnitker, who was born in Germany. In 1885 he purchased a farm in the old Patterson settlement on Old Halls Ferry Road, nearly 200 acres in the northeast of Survey No. 107 D. Brown Heirs. In 1910, he was farming about 300 acres, and specialized in fruit growing. Along with the farm came a big house, the former Douglass house at 15310 Old Halls Ferry Road. (See info about the Tunstall-Douglass house in Chapter 1.)

Herman C. and Eliza had nine children – Fred, Harry, Caroline, Emil, John, Robert, August, Alvin and Aurelia. Herman was active in township politics, served for fifteen years as road supervisor and for thirteen years as a member of the local school board. He was considered a progressive agriculturist and was a member of the St. Ferdinand Farmers Club.

> Daughter Caroline married Henry Krueger who owned a creamery in Black Jack.
>
> Daughter Aurelia married Ed Meyer. They owned a grocery, tavern and feed store in Shoveltown (North Hwy 67 and Old Halls Ferry Road), and lived above the grocery/tavern in a two-story brick building. Ed's brother, August Meyer, operated a Massey-Ferguson farm implement dealership behind Ed's businesses. The feed store is now Kitty's Corner.
>
> Son Harry (1884-1973) became the proprietor of the general merchandise store at Cross Keys -- New Halls Ferry and Hwy 67. He carried everything from general merchandise to farm implements, and was an agent for the International Harvester Company. Harry married Mathilda K. Gerling in 1907.

Other Rosenkoetters who lived in Old Jamestown:

Friedrich Wilhelm "William" Rosenkoetter arrived in New Orleans in 1849. William's wife, Elizabeth Homburg, arrived at New Orleans on board the ship "Julius" in 1852. It was a tragic coming for her. Arriving in St. Louis she faced the recent deaths, from dysentery, of her sister and brother-in-law. It is said her first reaction was to return to Germany. But Elizabeth felt obliged to care for her sister's little children. And, of course, she had come to see her future husband and on November 21, she and William were married.

William bought his first piece of land in 1856, 53.56 acres on Robbins Mill Road (Survey No. 360 Cumberland James). William was known as a good and honest man, and a hard worker. In 1871, William purchased an adjoining piece of property, 52.72 acres, which his descendants knew as Mueller's place. By this time, William and Elizabeth had three children of their own.

Ruegg – Portland Cement Company Town

[Photos 8-1 and 8-2]

Though most mid 1800s immigrants to Old Jamestown came from Germany, some came from other European countries. This story of John Ruegg whose father came from Switzerland is adapted from the 1883 "History of St. Louis County Vol 2." [154]

John H. C. Ruegg, was born in St. Louis on March 16, 1866, to John and Charlotte (Wiese) Ruegg. After coming to the United States, his father, John, Sr., a native of Zurich, Switzerland, worked his way up to superintendent in cotton mills and on his own time developed devices for use in the mills, including a cotton loom that he patented. Although his firm benefited financially from his inventions, he never received any financial reward, but was satisfied with the large salary. In 1870 he and a friend went to Springfield, Missouri, where they established a cotton mill. His partner, however, signed notes and papers in the east most indiscriminately, and as a result their business failed. John Sr. was a poor man when he died in August 1894.

John H. C. Ruegg attended Pea Ridge School near Spanish Lake until he was 14 years old. Despite the fact that his schooling was very limited he would pass anywhere as a well-educated man. A fine mind and scholarly instincts made him a wide reader and close observer, who possessed a large fund of useful information. At 14 he began working for grocers in St. Louis for 12 years. In 1895 he and his brother-in-law, Henry Borgman, purchased the business of Ferdinand J. H. Hartwig in Black Jack. It was a successful business that they sold in 1910 to Otto and Frank Hartwig.

In 1900 Ruegg married Fredericka Huhs, daughter of Henry Huhs, who was born in Germany and was one of the pioneer settlers of St. Louis County. They had an adopted son, John H. W.

In 1903 Ruegg and his partner established a branch store at the eastern end of Old Jamestown on the site of the Portland Cement Company's quarry. Mr. Ruegg became postmaster of the new town, known as Ruegg Post Office [which operated from 1905 to 1938[155]]. The village had at least nineteen houses and became a thriving settlement. In 1911 Mr. Ruegg sold his interest in the business there and focused on cultivating his farm.

In 1898 John Ruegg ran for the office of justice of the peace. He won the election in spite of a large opposition and held the office for twelve years, during which time he had a reputation as a man who upheld the law and enforced it regardless of the position or influence which the offender might have. He strove to make his a court of justice, using the law to protect the innocent rather than the unscrupulous. As a result he rid this section of the county of many undesirable characters, having arrested and brought to justice three horse thieves in one year. If there was an arrest to be made and the constable was not available Mr. Ruegg went in his official capacity and captured the offender. He paid careful attention to the enforcement of the speed law and never hesitated to arrest and fine to the limit any man whom he found running an automobile at an excessive rate of speed. Mr. Ruegg then became deputy constable. In 1910 he was appointed census taker. In addition to his other interests he was a stockholder in the Baden Bank.

Others

Robbins

Many wonder about the origin of the name Robbins Mill Road, which Hwy 67 was once named and a short stretch of which still exists east of Old Jamestown Road and north of Hwy 67.

The 1868 Pitzman Atlas shows property owned by "Wel. Robbins" at what is believed to have been Robbins Mill. Carlene Randolph who currently lives nearby said she had been told the mill was on the property that is now 6405 N. Hwy 67. She said there is a spring there and it still keeps a pond and creek filled with water.

Several properties in and near Old Jamestown were purchased by Welcome A. Robbins and his brother Frederick Robbins about 1840. While we don't have much information about Welcome Robbins in Old Jamestown, we learn a bit about him in the history of St. Charles County, where he had a home. From the First Capitol News Archives:[156]

> "In 1833 Robbins bought the home of John Orrick at 701 North Third Street in St. Charles in 1833. Captain Orrick was in the mercantile business and piloted the packet* Fayaway from here to St. Louis and back three times a week. This three story handmade brick home featured fireplaces in each of the 12 rooms and an ice cellar for food preservation.

> ".... Welcome and his brother Frederick constructed the extravagant marble and stone Robbins Tomb at Oak Grove Cemetery in 1865. It measures 900-sq. ft. and contains five iron, alcohol-filled caskets with glass face window plates. This unusual Pioneer burial technique eliminated the need for embalming. Mourning family members could also visit the tomb and view the faces of their departed loved ones."

> [*packet: a river or coastal steamer usually of shallow draft carrying mail, passengers, and cargo on a regular run[157]]

Welcome's father, Major Moses B. Robbins of Revolutionary War fame died in 1810 in Portage Des Sioux and is buried in Black Walnut Cemetery, just across the Missouri River from Musick's Ferry.

Veale/Vaile

[Photos 8-3 and 8-4]

So…..Patterson Road was the route from Old Town Florissant to the Patterson family properties. How about Vaile Avenue, which extends Patterson across New Halls Ferry to Old Jamestown Road? The most likely explanation is that it was the route to Jacob Veale's home. Vaile is an alternative spelling for Veale. Jacob owned several large tracts of land in Old Jamestown.

Findagrave.com provides some background on Jacob:[158]

> In 1840, Jacob Veale (1818-1886) married Lydia Patterson (1822-1910), daughter of William and Assenath Piggott Patterson and granddaughter of John and Keziah Hornaday Patterson. Jacob had been born to prosperous farmers in Cornwall, England, and came to the U.S. with his family as a two-year-old in 1820.
>
> After landing in Baltimore, the Veale family moved to Pike County, Missouri, where they intended to settle. However, soon after arriving in Pike County, Jacob's parents died of a mysterious black tongue disease.* Jacob and his brothers and sister were raised by a guardian and an executor. As a youth, Jacob went to Texas and then went back to England to claim an inheritance from his grandfather. He returned to the U.S. and settled in Old Jamestown. (John Patterson's brother, William, had moved to Pike County in 1817 and 'may' have told the Veales about the family's settlement in Old Jamestown.)
>
> After Lydia's mother Assenath was widowed in 1860, she lived with Lydia and Jacob. Sometime after her death in 1878, Jacob and Lydia moved to Barton County in southwest Missouri (birthplace of Harry Truman) where he bought and farmed more than 700 acres of farmland and where they are both buried.
>
> [*Black tongue disease: Black Tongue, which occurred anywhere that diets consisted almost entirely of corn, was perhaps the most acute vitamin deficiency the United States has known. The affliction caused diarrhea, mental confusion, loss of weight and strength, irritation inside the mouth and stomach lining, and painful lesions of the skin, especially areas exposed to sunlight. The affected tissue would darken, thicken, and become scaly; cases were some-times misdiagnosed as leprosy. Symptoms could progress to depression, stupor, and an irrational violence. Until foods containing niacin were determined a cure, as many as two of every three Black Tongue patients died of its effects. http://ncpedia.org/black-tongue]

Another Veale–Patterson connection: Jacob Veale's sister Mary was seven years old when the family came to the U.S. In 1829, she married Lewis James, son of Morris James and Cathy Sullivan. Lewis died not long after. In 1831 she married Joseph Patterson, brother of Lydia Patterson Veale. The marriage ceremony was performed by Rev. John Clark.

Buenger

[Photos 8-5, 8-6, and 8-7]

Buenger family members were longtime farmers in Old Jamestown and owned at least two historic houses.

One Buenger family house was at 14 Jamestown Farm Drive, which was described by Esley Hamilton in an historic inventory form from which this is adapted.[159]

The property was purchased in 1868 by William Buenger (1830-1899), a native of Germany, when the James Clemens, Jr., property was subdivided. James Clemens, Jr., was a St. Louis businessman, a relation of Mark Twain, and a son-in-law of John Mullanphy, St. Louis' first millionaire. Mullanphy purchased the land and gave it to his daughter and son-in-law. The land had previously been a Spanish land grant to Guy Seeley. (See more on Guy Seeley and James Clemens in Chapter 3)

William Buenger bought lots 13, 14, 23 and 24, and increased his farm in the early 1880s with 2 more lots bought from Clemens' children and 2 nearby tracts which brought his total to about 280 acres, a good amount for the time. Buenger's Clemens tract remained intact until 1978, when it was subdivided as Jamestown Farms.

The existing Buenger Farmstead on 17790 Old Jamestown Road is one of the very last farmsteads still possessing a house, barn, and other farm buildings though they are all now vacant. It was described in a November 15, 2011, letter written by Ron Buenger to St. Louis County, after a concern by someone else that the buildings were a problem.[160] The current farmstead is on 4 acres. 45 acres were sold to Behlmann Properties in 1987 and now comprise Parc Argonne Estates.

It is believed that this house was built in the early 1800s. There are two main original interior rooms of log construction, with the entire house covered with aged weather boards. The noticeable roof sag is a result of the fact the roof rafters are actual tree saplings that were cut from the woods in the local area. The appearance of the roof has remained unchanged during my lifetime at the property, some 68+ years. As recently as 2008, my son and I both scaled the entire roof and covered it with new roll roofing.

Henry Buenger, my grandfather, purchased the property in 1920 and raised four sons there, including my Dad. Two of those boys were born inside this very house. My wife and I built our current home directly across the county road from the farmstead in 1964 and intend to reside here for the rest of our lives. Our two sons, also both built homes in 2000, on lots across the street from the farmstead and are raising the fifth generation of the Buenger Family to live on this very ground. As a result, the existing homestead is of very significant sentimental and historic value to our family. We treasure the view of the homestead.

Meyer

St. Ferdinand Township had many residents with the Meyer surname. These are the stories of just a few of them, two who lived in Old Jamestown and one who lived in or near Old Jamestown.

The story of Charles Meyer was adapted from Volume 2 of the 1911 "The History of St. Louis County, Missouri":[161] Charles W. Meyer was born on what is known as the "Meyer Farm" (Morris James land grant, Survey 1960) in 1867, a son of Charles and Louisa Buenger Meyer. The farm had been purchased by his grandfather, Henry Meyer, shortly after his arrival in the United States in 1840. Because of his father's early death Charles W. Meyer left school when he was twelve years to become a wage earner. He left home, barefooted and with but one suit of clothing, to enter the employ of his uncle, William Buenger (Louisa's brother), a farmer who lived in Old Jamestown. He continued to work for him and other farmers in the township for several years. After his marriage he rented the farm of his mother-in-law, containing one hundred and forty-five acres of excellent land. Despite the fact that his schooling was limited to a few months' attendance prior to his leaving home, Mr. Meyer is anything but an uneducated man. A desire for knowledge prompted him to read and study at night after the long, arduous, physically taxing duties of the day had been discharged, and as a result he is well posted on current events, thinks clearly and decisively and expresses himself intelligently on all subjects of the day.   In 1892, Charles Meyer married Annie Haltmann, a daughter of Henry and Minnie (Wolff) Haltmann and an adopted daughter of William Buenger. They had five children: Emma, Louis, Edwin, Fred and Clarence.   Meyer was a member of the school board. A lover of outdoor life and hunting and fishing, he enjoyed a day in the woods with a rod or gun, and whenever he could spare the time from his farm indulged in such recreation, always returning with a nice bag of game or string of fish.

The history of the Meyer-Lindemann-Kahre House, 6700 Robbins Mill Road, constructed in 1857, has lots of familiar names, including Meyer. According to Esley Hamilton, longtime St. Louis County historian, the land on which the house stands was originally set aside for the benefit of the public schools. A 55-acre tract was sold to Lewis Patterson June 10, 1844, and he sold it two months later to Jacob Veale. Jacob and his wife Lydia Patterson Veale sold a 2.76 acre parcel in 1857 to Henry C. Meyer, who in 1855 had bought about 77 acres on the north side of Robbins Mill Road and east of New Jamestown Road. He paid $90.40 for this site and probably constructed the house soon thereafter. Tradition holds that Adolph Lindemann constructed the building's foundation using quick-lime mortar. In 1864 he bought the house and four larger pieces of land from Meyer for $7,000. Lindemann's daughter Wilhelmina married Henry George Kahre, the son of a neighbor and sometime between 1878 and 1893 the estate passed to them. Henry Kahre died in 1931 leaving his farm to his son Henry, Jr., who kept it until his death in 1970.[162]

It is not clear whether Herman Meyer ever lived or worked within the Old Jamestown boundaries but he lived close and had a unique, adventurous life so he is included here for interest. According to Volume 2 of the 1911 "The History of St. Louis County Missouri," Herman Meyer (1817-1887) was a successful farmer and a thorough business man, acquiring through his own exertions one of the most valuable farms in St. Ferdinand Township. At the age of 35 he came to St. Louis County from Germany and worked as a farm hand for three years. A great gold excitement was sweeping through the country and Herman joined a party that was crossing the plains for the Pacific coast. It took them six months to reach California. He was more fortunate than a majority of the gold seekers. After four years, he went aboard a ship at San Francisco and sailed around the Horn, landing at New Orleans, and then came up the Mississippi on a steamboat. Back in St. Louis County he purchased forty acres in St. Ferdinand township. From time to time he purchased land until he owned three hundred acres. In 1851 Mr. Meyer married Mary Ann, daughter of John H. and Mary Z. (Rickers) Schutte, and they had eight children: Barney, John Henry, Mary, Herman, William, John, Herman and Maggie. John inherited the farm and continued to work it.[163]

Wehmer

[Photo 8-8 and Photos with Appendix 10]

Descendants of Henry Wehmer have been a major part of the community and continue to live in Old Jamestown. Adapted from the 1911 The History of St. Louis County Missouri:164 Henry Wehmer was born in Prussia, Germany, in 1852. His parents passed away while he was yet a very small boy and he was reared in the family of Henry Niemeyer of Prussia, where he lived until at age 15 he came to the United States with a neighbor, locating in St. Louis, where he worked in a grocery store for a year. He then went to the country and for eight years worked as a farm hand. In 1876 Wehmer married Sophia Marie Louise Buhrmeister, also a native of Prussia and a former schoolmate of Wehmer, who had immigrated in 1867 to Washington County, Illinois with her parents. After his marriage he rented and farmed land on Douglas Road. A few years after the 1900 death of her husband, Sophia Wehmer and her family moved to their home on 40 acres adjoining the land he had previously rented. Henry and Sophia had eight children: Carrie, Edward, Fred, Henry (a stationary engineer of St. Louis), Louis (employed by Norman Shapleigh Hardware Company of St. Louis), Paul, Esther and Emily.

One grandson of Henry Wehmer was Norman, son of Henry. Norman and his wife Kelly still live near the Douglas Road home and are active in the community.

Other grandsons were Jim and Ralph Wehmer, two of the four sons of Louis and Aurelia Thompson Wehmer. Louis was a farmer and helped his father-in-law James Thompson work the threshing machine. Aurelia was a descendant of Walter Carrico (1818-1868). Aurelia shared her stories of Brown School with Gregory Franzwa for his "History of the Hazelwood School District." (See Chapter 7.)

Jim Wehmer was an agriculture graduate from the University of Missouri and was a Marine Corps night fighter pilot in the South Pacific during World War II. He was also on the School Board when Hazelwood School District organized and served as President for several years. A 1947 ©St. Louis Post-Dispatch article featured Jim and his father, Louis, using terracer equipment to create terraces on their farm to prevent soil erosion (See Chapter 10)[165].

Ralph's own very interesting stories of growing up in Old Jamestown were told shortly before his death to Olga Smith who was a BJC Hospice Lumina Project Volunteer.[166] Here are just a few of them: See Chapter 7 for Ralph's story of assisting a pilot during a Brown School recess. See Appendix 10 for all of Ralph Wehmer's stories with photos.

> "I have so many stories to tell you. Where do I begin? Well, I was born in a log cabin, one mile down from this house [Old Jamestown Road and Carrico Road]. Back then, our street was called Accommodation Road, and it was a dirt road. Now, the street is called Old Jamestown Road.

> "Growing up, my brothers and I would ride a corn grinder and it would go round and round like a merry-go-round. One afternoon, my brother and I were riding on it and Ed came out of the house and yelled at us: "Do not put your hands in there! Next thing I knew, I put my hand in the grinder and I lost part of my finger. Boy, did I cry -- for hours. Because the nearest doctor was in Florissant, we drove our Model-T car. Because the road was dirt, we hitched it to a team of mules and we headed down the street to Salem Baptist Church with the reins through the windshield opening. We left the mules at the church and drove on into Florissant to the doctor's office. Every time we went to the doctor's, this is how we traveled. I can even remember my doctor's name, Dr. Milmann.

> "At the age of 19, I earned a job at the Florissant Post Office, as a postal clerk and worked at that for 11 years. [Al Pondrom] was the Post Master. After that, I was a Rural Mail Carrier for 25 years. I truly enjoyed that job, because of all of the people that I met. I once received Missouri's Outstanding Rural Letter Carrier Award.

> "I will tell you that my brother Jim was a really honest person. He worked for Riverview Stone and Material for years. While working, his boss asked him, 'What are you paying those African American drivers?' Jim told him that he was paying them the same as the white men. And, his boss went on to say that he should dock the African American's pay. Well, Jim disagreed and said, 'No' and quit. He walked out of the office (and he had 12 kids!), but he disagreed with things like that. The Lord works in mysterious ways, because shortly after he quit, Jim found a job at Westlake Quarry with a better salary."

In 1943 Ralph married Rosemary Fuqua. Their oldest daughter, Susan Wehmer Kagy, lives on Wehmer Estates Drive in what began as the Louis Nolte summer home. Louis Nolte was the comptroller for the City of St. Louis. He built the lodge as a hunting and fishing retreat using materials & employees from the City. It was like a park and the public was allowed to have picnics on the lakeside. The Roosevelt era WPA (Works Progress Administration) appropriated funds for the project. The original building had no bedrooms but did have two murphy beds in a closet on the sun porch. It was built at the same time, with the same stone, as the Fort Bellefontaine bathhouses & staircase.

Susan's daughter Jennifer Welch Cudnik and her family live in the same home. See Chapter 9 for more about Jennifer and her husband, Christian Cudnik.

Many current subdivisions - Shamblin, Fountainebleu, Old Jamestown Estates, Afshari Estates, Wehmer Estates - are on land once owned by Wehmer family members. Joseph Afshari, home developer in Old Jamestown, built his home in the Afshari subdivision on the same spot as the log cabin in which Ralph Wehmer was born.

Thompson

[Photo 8-9]

Adapted from Volume 2 of History of St. Louis County Missouri by William L. Thomas, 1911[167]

> Aurelia Thompson Wehmer's father was James Thompson who was born in Glascow, Scotland, in 1843, son of Robert and Margaret Thompson. When he was two years old, he came to the United States with his mother, two brothers and one sister. His mother died six years later, leaving James an orphan. He remained in St. Louis until he was ten when he was taken by a farmer, Stokes Thorp, who was also a dealer in hides and furs on the corner of Commercial alley and Walnut Street. He remained a member of Mr. Thorp's household for five years and then went to an uncle in Stillwater, Minnesota. There he learned the machinists' trade and stationary engineering. Returning to St. Louis in 1860 he worked for another uncle, who was a lithographer, didn't like the work and soon went to the country.
>
> During the next two years he worked as a farm hand, and while in the field one day he was placed under arrest by an officer of the Missouri militia, on the charge of being a southern sympathizer. Despite his denials he was imprisoned for two months, at the end of which time he was found not guilty and discharged.

For five years Thompson worked at various occupations, all of them along agricultural lines. In 1877 his wife inherited forty-seven acres. He bought another sixty acres, but in 1908, he lost seventy acres of his land, through the Missouri River changing its course.

Before acquiring his homestead he began running a threshing machine, being among the first to engage in that activity in the county. The competition was very keen but he kept his customers and had all that he could do during the entire season because he has a well established reputation.

Margaret Carrico, James Thompson's wife, was born in July 1849. Her parents, Walter and Louisa (Downs) Carrico, owned and lived on the farm adjoining James Thompson's property. After their marriage in 1869, the Thompsons had 10 children. Those living in 1911 were: Eveline, wife of Julius Warren, an engineer for the Portland Cement Works; Margaret L., wife of John Patterson, a farmer; Amanda V., the wife of Otto Harder; Gilbert, husband of Grace Pritchard; Silas H., husband of Betty Hume; Sarah A., wife of Horace Wagner; Aurelia, later wife of Louis Wehmer; and Elmer L. Elmer and his wife, Marcella, lived in the Thompson homestead on Carrico Road. The family was active with nearby Salem Baptist Church.

Gerling/Albers

Don Gerling grew up in Old Jamestown and shared some history about his grandfather (Charles) and his brothers.

Three Gerling brothers had homes and property in Old Jamestown in the late 1800s – Henry, Charles, and Frederick. Another brother was killed in a wagon accident in 1868. Their father, Frederick Gerling, Sr., and his wife, Louisa Korte Gerling, had immigrated to Florissant from Minden Germany in 1856 and owned a 100 acre farm near Old Halls Ferry and Robbins Mill (now Hwy 67).

Henry Gerling owned several hundred acres of farmland and his home on Robbins Mill (now Hwy 67) near Old Halls Ferry. His daughter Matthilda married Harry Rosenkoetter in 1907 and they rented the farm from her father until 1914 when they opened the Rosenkoetter general store at Cross Keys.

[Photos 8-10, 8-11, and 8-12]

Charles H. and Caroline Niehaus Gerling purchased a 60 acre farm on Shackelford in 1892, which he gave to his son Louie (Franz Heinrich Ludwig) and his wife Ella in the early 1920s. This land is now Lexington Farms.

Charles also purchased 90 acres on New Halls Ferry (now next to the Boeing property) and gave it to his daughter Alvina (Alwine Louise Marie) and her husband Charles 'Carl' Albers in 1906. Alvina and Carl were married in 1904 and had three children: Carl, Edna, and Hilda. Two nephews, Martin and Otto, also lived with them on their farm.[168]

Hilda Albers Kuhn, who was a longtime leader of the Triple C (Coldwater Community) 4-H Club, was the last survivor of the Charles Albers family and inherited all the land. After her death it was sold and the proceeds used for a charitable foundation.[169]

Frederick Gerling, Jr., fought in the Civil War on the Union side. He was married to Anna Marie "Louise" Rosenkoetter, daughter of Friedrich Wilhelm "Adolph" and Anne Marie Wilhelmine "Charlotte" Homburg Rosenkoetter. Louise was four years old when her family immigrated to the U.S. in 1850. Frederick and Louise settled in Shoveltown at Old Halls Ferry and Robbins Mill (now Hwy 67) and along the road leading to the Sinks. They had eight children.[170]

Leber

The Pitzman 1868 Atlas shows 78 acres owned by John Leber on Robbins Mill. This is most likely Johannes Leber (1820-1877), who was married to Louise Hoffmeister (1831-1889). The Leber house on the property was torn down in the late 1970s by the Randolph family who then owned the property.

[Photo 8-13]

John Leber was a member of the school board in 1874 when it purchased land for the Vossenkemper School from Henry and Henrietta Hoffmeister Vossenkemper.

A Calico Jam article about Black Jack includes information about a "Carl Leber." Given the exact birth and death years and mention of a large farm, it is very possible Carl is another name for Johannes Leber's father, Alexander Leber, a blacksmith who came from Germany with his wife and children in 1836: "The blacksmith shop was owned by Carl Leber whose life spanned the period from 1792 to 1865. His brother soon joined him in the shop and Carl acquired a large farm in the area. A descendant of Leber relates when Leber acquired the farm he also acquired the black family of Mrs. Lily Winston Garth. Children of both families were educated by private tutors on the farm, and the children spoke both English and German."[171]

Lange

[Photos 8-14, 8-15, 8-16, and 8-17]

Gene and Mary Lange Stellhorn have lived on Douglas Road in the Musick's Ferry community since 1962 and raised their two children there – Gena and Glen. Their home was built by Mary's uncle and aunt, Orville and Frieda Lange, following Orville's return from the Navy in World War 2.

In an August 2013 interview, Gene and Mary shared some of their many memories of Old Jamestown:[172]

> "Gene was born in Nebraska and grew up near Old Halls Ferry and Hwy 66 (now Dunn Road). His family rented and farmed the land. When they started, there were lots of ditches on the land which were leveled when his dad got a tractor with a loader. They planted wheat and corn crops.
>
> "Gene's dad was Art of Art's Lawn Mower Shop in Black Jack. After he leveled the ditches on the land he was farming, he began repairing lawn mowers in his barn. He had access to lathes at his job at Keasbey and Mattison Co. on St. Cyr Road and used them to build clutches. He attached a clutch and a gasoline-powered washing machine motor to a reel-type lawn mower, converting it into a power mower. His neighbors soon wanted a power mower also. He built 75 power mowers for neighbors and friends. In 1951, Toro asked him to be a dealer and Art's Lawn Mower Shop was born. Art also was one of the first paid firemen for the Black Jack Fire

District. Gene's brothers eventually took over the lawn mower business, and it continues today at its location in Black Jack.

"Mary's parents, Earl Lange and Wilma Witte, were married in 1934 and had three children - Mary, Susan, and Melvin. As newlyweds, the Langes moved to a farm on Vaile Avenue that is now the Talisman subdivision. They rented and farmed the 70-acre property. They, too, had to fill in many ditches to make it useful to raise hay, corn, and wheat crops, orchards, and dairy cows.

"Mary's family also rented and farmed land owned by the Lemkemann family, which is now Sioux Passage Park. When it was threshing time, aunts and uncles would all show up to help, as they did for applebutter cooking, and beef and hog butchering. Mary says, "It was great!"

"In December 1946, when Mary was 9 years old, her parents bought farm property on Sinks Road. Following her dad's death resulting from cancer complications in 1953, Laclede Gas bought the 100-acre farm from her mom. (See Chapter 10 for more information about the Laclede Gas property and underground storage on Sinks.)

"Mary's widowed great-grandmother, Sophie Schnatzmeyer, married George Rau who owned property at the northeast corner of Old Jamestown and Hwy 67. Mr. Rau eventually sold off much of the property, and his son, Ed, became owner of ten acres on Old Jamestown just north of Hwy 67. After selling the Sinks Road farm to Laclede, Mary's mom bought the acreage from Uncle Ed, and built a house on it where she lived for the next fifty years. Her in-laws, Ed and Rosie Lange, sister of Uncle Ed, lived next door in a small house built on the property in the early 1900s. Mary's sister, Susan, married Ken Meyer, and they also built a house on the other side of the "little house". Ken's parents, Louie and Loretta, owned and operated a Standard service station for 27 years on the southeast corner of Hwy 67 and Old Halls Ferry Road in Shoveltown. Mary's brother, Mel, married a girl whose family's home was adjacent to the Lange's property. He and Connie raised their family in a house next to Mill Creek on Old Jamestown Road on acreage that had been part of the Lange's original farm home on Vaile."

Mary started school at Coldwater School, the one-room school house on New Halls Ferry Road. When the family moved to Sinks, she had to attend Vossenkemper School which was where Jamestown Mall is now. (See Mary's school memories in Chapter 7.)

Mary joined the Triple C's (Coldwater Community Club) 4-H Club in her teens. Hilda Albers organized the club in the 1930s – Hilda had the girls, Louis Wehmer, Jr., had the boys. Projects included canning, sewing, cooking, crafts, raising sweet corn, horsemanship, and woodworking. There were county-wide Achievement Days where projects were displayed and judged. Winning entries were then exhibited at the Missouri State Fair in Sedalia. Later, local Achievement Days were also held at Sioux Passage Park. Hilda led the club for more than 40 years. Following her retirement, other leaders were Rosemary Wehmer, Kathleen Newcombe, Mary Stellhorn, Connie Morgan, and Carolyn Rubsam.

Mary said she was told that "Shoveltown" at Old Halls Ferry and Hwy 67 got its name because when mud caused problems for vehicles trying to drive through that location, the neighbors came out with shovels to dig them out and get them on their way. Others have heard that it was named Shoveltown because there was once a fight with people using shovels. Of course, it's possible that residents came out to help and one time there was a fight.

Niehaus

Glen Niehaus who lives on Sinks Road recently retired….he is the last of the Niehaus carpenters.

Glen's great grandfather, Herman Niehaus (1884-1967), was one of the 11 children of Herman Henry Harmon Niehaus (1852-1908), who came to St. Louis County from Germany in 1867, and Marie "Mary" Gerling Niehaus (1852-1920), who arrived from Germany in 1856.

Herman married Caroline Kamp (1885-1973) in 1907 and they had three sons, Harvey Heinrich Herman, Elmer August, and Harold Edward. He built many homes in Old Jamestown. Members of his family were also carpenters.

Biographies of several more Old Jamestown area farmers (Gerbes, Jacobsmeyer, Pondrom, Eggert, Schutte, Grueninger, Lindemann, Nolte) are available in Volume 2 of The History of St. Louis County Missouri by William L. Thomas, 1911 http://cdm.sos.mo.gov/cdm/ref/collection/mocohist/id/11452]

Slavery and Divided Loyalties during Civil War

Cindy Winkler, Old Jamestown Association History Committee member researched records for the Civil War years in Old Jamestown and gave a presentation to the Old Jamestown Association meeting in May 2012, from which this is adapted.[173] See much more of Cindy's report on the impact of Slavery and the Civil War on Old Jamestown in Appendix 8.

> There were slaves in Old Jamestown for many years before the Civil War, some of whom came with the original land grantees. The 1860 Slave Schedules list the names of the slave owners, not the names of the slaves but they do list the slaves' ages, sex, whether black or mulatto, whether there were any slaves 'fugitive from the state,' the number manumitted (freed), and the number of slave houses. Those related to Old Jamestown show a total of 148 slaves, 31 slave owners, and 37 slave houses. (See Chapter 7 for speculation about an underground railroad operation at Musick's Ferry.)
>
> Reuben Musick (Chapter 6, Musick's Ferry) owned 12 slaves and had three slave houses. Michael Cerre (1803-1860)'s estate was shown on the 1860 Slave Schedule as owning one male slave, 60 years old. Mr. Cerre's will also includes reference to "A Negro man named Frank, around 60 years old." Cerre's family was Creole, and probably had been in the middle Mississippi River valley area since the 1750s. He had a paternal aunt married to Auguste Chouteau, and another married to Antoine Soulard. Soulard surveyed a large portion of St. Louis in its early settlement days, including the Old Jamestown area.
>
> Missouri did secede from the Union….or maybe it would be better to say that we were admitted into the Confederate States of America in November of 1861. Only the Confederate-sympathizing portion of the Missouri government seceded. The loyal Union portion of the state remained a part of the United States of America. It must have been a very confusing time to be a Missouri resident – and politician.
>
> Martial Law (Military Rule) was declared in St. Louis on August 14th, 1861.[174] And a Provost Marshal was in charge of the military rule. Citizens would report their neighbors as suspected secessionists to the Provost Marshal who would then investigate and arrest people.

An example of families being at complete odds during the war was the difference between Durrett and Lewis Patterson. Durrett Patterson, whose land was in or near Musick's Ferry, was a slaveholder. He was a son of Elisha and Lucy Patterson, and a grandson of John Patterson, Sr. Durrett had a rap sheet with the Provost Marshal. Durrett's brother, Lewis Patterson, on the other hand, gave a statement against a Reuben Carrico, alleging Reuben is a 'notorious rebel.' Reuben had to pay $1,000 bond and swear an oath of loyalty to be released from prison.

In the 1911 History of St. Louis County it was reported that James Thompson worked as a farm hand, and while in the field one day he was placed under arrest by an officer of the Missouri militia, on the charge of being a southern sympathizer. Despite his denials he was imprisoned for two months, at the end of which time he was found not guilty and discharged. (See more on James Thompson above.)

Henry C. Rosenkoetter's father, Henry [Casper Heinrich Samuel] was a farmer working his homestead when the call came for troops. "As a member of the fourth Missouri Cavalry, which he joined at the outbreak of the Civil War, he served three years and was given an honorable discharge. He returned home for a week and then rejoined his regiment. About six weeks later, while a member of a scouting expedition, he fell into the hands of the enemy at Union City, Tenn. They demanded his surrender; he refused and was shot to death on the 10th of July, 1863."[175] Henry's widow later married William Meyer. (See more on the Rosenkoetter family above.)

The Emancipation Proclamation did not free the slaves of states that did not officially secede. Freedom from bondage came with the 13th Amendment to the Constitution, which took effect in December 1865.

Some local stories:

Don Gerling, former Old Jamestown resident shared some Gerling family stories about the time of the Civil War. The Abraham Lincoln and Stephen Douglas debate was in Alton Illinois in 1858. Don says a group of people from Old Jamestown went to the event and probably got to shake Lincoln's and/or Douglas's hand or at least get close to them. Lincoln was only a U.S. legislator then and the security was probably not very strict -- the event took place in the fall, which made it easy for farmers to attend.[176]

According to Salem Lutheran Church's 1974 125th anniversary directory, ".... Shortly after the close of the regular Sunday service on April 9, 1865, news of the War's end reached the Church via horseback rider from the telegraph office in Ferguson. The elated members re-entered the Sanctuary and held an impromptu service of Prayer and Thanksgiving."

Chapter 8 Photos

Photo 8-1 Ruegg Post Office at Portland Cement Facility– George A. Warren Collection, Missouri History Museum of St. Louis

Photo 8-2 Workers at Portland Cement Facility – George A. Warren Collection, Missouri History Museum of St. Louis

Photo 8-3 Jacob Veale – findagrave.com

Photo 8-4 Jacob Veale tombstone – findagrave.com

Photos 8-5 and 8-6 – Buenger Farmstead Old Jamestown at Vaile 2014 -- Photos by Bev Girardier

Photo 8-7 Buenger Farmstead
Old Jamestown at Vaile 2016 --
Drone Photo by Chan Mahanta

Photo 8-8 Henry Wehmer, Photo 8-9 James Thompson
1909 Plat Book St. Louis County
Scans by History Museum of St. Louis

Photo 8-10 Charles Gerling House – 1909 Plat Book, St. Louis County, Scan by Missouri History Museum of St. Louis

Photo 8-11 Charles and Alvina Gerling Albers Wedding – Photo shared by Lois Farley, friend of Hilda Albers

Photo 8-12 Hilda Albers on Family Farm New Halls Ferry north of Shackelford – ©St. Louis Post-Dispatch July 1941, 1992, and 1998

End Note for 8-12[177]

Photo 8-13 Former John Leber House on Robbins Mill – Photo shared by Carlene Randolph

Photo 8-14 Cold Water Inn Hwy 99 (now 367) and Robbins Mill Road – Postcard shared by Lois Hoffman

Photo 8-15 Esther Lampe, Norma Witte, Selma Hartwig, Mildred Trampe, and Wilma Witte on Niehaus Farm overlooking Missouri River – Photo shared by Mary Lange Stellhorn

Photo 8-16 Earl and Wilma Witte Lange on Dr. Vilray Blair's farm on Portage Road in the 1930s (Earl worked for Dr. Blair.)
Photo 8-17 Earl Lange in his car on newly constructed Hwy 99 (367) bridge over Coldwater Creek in early 1930s
Photos shared by Mary Lange Stellhorn

Chapter 9 – Prominent Residents

Attraction of Old Jamestown.

As had American Indians and settlers before them, the wealthy recognized the Missouri River bluffs' wonderful environment. Those who could afford magnificent river estates began coming to Old Jamestown in the 1920s, 30s, and 40s, as roads and cars made it easier to travel so far from the centers of commerce.[178] The largest estates were located on the west at Musick's Ferry,(Desloge), in the center at Sioux Passage Park (Curlee) and on the east at the site of Phinehas James' plan for "James Town" (Mesker).

Desloge Family -- Vouziers Mansion

[Photos 9-1 and 9-2, Map 9-1]

The Desloge Vouziers Mansion on New Halls Ferry at Shackelford was built by Joseph Desloge, Sr., who owned hundreds of acres in and near Old Jamestown. Desloge descendants still own property in the Musick's Ferry area.

Joseph's grandfather, Firmin Rene Desloge (1803-1856), came from France to Ste Genevieve, Missouri, in 1823. Firmin Rene's son, Firmin Desloge (1843-1929), founded Desloge Lead Company in St. Francois County in 1873, and amassed a fortune. Joseph was born in 1889, served with the French artillery in World War I and received an award (Croix de Guerre) for defending the town of Vouziers in France.

In 1919 Joseph bought a large tract of land near the intersection of what is now New Halls Ferry and Shackelford roads and commissioned New Orleans architect Dennis McDonald to design a Louis XVI-style chateau, which he named Vouziers. The ten-bedroom, four-story manor was completed in 1926. A 4,000-square-foot ballroom, built into the hillside, is connected to a parking area through an underground tunnel. Joseph Sr. had four children who grew up in Vouziers and several raised their own families on adjacent properties. The family was active in the St. Louis social scene and his daughter Anne was a Veiled Prophet queen in 1946.

The property was sold in 1977 to Hal Kroeger who used the carriage house for his business and sold it in 1996 to McDonnell Douglas (now Boeing) for its Leadership Center. In 1992 Hal Kroeger talked about his property in a ©St. Louis Post-Dispatch article: "As he tours his estate…pointing out vistas of the Missouri River, downtown St. Louis and the Gateway Arch, the agricultural delta of St. Charles County, the distant bluffs of the Mississippi River – he adds quietly, 'The spirit of Vouziers is one of people coming together.'"[179] And even today people gather from all over the world to attend classes, meetings and other events' at the leadership center built by Boeing.

[Photo 9-3]

Another house on eastern side of New Halls Ferry was built by Desloge about 1930 or 1940. Building materials for the house were left over from other construction. Joseph Desloge, Sr., kept his horses in a barn and the family went riding from there. At one time Mr. Schuyler, employed by the Desloges to care for their horses, lived in the house with his daughter, Mary Alice and it was rented to others over the years.[180] [It is possible that Frazier Vincent's family (Chapter 7) was the first to live in the house.]

Three children of Joseph Desloge, Sr., donated 3/5 of Pelican Island to St. Louis County and the County received a federal grant to purchase the remainder. The County later turned the island over to Missouri Department of Conservation, which now owns it. The expectation of both the County and the Conservation Department was that foot access to the island from the mainland would be built but that has not yet happened (the island can be accessed on foot when the river is very low). See more about Pelican Island in Chapter 10.

See Appendix 10 for comprehensive newspaper articles about Vouziers and the Desloge family.

Shelby Curlee -- Curlee Clothing Company

[Photos 9-4, 9-5, 9-6, and 9-7]

In the 1930s, Shelby Curlee, co-owner of Curlee Clothing Company, owned property overlooking the Car of Commerce Chute and the Missouri River, which has since become Castlereagh Subdivision on Old Jamestown Road. Curlee had a 'mansion' or 'castle' and a very large orchard. The clothing company was begun in Corinth, Mississippi in 1900 and moved to St. Louis in 1903.

Shelby Hammond Curlee was born Corinth, Miss., Aug. 29, 1868. He was a son of William P. and Mary (Boone) Curlee and a great-grandnephew of Daniel Boone. In 1893 he married Luella Duncan and they had one son, S. H., Jr. Shelby began his business career as a traveling salesman for Janis, Saunders & Co., dry goods, St. Louis, covering Texas and Indian Territory, 1890-97. In 1900, he co-founded Corinth Woolen Mills, manufacturers of pants and children's clothing. In 1903, they relocated to St. Louis and eventually the company, renamed Curlee Clothing Company, became one of the most successful clothing manufacturers in the country, which during the 1940s was larger than Levi Strauss. In the very early 1900s, the clothing company was in the 1100 block of Washington Avenue and Shelby lived at 5736 Clemmons Ave.

During the 1950s, Hardesty Developments, Inc., purchased the nearly 500-acre Curlee estate and developed the Castlereagh subdivision. The still existing Curlee Mansion, built in 1931, was described in a recent real estate listing as a "handsome Federal-style limestone residence with its matching limestone stable block and outbuildings situated on a breathtaking Missouri River-bluff setting of 15 acres with incomparable views in every direction...."

A reference in Edward Charles Hume's story (Chapter 5) to his working at the "Shelby Curlee Possum Hollow Farm" probably explains why "Possum Hollow" has been identified by local residents in two different locations – at the end of Carrico Road and near Jamestown Farms. Curlee's large estate likely extended across both those locations.

Shelby died in 1944, leaving his brother Francis as the head of the Curlee Clothing Co. In 1925 Francis had purchased the Nathan Boone Home near Defiance, Missouri, and his life's work was the restoration of this historic site where Daniel Boone died of natural causes in 1820 at age 85. Francis eventually purchased 509 acres with a value of $250,000 (during the depression era). During his illness in the 1950s, the "Daniel Boone Shrine Association" was formed and opened the home to the public. Francis Curlee died in 1958.[181]

Mesker Family

David Mesker, Jr., owned most of the property on Portage Road where his parents built 19 Portage, now owned by brothers Chris and Mark Waier. Chris and Mark are restoring the home to its elegant past. Until his death in 2015, David lived at 6 Portage Road and owned Little's Island in the Missouri River as well as the land being used for the Central Stone quarry at Hwy 367 and the Missouri River. These two homes were described in 1988 by Esley Hamilton.

Francis Mesker House, Fercrest -- 6 Portage Road[182]

> Portage Road is a private development that was organized in 1931 by Marion Blossom, the owner of the land, and physicians Ellis Fischel and Vilray Blair. Marion was the daughter of Alfred Clifford of Westmoreland Place and the former wife of Dwight Bradford Blossom. Fischel and Blair were preeminent physicians. In 1933 they revised their indenture to include Francis A. Mesker, who acquired a site of 33.44 acres at the same time.
>
> Francis Mesker (1906-1981) was the elder son of Frank Mesker (1859-1952), who with his brother Bernard Theodore Mesker (1852-1936) had founded an iron company in 1879. Incorporated in 1912 as Mesker Brothers Iron Company, the firm was especially known for sheet metal work, including patented building fronts. They later made special windows and doors. Francis graduated from MIT in 1927 and joined the company, later becoming vice president. He retired in 1961, and the company went out of business in 1966.
>
> Francis' house is made of cast iron and was built as an experiment by Mesker Brothers.
>
> Behind the house the ground drops dramatically to the Missouri River. Just above the river was a most unusual construction, a three-story pool pavilion assembled from parts of retired riverboats, complete with two smokestacks, 45 feet of open deck toward the river, and a built-in steam whistle. The top deck toward the pool resembles a pilot house. The level below the pool has showers and dressing rooms. The pool is reached from the house by a funicular, which also stops at a tennis court flattened out of the lower part of the hill.

John B. G. Mesker House – 19 Portage Road – Being Renovated by Chris and Mark Waier[183]

[Photo 9-8]

> John B. G. Mesker bought this lot of 10 acres in 1936 from Marion Blossom, who was responsible for the whole Portage Road development. At the same time, he bought another 15.23 acres on the south side of the road. Mesker's brother Francis was building a house at 6 Portage at the time. John Mesker's house didn't get under way until 1939.

This house was extensively described in the ©St. Louis Post-Dispatch on May 28, 1939: "Construction has started on a country residence for Mr. and Mrs. John R. Mesker on the Jamestown road, on a site overlooking the Missouri river, with Study & Farrar as the architects. It has been designed in the French chateau style. An interesting feature of the owners' suite will be a sunken bathtub of marble. In order to utilize all the space economically the storerooms and servants quarters have been placed on the second floor above the garage wing."[184]

Brothers Mark and Chris Waier, who grew up on Old Jamestown Road, purchased the 19 Portage after a period of decline and have been painstakingly restoring the house and grounds to their former glory. As Mark says, "Even the colors we are using throughout the house are now accurate to the period of construction - 1939."

McNair Family –St. Louis Cold Drawn Steel

[Photo 9-9]

Lyle (1914-2004) and Nadine (1915-2005) McNair, founders of St. Louis Cold Drawn, Inc., built their home on the Missouri River at No. 4 Old Jamestown Lane in 1955. Their son, Bill, current owner of St. Louis Cold Drawn, built another home there in 1984 and still lives on the property.

Adapted from St. Louis Cold Drawn web site:

> Julia Nadine McNair was born in Ames, Iowa, to Hans and Tesse Ryan Hanson. In 1937 at the age of 22, she became the first woman ever to graduate from Iowa State University in general engineering. She then worked for several corporations in the St. Louis area including Carter Carburetor and Emerson Electric. Lyle McNair was born in Osceola, Iowa, to Robert Charles and Gertrude Wyatt McNair. He was a graduate of Industrial Engineering from Iowa State University.
>
> Nadine and Lyle, married in 1938, started Hazelwood Engineering and later opened aluminum plants in Murphysboro and DuQuoin, Illinois. They founded St. Louis Cold Drawn in 1971 as a start-up company making cold finished steel bars. Operations were held in a small industrial garage with annual production capacity of 2,000 tons. Now owned and managed by their son Bill, St. Louis Cold Drawn currently operates an annual production capacity of 250,000 tons in two states and in Mexico.
>
> Nadine and Lyle were both licensed Missouri professional engineers and licensed aircraft pilots. They were active in civic organizations and supported charitable causes.

Evarts Graham, M.D.

Evarts A. Graham, M.D., F.A.C.S. (1883-1957) and his family lived on the Missouri River bluff on Jamestown Acres in the 1940s and 1950s.

Esley Hamilton wrote about the Grahams in the 1988 Inventory of Historic Buildings Form:[185]

> Dr.Evarts A.Graham (1883-1957) was one of the most respected and honored physicians in St. Louis history. Professor of Surgery at Washington University from 1919 to 1951 and surgeon-in-chief of Barnes Hospital, he was called the dean of American surgery. Graham was born in Chicago, the son of a surgeon who taught at Rush Medical College there. He graduated from Rush in 1908 after obtaining his undergraduate degree from Princeton. During World War I he served as a major in the Medical Corps. As a surgeon he was particularly well known for the imaging test he developed for gall bladder disease and for being the first, in 1933, to remove an entire lung for the treatment of lung cancer.

After retiring, Dr. Graham concentrated his research on the relationship of cigarette smoke to lung cancer. His findings, published in 1953 in Cancer Research found positive evidence of such a relationship through studies of mice. A follow-up, reported in 1956, found similar evidence in rabbits. These studies form the cornerstone of subsequent research, legislation and public education on this still controversial subject. Ironically, Dr. Graham himself died of lung cancer in 1957.

Mrs. Graham, the former Helen Treadway, was an associate professor of pharmacology at Washington University and highly respected in her own right. Born in Dubuque, Iowa, she received her Ph.D. from the University of Chicago and became a specialist in histamine and its relation to allergies. She served as president of the St. Louis League of Women Voters and the St. Louis Branch of the American Association of University Women, and she was active in the ACLU. She retired from teaching in 1959 but continued to do research until her death in 1971 at age 80.

The Grahams' son, Evarts, Jr., was managing editor of the ©St. Louis Post-Dispatch from 1968 to 1979. Their other son, David, was a physician at the University of Wisconsin.

[Photos 9-10 and -11]

Bits of the Grahams' Old Jamestown experience can be seen in excerpts from the "Helen's Modern Home" chapter in the 2002 book "Evarts A. Graham."[186]

> In 1940 the Grahams sold their home on Westminster Place and for 3 years lived in a large grey, modern, limestone house at No. 10 Upper Ladue Road in a posh suburb of west St. Louis. ... During these years Evarts and Helen purchased seven acres on Old Jamestown Road that ran along the bluffs overlooking the Missouri River. Vilray Blair, a plastic surgeon, Alexis Hartman, chairman of pediatrics, and William Scarlett, bishop of the Episcopal diocese, were neighbors. Harris Armstrong, a leading St. Louis architect, designed a spacious house that showed the Frank Lloyd Wright influence – flat lines, open spaces, brick and wood interior, with uncluttered décor and no carpeting. It was both simple and elegant, and in 1943 Evarts, Helen, her father, Harry Tredway, Evarts Jr., and her housekeeper Tillie Hecht moved in.
>
> Helen and Evarts were very proud of the house and its view. ... It permitted Helen and Evarts to expand their interest in growing vegetables, flowers, and shrubs; they would take guests on a walk around the property to look at the plants. Evarts was interested in the esthetic effect of the garden, whereas Helen was more interested in the science of growing, whether it be trees, shrubs, flowers, or tomatoes, and she was proud of her compost pile, which she had decades before most people had heard of them. ...
>
> ... The Missouri River house was tailor-made for the dinners and receptions that had become a way of life, and Helen meticulously kept a card file of all visitors, the date of the visit, and the food she served. She and Graham bought a small ride-on tractor, and after his death, the tractor remained Helen's connection to the land; her connection to St. Louis was a red Karman-Ghia that she drove until she moved into the city.
>
> ...In 1953[] the Laclede Gas Company planned to store natural gas in the limestone strata under the corner of [Sinks] Road and Old Jamestown Road, one-quarter of a mile underground and about a mile from the Graham home. In an effort to block the scheme, Drs. Graham and Dr. and

Mrs. Alexis Hartman formed the Osage Gas Company, incorporated with $500 as capital, and an announced purpose to compete with Laclede. By using a special section of Missouri law, they went to court in early 1955. It was a contest of David-and-Goliath proportions, eagerly followed by newspaper coverage. In September 1955, a settlement was reached that approved the Laclede purchase of the Osage Gas Company for an undisclosed sum and permission to store its gas underground. (See Chapter 10 for more on the Laclede Gas Underground Storage Facility.)

On January 27, 1955, while Evarts was in Princeton attending a National Institutes of Health subcommittee meeting on lung cancer, two burglars broke into the house and ransacked it for money. Using the cut telephone lines, they tied Helen and Tillie to the furniture, while Helen called out that their money was not in the house, that it was in the First National Bank and they should look there. The burglars took more than $2000 in cash (Tillie's savings of 3 years), clothing, jewelry, and a quantity of liquor before escaping in the Graham station wagon. The entire episode lasted more than 2 hours. After the burglars departed the two women remained tied for about 20 minutes before Helen managed to work free and call for help on another telephone. In the succeeding months, Evarts made three appearances before the County Council to protest inadequate police protection. "Crooks know we have no protection" was his plea for an enlargement of the force. Nine deputy sheriffs were added, but the robbers were never caught.

Evarts died in 1957. In 1966, Helen and Tillie moved from Old Jamestown to the Montclair apartment building on South Kingshighway, five blocks from the Medical School where Helen still worked.

Alexis Hartmann, Sr., M.D., and Alexis Hartmann, Jr., M.D.

Alexis Hartmann, M.D., and later his son, Alexis Hartmann, Jr., M.D., had a summer home on Jamestown Acres.

The senior Hartmann was Chief of Pediatrics at Washington University and was part of a group who developed a technique to measure sugar in patients' blood, an important step in the discovery of insulin. He is also well known for creating a fluid and electrolyte replacement therapy for infants, known as Lactated Ringer's solution, or Hartmann's Solution. A native St. Louisan, he spent his entire academic and medical career at Washington University, earning a bachelor's degree in 1919, master's and medical degrees in 1921 and later heading the Department of Pediatrics from 1936-1964. He also was physician-in-chief of St. Louis Children's Hospital. He became emeritus professor of pediatrics in June 1964 and died in September 1964.[187]

His son, Alexis Hartmann, Jr., was a pediatric cardiologist at St. Louis Children's Hospital and a faculty member at Washington University's School of Medicine. He was the first to recognize the double-chambered right ventricle in the heart, a form of septated right ventricle caused by the presence of abnormally located or hypertrophied muscular bands.[188]

Vilray Blair, M.D.

[Photo: 9-12]

Vilray P. Blair, M.D., (1871-1955) lived at 16 Portage Road, which was constructed in 1931-32, but was torn down in 1988.

Adapted from 1988 Historic Inventory, Missouri Office of Historic Preservation[189]

> Blair was a descendant of Pierre Laclede through the Papin family. "During World War I he was in charge of plastic and oral surgery in the U.S. Army and startled the world at that time with extraordinary work done in restoring shattered faces and skulls," according to The "Founding Family of St. Louis." He served as chief of the Division of Plastic and Reconstructive Surgery at Washington University from 1925 until 1955 and is recognized as a premier American pioneer in plastic surgery.
>
> Blair and his wife entered into an agreement with Marion C. Blossom and Ellis Fischel in 1931 to form the private enclave on Portage Road. Another agreement in 1933 confirms that this residence had already been erected. In 1985 the house was purchased by Pauline C. Mesker, who lived next door. By 1988 the house was demolished.
>
> The Blair home had 14 rooms, including 6 bedrooms, 4 full baths and 2 half baths. Most of the house looked like the Early American revival of the 1930s, but the oldest section is supposed to have been built in 1850 with an addition in 1880. The lot has 390 feet of frontage on the Missouri River and is on a high bluff with a view north to the Mississippi River. Support buildings included a stone barn with a courtyard bounded by a serpentine brick wall, dog kennels with runs, servants quarters, and a 5-car garage with living quarters.

Ellis Fischel, M.D.

This information about the Ellis Fischel Guest House, 20 Portage Road, is adapted from the 1988 Historic Inventory, Missouri Office of Historic Preservation[190]

> The present lot [1988] is half the original 10 acre tract set off for Ellis Fischel in 1931 as part of an agreement between himself, Vilray Blair and Marion Blossom to establish a private enclave on these bluffs. The lot is long and narrow but has at the north end a fine view of the Missouri River, seen from a steep hillside.
>
> Fischel intended to build a large house overlooking the river, but the effects of the Depression intervened, and this guest house, constructed in 1932, was all that was finished. Fischel was a noted surgeon and leader in cancer research and treatment, the son of Washington Emil Fischel, another physician, and the former Martha Ellis.
>
> A graduate of Harvard (1904) and Washington University Medical School (1908), he began private practice in 1913. He was on the staff of the Barnard Free Skin and Cancer Hospital and taught at St. Louis University and Washington University. He led a campaign to establish a state cancer hospital which led to the enactment of such legislation in 1937. He was appointed chairman of the State Cancer Commission to locate, plan and construct a hospital, but he was killed in an automobile accident near Linn, Missouri, on May 14, 1938. The Ellis Fischel State Cancer Hospital, named in his memory, opened in Columbia, Missouri, in 1940. It was the second of its kind in the U.S., and the first west of the Mississippi. The hospital attracted many scientists and physicians of international renown over the years and in 1981 was reorganized as a Center.

Fischel's family was well-connected socially. He married Marguerite Kaufman, daughter of John Kaufman whose home had been the site of the Chase Hotel. She was an expert on spastic children and a composer. After her husband's death, she moved to New York to teach nurses and physicians, and died there in 1950. Fischel's sister Edna married George Gellhorn and was the mother of Martha Gellhorn, the reporter who married Ernest Hemingway.

The guest house was used in the 1940s as a summer house by Frank Mesker, whose sons Francis and John had both built houses on Portage Road. (See above.)

Episcopal Bishop William Scarlett

From a ©St. Louis Post-Dispatch article, December 1952: Bishop William Scarlett was praised last night by Associate Justice Felix Frankfurter of the United States Supreme Court as "the highest representative of the tradition which binds us together and makes us a nation."

When Bishop Scarlett retired November 1, 1952, as bishop of the Missouri Diocese of the Episcopal Church, the ©St. Louis Post-Dispatch reported that Bishop Scarlett would continue to live on Old Jamestown road, on the northern rim of St. Louis County, in a house that overlooks the Missouri river. The article also included information about his background:

> Bishop Scarlett cannot remember when he first decided to be a priest in the Episcopal Church – he recalls preaching sermons to his father and mother when he was 6 years old. He graduated from Harvard University in 1905, and from the Episcopal Theological Seminary, Cambridge, Mass., in 1909. He was ordained a priest in 1910. He was dean of Trinity Cathedral, Phoenix, Arizona, from 1911 to 1922, and dean of Christ Church Cathedral in St. Louis from 1922-1930. In 1930 he was elected bishop coadjutor and three years later became bishop of the diocese.
>
> During his 30 years' ministry in St. Louis he has been a leader of liberal Protestantism, always outspoken in his views. He was president of the Urban League for 16 years. He was one of the organizers of the Social Justice Commission. He has been chairman of the Joint Commission on Social Reconstruction of the Episcopal Church since 1940, and chairman of the Department of International Justice and Goodwill of the National Council of Churches since 1948. He has been a national leader in promoting church unity.

Henri Chomeau

Henri Chomeau, founder and president of the St. Louis County Land Title Company, spent part of his youth living in Old Jamestown. His wives, Mary "Mollie" and Virena, who were daughters of Nicholas and Margaret Patterson Douglass, grew up in the Tunstall-Douglass House on Old Halls Ferry. Mary died in childbirth. Henri later married Virena and they had three children, including Adele Chomeau Starbird. Both wives taught at Brown School.

[Photos 9-13, 9-14, and 9-15]

Adapted from the 1911 History of St. Louis County:[191]

> Chomeau was born in St. Louis in February 1848 to Henri and Adele (Williams) Chomeau. His father was born in the south of France and his mother was born in Normandy, but of Scotch

parentage. In the early 1840s, they came to St. Louis County. The senior Henri was a chemist and opened the first dyeing establishment in the City of St. Louis. Later he and his wife moved to Old Jamestown. They had three children: Celine, the wife of Joseph Aubuchon; Marie, the widow of Dr. Pondrom who was a surgeon in Jefferson City; and Henri.

The younger Henri was educated in an old log schoolhouse and majored in civil engineering in the "State University." In 1877 he was appointed as county surveyor and road commissioner and he laid out the original town of Clayton. His position gave him a comprehensive knowledge of land values and real estate conditions. In 1880 he organized the St. Louis County Land [Title] Company. After the death of his first wife, Mary "Mollie" Douglass in 1882, in 1890 Henri married Virena B. Douglass and they had three children: Adele, Henri and Richard. The family lived in Clayton.

Famous in her own right was Henri's daughter Adele Chomeau Starbird, born in 1891. From 1931 to 1959, Adele was dean of women at Washington University. From 1946 to 1979, she wrote a popular newspaper column, which appeared in the Star-Times for the first five years and then in the © St. Louis Post-Dispatch.

In a 1988 ©St. Louis Post-Dispatch article, Patricia Rice wrote about Adele: Adele met her husband, Robert Starbird, a Washington U. professor, at the university and married him in 1912 when she was studying music at the Conservatoire in Strasbourg, France. He was 38 and she was 21. Within a few years, Robert developed paresis and died in a sanitarium in Chicago in 1916. In the last 20 years of her life, Adele became a model to neighbors in her retirement residence, the Gatesworth Manor on Union Boulevard. When her eyesight dimmed, her passion for good literature did not. She hired students to read to her in English and in French. In her late 80s, she became too frail to attend symphony concerts and opera performances, so she arranged her days around music programs on radio and television. Adele died in 1987 and is buried with her parents in Cold Water Cemetery.[192]

Oscar Hammer

Oscar and Velma Wood Hammer bought the Tunstall-Douglass House at 15310 Old Halls Ferry Road and the 100 acres surrounding it in 1940. The couple renovated the two-story, white brick house. It had 12 rooms, each with a fireplace of bricks made on the property. The home was considered an unusually well-preserved example of 19th-century brick farmhouses. Starting in the 1950s, the Hammers owned and operated the Old Halls Ferry Stables on the property, raising and boarding thoroughbred horses.[193]

Adapted from 1997 ©St. Louis Post-Dispatch article:[194]

> During World War II, Oscar was vice president of materials with Curtiss Wright Aircraft Company and later held a similar post with McDonnell Douglas Corporation., where he retired in 1965. Oscar was born in Goldfield, Nevada, and reared in Lexington, Mo. He attended Wentworth Military Academy High School and Junior College. Velma was a native of Eldon, Missouri. She was a founding member of Ferguson Baptist Church and later a member of Salem Baptist Church. Velma died of a heart ailment in 1995 and Oscar died in 1997. Among the

survivors are two daughters, Rosann H. Stegall of North County and Nancy Sue Traad of Miami; a son, Oscar Lawrence Hammer II of Chicago; five grandchildren; and a great-grandson.

In 1992, an electrical fire had nearly destroyed the Old Jamestown house. After her parents' deaths, Rosann Stegall moved back to St. Louis to rebuild the family farm. "She loved that house," said the Rev. Jeff Logston, former pastor of Salem Baptist Church. "I think it was a link to her past and to simpler times."

In 1999, when Rosann Hammer Stegall was 65 years old she disappeared and her body was later found fatally shot and weighed down with a concrete block about 20 miles off the coast of New Orleans. A suspect and motive have not yet been identified. [195]

See Chapter 1 for other history of the Tunstall-Douglass House

Adela R. Scharr

Adela Riek Scharr and her husband, Harold, lived on Old Jamestown in Black Jack. Her parents lived on the Old Jamestown side of Coldwater Creek. During World War II Adela delivered military planes for the Women's Airforce Service Pilots (WASP). In a 1989 ©St. Louis Post-Dispatch interview, excerpts of which are adapted below, Adela shared some of her aviation experiences.[196]

> While teaching at an elementary school in St. Louis in the 1930s, Scharr took streetcars and busses to Lambert Field to take flying lessons. "My master's degree at the University of Missouri was in educational psychology and history, and my reading convinced me that Hitler wouldn't be stopped without war. I knew that when it came, I wanted to be part of it, and flying seemed to be my best bet."
>
> Q. Was it difficult for a woman to learn to fly in the 1930s? A. When the men at Lambert became convinced that I was serious about learning to fly, they accepted me. I could only afford one half-hour of air time a week, so it took me five years to get my license. Eventually, I married one of the guys, Harold Scharr.
>
> Q. And then? A. The St. Louis Board of Education forced all women teachers to resign if they married. I taught ground school at St. Louis University five nights a week. I flew passengers for joy rides on weekends, kept house and continued to learn until finally I had a flight instructor's rating. The pay for teaching people to fly was $2 an hour.
>
> In September 1942, Adela was one of the women pilots recruited to ferry planes within the United States. The group of women, called WAFS (Women's Auxiliary Ferrying Squadron), were civilians in the early years. They paid for their own uniforms and other expenses out of their $250.00 monthly salary. The planes they transported usually didn't have radios, so she paid $40 for a TransLear radio so she could listen to the tower communicate with big planes while landing at an airport.

During the war, Scharr wrote hundreds of letters to her husband, the late Harold Scharr, and these became the basis of a two-volume set of books, "Sisters in the Sky" The following excerpt describes flying over her parents' house on Old Jamestown.[197]

> "I thought I was to go by myself and was surprised when I picked up my orders to find that I would fly with a young 2nd lieutenant. Operations evidently decided that I'd make a good aerial babysitter for this newly-graduated cadet….
>
> "Before we took off for St. Louis, I said, 'We'll fly right over my parents' home before we reach Lambert.' I showed him where that would be on the chart. 'I'll get down to 500 feet and cut out my engine a couple of times to attract their attention and then we'll go on and land.' I didn't invite him to anything but to circle and wait for me.
>
> "When we reached my parents' house south of the Missouri River, I let down a bit, pulled back the throttle and then pushed it forward again several times. The old folks came out, I dipped my wing and started on up.
>
> "But I had not reckoned with Mr. Smart Alec. When I went down to 500 feet, he decided to follow, but he went down to the treetops and buzzed the neighborhood again and again. I had to fly around upstairs, waiting for him to stop. That I was angry with him for that silly demonstration was evident to him when we got down. I blistered his ears.
>
> "When I closed my flight plan over the phone, Paul Dobbins said, 'Someone up by the river called us and said you were buzzing dangerously low. I told them I knew you and I was sure you wouldn't do anything like that.'
>
> "I told him what happened. He said he wouldn't report it."

After the war, Adela taught flying at Lambert Field.

Behlmann Family

Many members of Behlmann family, who were business owners and community leaders, have lived in Old Jamestown. Brothers Paul and Lee and their nephew Ken owned the very large GMC/Pontiac dealership at I-270 and McDonnell Douglas Boulevard. Brothers Mark and Al were builders and built Parc Argonne near Old Halls Ferry and Hwy 67. Mark's son Mark was also a builder and built Parc Argonne Estates at Vaile and Old Jamestown Roads. Other members of the family owned businesses in Florissant and many were active in civic and charitable organizations.

[Photo 9-16]

Adapted from Paul Behlmann obituary in the ©St. Louis Post-Dispatch:

"Paul Behlmann died in 2013. He had grown up the youngest of 12 children in a family of self-described "dirt farmers." His grandparents emigrated from Germany and Paul grew up on his parents' 82-acre vegetable farm in Florissant. After graduating from the old McBride High School in 1953, he, his brother Lee and their nephew Ken Behlmann opened the Florissant Tire Center in the Old Town district. The business was very successful and continued to expand. In the early 1970s, the local GMC dealer moved to Rolla. GM asked the Behlmanns if they wanted the dealership. The Tire Center became the first of the family's auto dealerships. In 1990, they moved to a bigger operation on 15 acres at Interstate 270 and McDonnell Douglas Boulevard in Hazelwood. From 1992 to 1996, they were the largest volume dealer GM had for GMC trucks and Pontiacs. Ken was owner of the "Behlmann Mansion" on Hwy 67 in Old Jamestown – the mansion was torn down and the property was developed as the Estates at Behlmann Farm."[198]

Al and Mark Behlmann, builders of Parc Argonne, were two of the thirteen children of Bernard Behlmann and Adela Rose Ebbesmeyer.[199] Al and Mark and their wives, Betty and Louise, were very active in Florissant/Old Jamestown area civic organizations and institutions, including Christian Hospital and Pallottine Renewal Center. Their great grandfather, Henry J. Behlmann, immigrated to the United States as a young man, coming directly to Florissant. He arrived there penniless and went to the home of a brother who had arrived earlier. After working as a farmhand, he eventually managed to save enough to purchase two and a half acres of land and was later able to add another sixty-five acres.[200]

Another son of Henry J. Behlmann was John, who owned a sixty-acre farm in Old Jamestown. John was born in Florissant in 1867. His early years were spent on the homestead with his father. In 1885 he began a position as a farm hand. By age 21, he was able to purchase his farm where he raised wheat and potatoes. "Mr. Behlmann, who is an intensive farmer rather than an extensive one, is progressive in his methods and gives a great deal of time and attention to the preparation of the soil for the seed, the same care extending through the entire period of development until the harvest time. Thus he makes each acre of his land yield the utmost." In 1888 John married Annie M. Gerbers who was born on a farm near Florissant. She was a daughter of John B. and Mary A. (Seaver) Gerbers. John and Annie had five children: John H., Mary A., Elizabeth G., William B., and Henrietta. For sixteen years John served on the school board in his district. Mr. Behlmann was involved with the Farmers Mutual Insurance Company and was a stockholder and director of the Citizens Bank of Florissant.[201]

Zykan Family

[Photo 9-17]

Members of the Zykan family, whose primary business was trash hauling, lived in Old Jamestown and were active in Florissant area business and civic organizations. Don Zykan, Jr., currently lives on Jamestown Acres in the house built for Episcopal Bishop William Scarlett. Don's parents, Don Sr. and Grace Zykan, once lived on Old Jamestown Road.

John Zykan, father of Don, Sr., started the trash hauling business in Ferguson in 1932. He later moved to North Hwy 67, where Walmart is now. John's three sons, Ed, Joe, and Don R., grew the company from there (Zykan Brothers Hauling). They sold it to BFI in 1986. Ed Zykan was first president of the Florissant Chamber of Commerce in 1952.

Don Zykan, Jr., vice president of Zykan Brothers Hauling, from 1968 to 1986, and his wife Micki owned the Valley Bistro Café in Florissant from 2000 to 2005. Don remains very active in the Florissant/Old Jamestown community.

Christian and Jennifer Welch Cudnik

Since 2003, Christian and Jennifer Welch Cudnik have lived on Wehmer Estates Drive with their two daughters, Elsa Rosemary and Mira Sophia. Jennifer is the daughter of Susan Wehmer Kagy whose family has deep roots in Old Jamestown (see Chapter 8 stories of Wehmer, Thompson and Appendix 9 memories of Susan's father Ralph). Jennifer is a ballerina and teaches ballet. Christian is a long time broadcaster and two time Emmy winner and has worked at the Missouri History Museum since 2011. Christian assisted with development of the recently opened National Blues Museum in St. Louis.

Christian attained the number-one-ranked afternoon radio program in Philadelphia, and was nominated for two AIR Awards including, "Best Field Reporting" and "Best Evening Program-Host." In 2003, he moved to St. Louis where he hosted programs on St. Louis Public Radio for a decade. He was awarded two Regional Emmy Awards and three Telly Awards for his television work. His documentaries have aired on PBS, and include "Enduring Tradition: Ballet in the Heartland", "Collective Improvisation: The Story of Jazz in Saint Louis", "Seeking Freedom", "Uncovering Ancient Saint Louis", "Wallace Herndon Smith: Artist Without Boundaries", and "Footsteps into the World Beneath". In 2009, Christian co-founded the nonprofit art organization, Ballet Initiative. Ballet Initiative trains dancers to dance and works to raise the profile of ballet. In August 2013, he created the first audio podcast devoted to the art of ballet. [202]

Jennifer teaches ballet at COCA (Center of Creative Arts in St. Louis. She has been a guest artist with the Saint Louis Symphony and Montana Ballet, as well as a teacher with Saint Louis Ballet School and various schools in Pennsylvania. She danced professionally with Pennsylvania Ballet, Stamford City Ballet, and Saint Louis Ballet where she performed principal roles in numerous classical and neo-classical works. At age 15 she had moved to New York City to study on full scholarship at the School of American Ballet where she performed in ballets by Balanchine and Bournonville, and originated roles in ballets by Wheeldon and Woetzel. Cudnik spent summers training on full scholarship with SAB, Pacific Northwest Ballet, and the State Ballet of Missouri. She is the co-founder and director of the nonprofit organization Ballet Initiative. [203]

Eddie Moss

Eddie B. Moss lives on Eagle Estates Court off Vaile. Eddie was born September 27, 1948, in Dell, Arkansas and is a former National Football League running back, playing for the St. Louis Football Cardinals and the Washington Redskins. He played college football at Southeast Missouri State University and was drafted in the 13th round of the 1972 NFL Draft.[204]

"Bubbleheads"

The Bubblehead story is included because it is often mentioned when people learn the history of Old Jamestown is being researched. The legend seems to be known far and wide. A 2012 Riverfront Times Article describes the stories and offers the most likely explanation:[205]

The Bubblehead Family of North County

"On a windswept October evening, Carrico Road seems like the sort of place plucked right out of a Grimm fairy tale. The winding stretch of asphalt disappears from one bend to the next. Fallen leaves swirl across the pavement, and at least eight signs along the shoulder of the roadway carry the same ominous message: No trespassing.

"Somewhere in the thick woods beyond those signs, according to local lore, live the Bubbleheads. Some say they are a family who took experimental drugs that caused their heads to swell to the size of large pumpkins. The government — or the pharmaceutical company — bought them off and hid them away on this isolated road just south of the Missouri River in unincorporated [St. Louis County]. Others say that the Bubbleheads are an old St. Louis family with physical deformities from years of inbreeding. They keep to themselves, or they attack trespassers in a flurry of rage. Some stories about the area reference "hook men" who stalk the night, mysterious hitchhikers from the great beyond or simply ghosts with big, swollen heads.

"Yes, Carrico Road is the kind of place where urban legends are born, though ask local thrill seekers for directions there, and you will likely get blank stares. People know it better as Bubblehead Road, and they've been coming here for at least 40 years — much to the dismay of residents….

"John Goessmann, who inherited an old farmhouse on Carrico…six years ago, suggests there could be [a kernel of truth to the stories]. He remembers a boy who lived at the far end of the street a long time ago. The boy had hydrocephalus, a medical condition that leads to swelling of the brain. Supposedly he would play outside wearing a helmet to protect his sensitive skull. Goessmann and others say the family moved away a long time ago — probably to seek privacy…."

Chapter 9 Photos and Maps

Photo 9-1 Desloge "Vouziers" Mansion
Photo by Peggy Kruse

Photo 9-2 Underground Ballroom on Desloge Estate, now part of Boeing Leadership Center
1999 ©St. Louis Post-Dispatch

End Note [206]

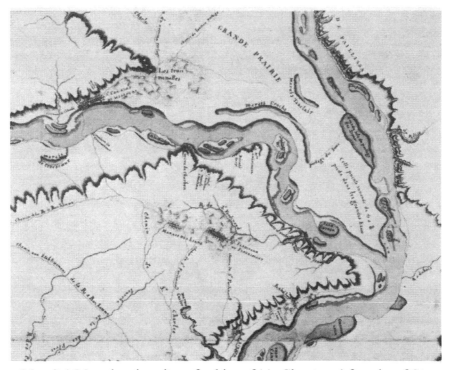

Map 9-1 Map showing sites of cabins of 'A. Chouteau,' founder of St. Louis, and his son, 'Cadet Chouteau,' on current Desloge property just west of Old Jamestown [adjoining properties in center, above R. de St. Ferdinand (Coldwater Creek) and west of Musick's Ferry]
Map obtained by Wesley Fordyce from ©2005 St. Louis Mercantile Library at the University of Missouri St. Louis

Photo 9-3 Brick house on Desloge property across from Vouziers
Photo by Peggy Kruse

Photo 9-4 1940 Aerial photo of Shelby Curlee property.
Photo 9-5 1956 Aerial photo of previous Curlee estate just prior to Castlereagh development
Photos courtesy of Castlereagh Estates subdivision and neighborhood residents

Photos 9-6 and 9-7 Curlee mansion in a realtor listing

Photo 9-8 Back of John B. G. Mesker House on Portage – Photograph by Mark Waier

Photo 9-9 McNair Estate on Old Jamestown Lane – Aerial photo by Chan Mahanta

Photos 9-10 and 9-11 Dr. Evarts and Mrs. Helen Tredway Graham at their home on Jamestown Acres and Christmas Note sent by Mrs. Graham in 1965
Photos courtesy of Becker Medical Library, Washington University School of Medicine

Photo 9-12 Dr. Vilray Blair residence on Portage Road – photo shared by Bev Girardier

Photo 9-13 Henri Chomeau – 1909 Plat Book of St. Louis County
Scan by Missouri History Museum of St. Louis
Photo 9-14 Douglass/Chomeau Gravestone in Cold Water Cemetery
Photo by Peggy Kruse
Photo 9-15 Henri's daughter, Adele Chomeau Starbird -- ©St. Louis Post-Dispatch

End Note[207]

Photo 9-16 Paul Behlmann -- ©St. Louis Post-Dispatch

Photo 9-17 Zykan Brothers
Photo shared by Don Zykan

End Note: [208]

Chapter 10 – Land/Water (Environment)

Attraction of Old Jamestown

Though the Old Jamestown environment has changed some across the ages, it continues to be attractive. The Missouri River can be seen from many homes and several public locations; it can also be accessed from the Sioux Passage Park boat ramp. Subdivision development is limited because of the karst geology through much of Old Jamestown so much of the area remains unusually open and spacious. It is a truly unique area in St. Louis County.

Karst – Old Jamestown Association Efforts to Protect

[Maps 10-1 and 10-2]

Karst geology is characterized by underground rivers, caves, springs, losing streams, voids, and fissures, which are the result of millions of years of water dissolving limestone formations that eventually result in surface collapse and visible sinkholes on the surface. The "Florissant karst," an area of four square miles within Old Jamestown is well known by geologists worldwide. All storm water runoff discharges directly into sinkholes and then to the network of underground water aquifers. The earliest written record of the area dates back more than 200 years to 1797 when the "sinkhole area" was a part of the original Patterson Settlement.[209]

An excellent description of the karst geology in Old Jamestown and its effects was described a Missouri Resources Magazine 1995 article, "Living with the Sinks."[210] See Appendix 3 for the full article.

The author of the article, Jim Vandike, was a staff geologist for the Division of Geology and Land Survey of the Department of Natural Resources. He had visited the Old Jamestown area for a one day field trip in February 1988. Vandike's field trip included a one mile walk along the Missouri River and visits to known springs, caves, and major sinkhole formations in the area.[211]

The following excerpts are taken from the four page follow-up letter of the field trip. See the Old Jamestown Association 1988 Newsletter in Appendix 1 for more information about circumstances surrounding his trip.

> "The Florissant Karst area is different from other regions of intense sinkhole development in eastern Missouri. It even differs from the karst in south St. Louis County, even though only a few miles separate the areas and they are developed in the same stratigraphic units."

> "One of the key differences between the type of sinkhole development in south St. Louis County and that of the Old Jamestown area is the size of the sinkholes. …urban development in the Oakville [south] area has taken place in sinkhole plains. Some of the sinkholes were plugged and filled; drainage wells were installed in others. However, [in Oakville] the sinkholes were mostly 10 to 20 feet deep and relatively small diameter. Sinkholes in the Old Jamestown area,…are quite different. The sinkhole development is more intense here, sinkhole density is greater, and the sinkholes are deeper. Many shallow sinkholes are present, but there are also many that are 30, 40, and even 50 feet or more deep. Sinkhole diameters range from less than 100 feet to more than 1,000 feet."

"It is difficult to imagine intense residential development in the sinkhole plain of the Old Jamestown area. Parts of the sinkhole plain in the area between sinkhole sub-basins, where sinkholes are shallower and fewer, could be selectively developed using techniques similar to those used in development in south St. Louis County. Much of the area, though, contains steep-sided, deep sinkholes and high sinkhole density. Where these conditions exist, I feel low-density residential development similar to that already existing in the Old Jamestown area is a far wiser and more environmentally sound choice. The karst area is so unique; preserving its natural state as much as possible would certainly be desirable."

"….A major reason why the Old Jamestown area has not been extensively developed is its karst geology-- more than 56 percent of its landscape is drained by sinkholes. Karst is a term that describes features formed by the disintegration of soluble rocks such as limestone and dolomite. These rocks can be "eaten away" by the carbon dioxide in rain water and groundwater, which reacts with the calcium carbonate in the rocks to form carbonic acid…."

"….Most roads in Old Jamestown are serpentine by necessity. Sinks and Old Jamestown roads, the major transportation arteries through the area, narrowly miss dozens of sinkholes as they snake through the pockmarked surface of the karst plain overlooking the Missouri River. Evidence of ground movement can be seen by the pavement deterioration on the inside of every curve adjoining a sinkhole along these two roads…."

"….Because of its geologic makeup, the sinkhole plain in the Old Jamestown area cannot safely support intense urbanization as other parts of the county can. Many of the individual sinkholes are too steep and too deep to allow development anywhere except on the rims between adjacent sinkholes. Many of the area's residents still rely on relatively shallow private water wells and private waste disposal systems…."

"…. In 1987, Old Jamestown was recognized as an environmentally sensitive area by the St. Louis County Department of Planning. To cope with problems presented by the karst terrain, an area study was commissioned in 1988…. The study recommended low-density residential development in the sinkhole plain…."

After the study, Old Jamestown Association worked with St. Louis County planners to protect sinkhole areas from improper development. In March 2009, St. Louis County enacted environmental legislation to preserve part of the Old Jamestown area's unique geological karst formations. The karst zoning is similar to the Non Urban (3 acre) zoning with some other restrictions.[212]

"The lesson we must remember is that we are recent tenants of this delicate and slightly mysterious environment… There is a limit to how much we can alter what has taken ages to evolve in the earth beneath our feet…."[213]

See Appendix 3 for the Missouri for the Missouri Resources Magazine 1995 article with photos, "Living with the Sinks."[214]

Missouri River – Changes over the years

[Photos 10-1 and 10-2]

The northern border of Old Jamestown is about seven miles along the Missouri River as it arcs over north St. Louis County, just a few miles from its confluence with the Mississippi River. The river provides great opportunities for nature lovers in St. Louis County and for recreational and commercial river traffic.

The Missouri River originates in southwestern Montana and flows to the southeast about 2,315 miles to join the Mississippi River. Its history is well summarized in an article on the U.S. Army Corps of Engineers web site, adapted here.[215]

> Throughout its history, the Missouri River has offered an interior access way to the upper Midwest. American Indians built canoes and dugout boats from trees. Captain Meriwether Lewis and Captain William Clark traveled from St. Louis, Mo., to Washington State and back along the Missouri River launching their journey in May 1804 with a 55-foot long keelboat and two 40-foot pirogues…..
>
> From the mid-1800s, steamboats, ferries and barges were busily carrying commerce, produce and people along the river. Ships carried supplies for rail construction, groceries, whiskey, furs, tobacco, rope, wood, corn, wheat, etc.
>
> But the Missouri River we know today was very different back then; the river's waters were shallow with many bends, currents and sandbars. Boats were specially designed to travel the Missouri with flatter bottoms and powerful engines to fight the current.
>
> Often, the river and its snags (trees, sandbars, ice jams, shipwrecks, etc.) won the battle between river and boat. The typically shallow river rose during the spring thaw and in early summer with final snowmelt runoff and upper basin rainfall. An early spring could send ice chunks downstream damaging boats that were tied up for winter.
>
> An 1897 Report of the Chief of Engineers included a report of the Missouri River Commission, which included a list of steamboat wrecks on the river from the opening of steamboat navigation up to 1897. The list totaled nearly 300 wrecks and about 275 boats lost to the Mighty Mo'.
>
> But, many of the Missouri River's shipwrecks are no longer in the river – at least today's Missouri River. As the Missouri River rose and fell, it meandered in different locations sometimes more than a mile from today's river channel.

As reported in the St. Louis County Watchman in 1883: "It would be hard to estimate the damages done by the ever changing channels of the Missouri and a small part of the Mississippi Rivers. Within the past 12 years St. Louis County has lost thousands of acres of its best land, and many a farmer his entire farm, and the losses have not yet ended. Farms, which were the owners' pride a few years ago, are now the main channel of the Missouri…."[216]

The river's channel changed also in the Old Jamestown area. For example, Jean Baptiste Warren lost over 30 acres of his land (Chapter 6) and James Thompson lost 70 acres (Chapter 8) when the river's course adjusted in the late 1800s.

And just to the west at Charbonier Bluff: "Toward the 1850s, as the period of river exploration began to wane, the Missouri River also began to change its course, moving away from the bluff...." Charbonier Bluff National Register Application – Sec 8, page 1

The Corps of Engineers now has the responsibility for the construction, operation and maintenance of the Missouri River for navigation, flood control and related purposes, including flow regulation and bank protection. The 1945 Missouri River Bank Stabilization and Navigation Project provides for a 9-foot deep, 300-foot wide navigation channel for the 734 miles from Sioux City, Iowa, to the mouth at the Mississippi confluence.

The commercial navigation season is normally from late March to early December. Specific minimum flow rates are required during the navigation season to provide adequate depths and width. A flow of 30,000 to 35,000 cubic feet per second is generally maintained at Sioux City and Omaha. During insufficient natural flows, water is released from the upstream Mainstem Reservoir System of six reservoirs from northeastern Montana to Southeastern South Dakota and northeastern Nebraska.

Quarries

Musick's Ferry Quarry

[See Photo 6-9 in Chapter 6]

The quarry at Douglas Road and the Missouri River in Musick's Ferry, is now owned and used by John Lueke for his hauling service – Luecke's Hauling, Inc. It has a footprint of about 67 acres, the total property is about 100 acres.

This quarry was being used as least as early as the mid 1800s when its stone was used for the Musick's Ferry Inn (Chapter 6). Later owner John Warren continued to work the quarry through the turn of the century. John Heins, owner of the Musick's Ferry Inn building in 1931, also then owned the quarry from which stone was taken for Old Halls Ferry road. Heins said he would open the quarry again, as he had the contract to furnish macadam for the completion of Accommodation [now Old Jamestown] road and the improvement of Charbonier road. [217]

Still later, Bill Meyer owned and operated the Riverview Quarry there – he leased the land from several property owners.

In the 1980s Zykan Brothers Hauling (Chapter 9) wished to use the quarry for a landfill. Before the landfill began operation, Zykan Brothers was sold to then BFI (Browning-Ferris Industries) waste management company. Despite opposition from residents and organizations, including Old Jamestown Association, about air and water pollution, odor, and truck traffic, the 38-acre landfill was approved by St. Louis County. However, for other reasons BFI soon decided to stop using the landfill so the site was cleaned up and closed. [BFI was unable to buy the adjoining property, which it wanted to expand the landfill, so it closed. BFI preferred larger landfills. Per Don Zykan]

Portland Cement (now Central Stone) at Hwy 367 and the Missouri River

[See Photo 8-2 in Chapter 8]

The quarry at Musick's Ferry is at the far western end of Old Jamestown. On the far eastern end is another quarry where Old Jamestown connects with St Charles County and Illinois (Alton) via a Burlington Northern railroad bridge as well as MO-367/U.S. Hwy 67 across the Missouri and Mississippi Rivers.

As described in Chapter 9, from 1903 to 1911, John H. C. Ruegg operated a store and post office on the site of the Portland Cement Company's quarry. The village at the quarry had at least nineteen houses and became a thriving settlement, the children of the workers attended Vossenkemper School (Chapter 7).

Portland Cement Company owned property on both sides of Hwy 367 and the railroad line. Its quarry on the east side was used to provide rock for its cement plant on Riverview Boulevard in the City of St. Louis. The cement plant shut down in 1981 and Portland no longer took rock from its quarry. After several land transfers, the quarry was separated into two tracts, the east tract was owned by Central Stone and the west track by Bellefontaine Quarry.[218]

In 1998, Bellefontaine Quarry, Inc., asked St. Louis County for rezoning so they could expand the rock quarry. Many residents opposed the project because they were concerned that the enlarged quarry would turn into a landfill and that blasting would crack wells and foundations.[219] In December 1999, a decision was postponed.[220] It is not clear whether any or all of it was ever approved.

Both tracts currently seem to be completely owned by Central Stone.

Laclede Gas Underground Storage Facility – OJA Efforts

[Photos 10-3, 10-4, and 10-5]

Another unique feature of Old Jamestown is the Laclede Gas Underground Storage facility.

The Laclede Gas Co. stores natural gas in wells far beneath sinkholes and other karst features. A domelike rock formation prevents the gas from escaping. The Laclede Gas underground storage facilities and the surrounding 550 acres are situated just south of Old Jamestown Road along Sinks Road. The entire Laclede Gas holdings lie in the karst region.

"County aquifer is perfect site for Laclede gas" – These excerpts are from a 2001 ©St. Louis Post-Dispatch article.[221]

> "Nearly 50 years ago, when Laclede Gas Co. geologists were studying land formations as they sought a place to store natural gas underground, they began drilling on a promising uplift of hills in north St. Louis County.

"Soon they struck oil. The strike was a couple of miles north of Florissant, in an unincorporated area of the county, and about a half mile south of the Missouri River. "When they drilled their first well, they hit oil," said Scott Mirly, superintendent of Laclede's Lange storage facility and a petroleum engineer. "They knew that if it holds oil, it will hold gas."

"Some gas companies had been using aquifers - sandstone formations that hold underground water - as safe and secure storage areas for gas since the early 20th century….

"Today [2001] the gas company can store up to 5 billion cubic feet of gas in the underground aquifer by injecting it under pressure - between 300 and 630 pounds per square inch - into the sandstone. Injecting the gas drives out the water. If you look at a core sample of the sandstone, you would not see how the gas can be held between the particles. It seems too dense, but looks are deceiving. Joan Levick, a geological engineer for Laclede, explained that the sandstone is 17 percent air - and that's where the gas goes when it's forced into the aquifer under pressure….

"The Lange field runs north under the Missouri River to underlie about 110 acres in southeastern St. Charles County. Laclede holds underground leases on an additional adjacent 12,390 acres around its rustic stone service buildings at 14905 Sinks Road….

"There's no danger to people living above the storage field, Mirly said, because the sandstone is capped by a layer of non-porous shaly dolomite, which lies 300 feet below the surface. The entire field, sandwiched between varying layers of sedimentary rock, lies on top of a Precambrian layer of granite formed about 2.5 billion years ago.

"Today, the area is quiet. Farmers have planted soybeans, corn and wheat on the gentle slopes. You have to look closely to see evidence of Laclede's presence, such as a small sign on Sinks Road and a few company trucks.

"But when Laclede began eyeing the area 50 years ago, some landowners and Florissant residents fought the gas company with all they had. Many did not want a natural gas field under their homes because they feared an explosion. (In 1963, their fears were validated in part when gas under pressure blew a cap off a pipe at the surface [and continued to escape. No fire started.] The dangerous situation was not corrected for days, until Paul "Red" Adair, the legendary oil-and-gas-well emergency specialist, came to recap the pipe.) The gas company went to the Missouri Legislature for a law to condemn the subsurface rights of the resistant landowners for the storage facility. The Missouri Supreme Court eventually cleared the company's right to take the aquifer…. [See Chapter 9 to learn about Dr. Evarts Graham's efforts to stop the storage.]

"…The Mississippi River Transmission pipeline from the Gulf Coast is the feeder line that provides gas for the Lange facility. The utility first withdrew gas from the Lange facility in the winter of 1957-58 and has in varying amounts every winter since then….

"Today, oil is a bonus and byproduct of this procedure. Twenty-two stripper wells are sited throughout the wooded hills and draws that are home to deer, turkey, coyotes and foxes, as well as a few isolated Homo Sapien families.

"Those wells produced about 7,700 barrels of good quality crude last year [2000], according to state figures. That is 7.2 percent of Missouri's oil production, which is strongest in the western part of the state, Mirly said...."

"We were working on our house when that gas well blew. It was on Hwy 67 at Old Jamestown. The well was just being tested and it blew and Laclede could not stop it. At our house, it sounded like a jet engine. They called in Red Adair and he got it shut down. All roadways were closed down and we had to come to our 'lot' over Sinks Road." – Long time Old Jamestown resident Olga Smith.

Parks – Sioux Passage, Briscoe, Champ

Several St. Louis County Parks also preserve the natural beauty of Old Jamestown.

Sioux Passage Park

[Photo 10-6]

Sioux Passage Park, 212 acres, is at the far north end of Old Jamestown, alongside the Missouri River and the Car of Commerce Chute around Pelican Island. It was described in "St. Louis Parks," by NiNi Harris and Esley Hamilton: "The land that has become Sioux Passage Park was purchased in 1965 with money from a bond issue, but its history goes back to the Late Woodland and Mississippian periods. Sioux Passage Park Archaeological Site was listed in the National Register of Historic Places in 1974. The park is one of few places in the county with a wide public access to the Missouri River. Early explorers passed here, and the journal of Zebulon Pike refers to camping in this vicinity."[222]

See Chapter 2 for the history of American Indians in the Sioux Passage Park area.

Visitors to Sioux Passage Park today will find a boat ramp to the Missouri River, horseback riding trails, fishing, primitive camping, and winter sports (snowmobiling, sled riding and cross-country skiing). (See the St. Louis County Parks Department web site for more information about these activities.)[223]

A 2010 ©St. Louis Post-Dispatch article described a trail in Sioux Passage Park: "Within Sioux Passage Park is the Black Buffalo Trail, which runs near the picturesque Missouri River chute that cuts off Pelican Island. The rest of the trail loops through a rich stand of trees. The trail is 2.54 miles and can be used for hiking, bicycling, and horseback riding...."[224]

The Great Rivers Greenway project to connect the St. Louis region with walking and biking trails along the rivers includes the Sioux Passage Park area along the Missouri River. However, this section of the greenway is not yet in planning stages.

John D. Briscoe Park

John D. Briscoe Park was described in "St. Louis Parks," by NiNi Harris and Esley Hamilton: "John D. Briscoe Park is a tract of thirty-three acres adjacent to the entrance to Sioux Passage Park on Old

Jamestown Road and almost indistinguishable from it. John Briscoe bequeathed the property to the county as an act of civic generosity in 2002."[225]

Mr. Briscoe, who was born in Sullivan, Missouri on September 24, 1913, died on February 27, 2002, and the property was turned over to the county in July 2002. Briscoe and his wife, Mary, paid $7,650 for the property in 1951. They bought the property from the nine children (and their spouses) of Mrs. Briscoe's grandfather, John C. Hughes, who had owned the tract since the turn of the century. Some of the three barns and five other outbuildings on the property may have dated from the Hughes era or earlier. The Briscoes farmed the property, and Mr. Briscoe also had a private business fashioning hand-made prosthetic limbs. The couple built a brick ranch-style house about 1956. The Briscoes had no children, and after Mary Briscoe's death, John decided to give the property to the County.[226]

A large communications tower was recently erected on Briscoe Park land, which will be used to facilitate emergency communications in St. Louis and surrounding counties.

A Disc Golf Course covers parts of Sioux Passage and Briscoe Parks. For more information see: http://www.dgcoursereview.com/course.php?id=6878

Champ Park

Champ (Norman B.) County Park is a heavily wooded 101-acre park, at 3991 Grand National Drive (Barrington Downs subdivision).[227] It has not been developed and is used for walking and nature study. In 2013 the ©St. Louis Post-Dispatch described the 1.3 Champ County Park Trail as a short, isolated nature walk near homes, which is a convenient place to get in a lap or two especially with fewer bicycles on the trail. It's best-known for its wildflowers in the spring and its quiet in the cooler months. This trail may offer a bit more solitude than others, because it's relatively remote, and the route to the park requires winding through subdivisions.[228]

Forty-nine acres of the park site was donated to St. Louis County Parks and Recreation by brothers Joseph C. Champ and Norman B. Champ, Jr., in 1971, and was named for their father, Norman B. Champ, Sr., who was the founder of Champ Spring Company and of Champ-Goodwood Farm in Elsberry, Missouri. The Village of Champ in St. Louis County is named for him. The brothers grew up in the grand estate of Goodwood. The house and the building and land surrounding it were bought by eminent domain to make way for an expansion of Lambert Airport. The Barrington Downs property was once owned by Norman B. Champ, Jr., but he never lived there.[229]

Pelican Island

[Photo 10-7]

Pelican Island is located in the Missouri River and occupies much of the far north portion of Old Jamestown. It is separated from the mainland by the Car of Commerce Chute, which was named for a steamboat that sunk there in 1832. "Car of Commerce" was actually a fairly common steamboat name; at least five boats with that name did trade along the western rivers. Before the age of automobiles, 'car', from the Latin carrus, was a poetical word meaning 'chariot'.[230]

According to Joseph Desloge, Sr.,'s grandson, Wesley Fordyce, Pelican Island in the mid 1900s had 300 acres that had been cleared and used by farmers.

3/5 of Pelican Island was donated to St. Louis County Parks by three children of Joseph Desloge, Sr., in 1976. The Parks Department received a federal grant to purchase the remaining part of the island and had plans to have a walkway to it from Douglas Road. In 1990, St. Louis County Parks gave the island to the Missouri Department of Conservation as part of a deal involving another tract of land on I-44 and the lease of St. Stanislaus Park to MDC. The Conservation director again mentioned building a walkway to the island, this time from Sioux Passage Park. The walkway has not yet happened. During times of low water, the island is accessible from Sioux Passage Park and Musick's Ferry on foot, but most of the time it can only be accessed by boat.[231]

Pelican Island is well described on the Missouri Department of Conservation web site:[232]

> This site is considered to be the best remaining example of a mature floodplain forest in the Missouri River floodplain of Missouri. An 1878 map showed two islands in the Missouri River that included what is part of Pelican Island today. In 1945 Congress passed an amendment to the 1912 Missouri River Bank Stabilization and Navigation Act which made provisions for a nine-foot deep, three hundred foot wide channel. Man-made changes to the river since 1945 have indirectly produced the one large island, Pelican Island, of today.
>
> Today the island is comprised of a mix of riverfront forest, slough, shrub swamp and old-field habitat. The floods of 1993 and 1995 killed a number of trees but riverfront forest is a dynamic community type and new trees have grown back in. Cottonwood, black willow, sycamore, hackberry, sugarberry, silver maple, box elder and red mulberry form forests ranging from thickets of young trees to more mature stands. Vines are common including raccoon grape, other grape species and poison ivy. Unfortunately due to the dynamic nature of this ecosystem a number of invasive, exotic species occur in the understory including the exotic vine species, Japanese hops.
>
> In the spring, just as the forest is greening up, look for migrant warblers including the American redstart, Nashville warbler, magnolia warbler, black-throated green warbler and the bay-breasted warbler. In the Car of Commerce Chute and other riverine habitats around the island are important areas for big river fishes such as sturgeon chub, sicklefin chub, channel catfish, and flathead catfish. The island's forested wetlands provide habitat for large numbers of gray treefrogs.

Coldwater Creek Cancer Issues

Unfortunately, one of the assets of Old Jamestown, its southern boundary, has more recently been associated with cancer among residents who lived along it after World War II.

These excerpts are from a 2014 article in the ©St. Louis Post-Dispatch.[233]

"An informal survey of 3,300 current and former residents of north St. Louis County shows that more than one-third have developed cancers, a rate the residents blame on radioactive contamination of Coldwater Creek, which runs from St. Ann to the Missouri River....

"Cancer is second to heart disease in leading causes of death. One in two men and one in three women will develop cancer at some point in their lives. But the Coldwater Creek group says it's the rarity of their illnesses, and the young ages at which they strike, which have them questioning the creek. Its water flooded their basements and lured them to play on its banks as children.....

"A year ago, the leaders launched the survey, which counted 1,242 total cancers among 3,300 people who had lived around the creek. Survey participants reported 202 thyroid cancers or conditions, 113 brain tumors, 37 appendix cancers and 320 auto-immune disorders, the group announced Wednesday. The group did not release further details, including the ages of the survey participants or the dates of their illnesses.

"Appendix cancer is especially rare, affecting fewer than 1 in 314,000 Americans each year. Dr. Graham Colditz [Deputy Director of the Institute for Public Health at Washington University] said last year that the number of appendix cancers in North County, then counted at 22, was larger than expected for the population....

"At least 50 people from North County have sued Mallinckrodt and other companies for their role in nuclear waste production in St. Louis in the World War II and Cold War eras. The plaintiffs claim they were sickened by growing up in housing developments built near the creek in the 1960s and 1970s....

"Those suing the companies include the father of Jenny Steinmann, who lived in Florissant and crossed Coldwater Creek on her way to school every day. Steinmann died in 2009 at age 23 after cancer spread to her lungs and back. Lead plaintiff Scott McClurg, a professor at Southern Illinois University, ate vegetables grown in his backyard in Florissant and developed a brain tumor in his 30s. Holly Coil has had more than five addresses in Florissant and was diagnosed with ovarian cancer at 18....

"[Mr.] Visintine, one of the leaders of the Coldwater Creek activist group, said their main goal was to alert residents and area doctors. 'We need our community to go to their health care providers when they don't feel right and we need our health care providers to recognize the signs and symptoms of radiation exposure.'"

Residents' Environmental Efforts

Combatting Soil Erosion in 1947

[Photo 10-8]

Old Jamestown farmers have practiced advanced farming techniques over the years. A 1947 Post-Dispatch Pictures Section describes Louis Wehmer and his son, James, (Chapter 8) terracing their farmland to prevent soil erosion:[234]

"Soil, the nation's basic heritage, is being washed from cultivated fields to streams and rivers in alarming quantities. It is estimated the recent heavy rains and resultant floods carried away enough topsoil from Missouri, Iowa and Illinois farmlands to cover all of St. Louis and St. Louis County to a six-inch depth.

"The unchecked force of water not only sweeps away rich topsoil but soon tears gullies in the land. These jagged ditches make operation of farm machinery difficult, endanger livestock, and often make land useless for agriculture. To prevent such destructive erosion, water control is vitally necessary. In recent years, many farmers have come to realize the value of terracing, a method of land preservation used for centuries in the Orient. Terraced fields produce better crops because they hold more moisture, slow down water runoff to a non-erosive velocity.

"Grass waterways form the basis of erosion control practices. A broad, shallow channel running from top to bottom of a hill or slope, the waterway confines runoff water to a definite course. Excess water is carried to the waterway by terraces, which divide a hillside into small watersheds.

"Terraces are constructed at approximately right angles to the land slope, are made by piling earth above the ground line in a ridge that runs along the contour of the hill. A channel is cut below the original ground level on the uphill side of this ridge. Held in this channel by the hill on one side, the terrace on the other, water flows slowly to the waterway, thence downhill. Waterway empties into natural water course.

Photo captions of James Wehmer using a whirlwind terrace: "…. The waterway, designed and surveyed by [Louis Wehmer's son, James], a University of Missouri agriculture graduate, will drain a 15-acre hillside, now streaked with gullies." "Terracing in Missouri often is done by contract because most farmers are unfamiliar with technical details of terrace and waterway construction…."

Cultivating Native Plants

Several Old Jamestown residents, Mahanta, McNair, and Mesker, who own large lots on the Missouri River have transformed their yards by planting them in native plants. Sioux Passage Park also includes 17 acres of native wildflowers and grasses. The work of Chan Mahanta, past president of Old Jamestown Association, was the subject of a 2010 online North County newspaper, nocostl.com.[235]

[Photos 10-9, 10-10, 10-11, and 10-12]

"Chan Mahanta's colorful prairie garden is a gem of the Old Jamestown area. He doesn't flinch about a tour bus dropping off more than 40 botanical garden professionals in his driveway. Visiting groups from the Perennial Plant Association or even famed garden writer and designer Noel Kingsbury don't worry him either. Chan can stand his own ground (literally!) with elite horticultural visitors from all over the globe, mostly because he has worked incredibly hard on his Old Jamestown property and it shows. The 1.5-acre prairie in his front yard was awarded the top prize for an amateur in the 2004 ©St. Louis Post-Dispatch Great Garden Contest, serving as an exquisite example of native plant use in a residential environment.

"An architect by trade, Chan designed his impressive home overlooking the Missouri River in 1997, moving there with his wife, Banti, from Creve Coeur. Originally from India, he was fascinated at an early age by the American landscape, often thumbing through comic books featuring American Indians, cowboys and bison herds that roamed the early prairie. During college he also saw The Vanishing Prairie, a 1954 Disney nature documentary, and it became etched in his memory. But it wasn't until moving from California to St. Louis (and ultimately north St. Louis County) that Chan realized he could finally fulfill his dream of creating his own native prairie. In 1999, he started his current garden entirely by seed.

"Looking back, he admits he should have prepared the site better, as a few areas had to be reseeded twice. But by three years in, the prairie gradually became established, and today it's a showpiece with more than 60 varieties of wildflowers, warm season grasses and native plants. June and July are peak bloom times, but prairie gardens hold year round interest. In winter, the dry grasses and seed heads are not only aesthetic, but provide wildlife food and habitat, proving that the prairie isn't just a 'garden' but an entire ecosystem….

"Active in the Old Jamestown Association, Chan would love to see more native plants and prairie plantings in the area. Always willing to share his experience, he has already assisted neighbors in establishing prairie gardens nearby, and his newest endeavor is beekeeping – another important aspect of the prairie ecosystem…."

Waier's Geothermal Heating/Cooling

The heating and cooling systems in two historic Mesker homes on Portage Road have been upgraded to geothermal. We learn about these systems from Mark Waier, who with his brother is renovating 19 Portage Road. (Chapter 9)

The Waier brothers were faced with a dilemma when they purchased the John B.G. Mesker residence. The house is made of steel and stone and windows are single pane and metal. There was no air conditioning in the house and the furnace ran on oil. There were two 500 gallon drums of oil storage in the basement and you could see the remnants of soot around the air vents. They needed a new HVAC system. They searched for a solution to provide efficiency, eliminate noise around the property because the views from the front and back yard are impressive and provide a clean source of HVAC. Geothermal was the best solution and it has turned out to be a solid investment. Their energy bills are a fraction of what they were.[236]

From the WaterFurnace web site, an explanation of how the Waier's geothermal system works:[237] "In all climates, the temperature throughout the year varies. However, the temperature below ground stays fairly consistent all year. The ground is able to maintain a higher rate of temperature consistency because it absorbs 47% of the Sun's energy (heat) as it hits the Earth's surface. WaterFurnace geothermal systems are able to tap into this free energy with an earth loop…. During the heating cycle, the geothermal heat pump uses the earth loop to extract heat from the ground. As the system pulls heat from the loop it distributes it through a conventional duct system as warm air. The same heat energy can also be used for a radiant floor system or domestic hot water heating. In the cooling mode, the heating process is reversed - creating cool, conditioned air throughout the home…."

Chapter 10 Photos and Maps

Maps 10-1 and 10-2 Sinkholes in Old Jamestown area
Google Earth map -- prepared by Department of Natural Resources

Photo 10-1 Ice on Car of Commerce Chute between Sioux Passage Park and Pelican Island, 2014 – Photo by Mark Behlmann

Photo 10-2 Missouri River looking West, Little Island on right, 2016
Drone Photo by Chan Mahanta

Photo 10-3 Oil well on Laclede Gas property, Sinks Road
Photo by Peggy Kruse

Photo 10-4 Laclede Gas Office on Sinks Road
Photo by Peggy Kruse

Photo 10-5 Inside Laclede Gas Facility on Sinks Road -- Photo by Peggy Kruse

Photo 10-6 Sioux Passage Park toward Pelican Island, Missouri River and Car of Commerce Chute – Drone Photo by Chan Mahanta

Photo 10-7 Pelican Island, Car of Commerce on Left, Missouri River on Right
Drone Photo by Chan Mahanta

Photo 10-8 James Wehmer creating terrace on his father Louis Wehmer's farm (now Shamblin) ©St. Louis Post-Dispatch 1947
End Note[238]

Photo 10-9 Native Grass section of Sioux Passage Park

Photo 10-10 (see next page)

Photos 10-10, 10-11, and 10-12
Across the Seasons in Mahantas' Native Grass Prairie on Old Jamestown Road
Photos by Chan Mahanta

Chapter 11 - Current Organizations

Attraction of Old Jamestown

Residents and others continue to come to Old Jamestown, drawn to bluff homes overlooking the Missouri River, the beauty and serenity of the large open spaces, and the well maintained subdivisions. Home buyers come from other areas of St. Louis and beyond. Boeing Leadership Center, Pallottine Renewal Center, and Paul Artspace draw visitors from all over the country and world.

Old Jamestown goes forward with an abundance of nonprofits, governments, businesses, churches and subdivisions:

Nonprofits

Old Jamestown Association

[Photos 11-1 and 11-2]

The Old Jamestown Association (OJA) was incorporated in 1942 as a benevolent organization and continued to operate during the 1950s, often responding to such issues as the threat of "being gobbled up by Florissant," the proposal to install a marine transmitting station for riverboat communications, and the project by Laclede Gas to store natural gas in a porous rock formation 1200 feet below the ground. The Association became inactive in 1963 and remained so until 1987 when St. Louis County announced the formation of the "New Jamestown" Area Study committee, to "help draft a plan for developing one of the County's few areas that remain largely undeveloped." Concern by Old Jamestown residents that no one from the area was included on the study committee led to the reactivation of the Association in October 1987. The Association worked with the County on the study and then continued to coordinate with the County Planning Department on the suitability of proposed new developments and eventual enactment of the Karst Area Protection District. In 2013, OJA became a 501.c.3 organization.

See Appendix 1 for more information about the Old Jamestown Association and the significant development activity in 1988.

Pallottine Renewal Center

[Photo 11-3]

Pallottine Renewal Center is on 83 acres at 15270 Old Halls Ferry Road. Many in the neighborhood recognize it only as the place where cows could once be seen grazing in front of the property or where pancake breakfasts were held several times a year. The Center is a ministry of the Pallottine Missionary Sisters, an order of Roman Catholic religious sisters founded by St. Vincent Pallotti. The Sisters broke ground on the Pallottine Renewal Center in 1968. The building was constructed to serve as a novitiate and formation house for incoming sisters as well as a residence for the retired sisters. With the changes of the Second Vatican Council, the Sisters realized that they would not have the number of novices they anticipated. As St. Vincent taught that we should use "any and all means possible" to share the Good News, the Sisters discerned that the facility could serve as a retreat center where all people could come to grow in faith and sense of mission. The Pallottine Renewal Center opened its doors in 1969 as a retreat center and has welcomed people from nearly all ages, backgrounds, and nationalities for retreat over the past decades. The center provides a welcoming place for groups to come for retreat, conference, or other types of gatherings. They welcome small and large groups who wish to host a one-day event or stay overnight.[239]

Jamestown New Horizons

[Photo: P11-4]

Information provided by Bonnie Grueninger, founder of Jamestown New Horizons:[240]

> Jamestown New Horizons (JNH), a special combination of people with disabilities, dedicated volunteers, physical and occupational therapists, experienced riding instructors and gentle horses, was founded in 1985 to promote the health and quality of life for people with a broad range of mental, physical and emotional disabilities. From the first of March until the end of November, young riders gather three days a week for riding lessons designed to help them "sit up tall."
>
> In 1984, the North American Riding for the Handicapped Association asked Bonnie & Oliver Grueninger, owners of the Jamestown Riding School located at 15350 Old Jamestown Road, to start a therapeutic riding center based upon their safety record of working with typically developing children. JNH trained 30 volunteers to serve as horse leaders and side-walkers to ensure the safety of riders with disabilities. The riding school's horses were introduced to wheelchairs, walkers and crutches. JNH had a garage sale, a bake sale, a raffle, a dog and pony show, five all-day car washes, and an auction to raise funds for insurance and a wheelchair mounting ramp – the first one built to ADA standards at a therapeutic riding center. Members of American Legion Post 444 made a generous donation to help cover student scholarships.
>
> Since 1985, they have provided over 35,000 hours of therapy for toddlers to adults with disabilities. With classical music playing in the background, the rider is taken through a complex series of movements that consciously and unconsciously use all the body's muscles while stimulating cardiovascular conditioning. Stronger arms and legs, increased torso strength, improved balance and greater physical endurance positively affect a disabled person's general health, decrease the likelihood of accident or tangential illness, enable them to get out of the bathtub or car, and be less dependent on others.
>
> When students arrive at the valley at Jamestown New Horizons, a whole world of nature opens to them – the rolling hills, the ponds, the Canada geese, the deer, and even foxes, in addition to the horses. It's quite a different world from special schools, clinical therapy, sheltered workshops, asphalt playgrounds and concrete sidewalks. At Jamestown New Horizons "the sidewalks end." As a five-year-old rider tells her mother each time they come to Jamestown New Horizons, "We are at the beautiful place."

Paul Artspace

A newcomer to Old Jamestown is Paul Artspace, 14516 Sinks Road. "Paul Artspace serves as a platform for creative exchange and impact. It is located on a beautiful and serene six acres in north St. Louis County. Since opening in July 2013, Paul Artspace has hosted more than 25 local, national, and international artists, writers, and curators in various stages of their careers. Selected applicants are provided housing and studio space for a period of 1 to 3 months. Residents enjoy a private room, private studio space, communal kitchen and bath, and access to the tool room, wood shop, library, and etching press. The facilities at Paul Artspace permit up to 3 individuals to work and live on the property, and this scheduling occurs on a rolling basis."[241]

American Legion Post 444

Post 444, 17090 Old Jamestown Road, was chartered in 1946 by 77 veterans returning home from World War II. The Post's home is located on seven and a half acres overlooking the Missouri River. It has two major buildings and several smaller buildings. The Post Hall is used for post meetings, social functions, fish fries, bingo, and rental space for weddings and other private parties. This building contains a primary 2500 square foot meeting room or hall. In addition the facility has a kitchen, bar, restrooms, and a store room.[242]

Florissant Elks

In 1965, the North County Benevolent and Protective Order of Elks Lodge 2316 was organized. When members outgrew their facility in Florissant in 1984, they built a new facility in Old Jamestown at 16400 New Halls Ferry Road. The Florissant Elks Lodge is used for meetings, social functions, fish fries, and bingo, and the Elks rent their hall for weddings, etc.

Governments

St. Louis County

Old Jamestown is an unincorporated area of St. Louis County, Missouri. As such, its planning and other municipal type services are received from St. Louis County.[243] Since 2010 Old Jamestown has been a Census Designated Place (CDP), which the Census Department treats as a municipality for statistical collection and reporting purposes.[244] The Old Jamestown Association[245] has worked with County staff on many issues over the years. (See Appendix 1 for more information about the association's activity with the County.)

Jamestown Bluffs Library

[Photo: P11-5]

Jamestown Bluffs, the 19th branch of the St. Louis County Library, opened on May 28, 1998. Named for the historic "Old Jamestown" area and the nearby Missouri River bluffs, the branch serves an area of the County that had seen dramatic increases in population during the 90s. The branch was renovated in 2015 and is now offering even more services to residents in the Old Jamestown area. The branch was awarded the Old Jamestown Association "Citizen of the Year" award in May 2016.[246]

Public Schools

Barrington Elementary School on Old Halls Ferry Road and Hazelwood North Middle School on Vaile are the only public schools currently in Old Jamestown. A current teacher at Barrington shared the following: Barrington was built in 2004 for children moving into new housing developments within the Old Jamestown area. One of these new developments is called Barrington Downs. The school contained kindergarten to 6th grades. Due to increased population growth and Hazelwood School District moving into a more middle school format the 6th grade moved to the newly built North Middle in 2008. Barrington currently holds 350 to 375 students. Unlike most of the Hazelwood School District, Barrington departmentalized 3-5th grades. This means in theses grades one teacher teaches math grade wide, another teacher only teaches reading and one teacher teaches science and social studies. The school has a very active Family and Community Committee. It has a yearly fall festival and it celebrates, with great turn out, Nation Walk to School Day. Barrington rates very high statewide on State testing.

Hazelwood Central High School and the Hazelwood School District Administration Building are across New Halls Ferry from Old Jamestown on the same property as the historic Coldwater School building.

Black Jack Fire Protection District

[Photo: P11-6]

Old Jamestown is part of the Black Jack Fire Protection District, which began in 1929 when a fire destroyed a house on Mehl Avenue. A crew of Volunteer Firefighters from Florissant Valley responded to a frantic call for assistance but could not save the house. Within days, several of Black Jack's community leaders held a meeting and started a plan in motion. Their proposed fire engine house was to be 20 feet wide, 35 feet deep and 10 feet high at a proposed cost of $1,097.00. The building was constructed in the rear of the Hartwig Brothers Saloon and General Store at Old Halls Ferry Road and Parker Road. The old fire house once stood in what is now the parking lot of the Walgreens Store, and served the community for nearly 28 years.[247] Current stations are House No. 1 at 12490 Old Halls Ferry Road, House No. 2 at 18955 Old Jamestown Road near Sioux Passage Park, and House No. 3 at 5675 North Hwy 67, which also houses the Administration Building.

Businesses

El-Mel

El Mel, Inc., 6185 N. Hwy 67, was started in 1961 by Elmer and Melba Wolff. Elmer grew up on the Wolff Farm at Portage Road and Old Jamestown. Melba grew up in Baden. In an online newspaper, nocostl.com, Shannon Howard in 2010 described the store, "The back half of the store is for lawnmower sales and service. In the front half El-Mel stocks nearly everything that chain pet stores sell, except often at better prices. Colorful bird feeders hang from much of the ceiling, and there are two aisles devoted to wild birds. You can also find all-natural dog treats, leashes, pet toys, and premium food for cats, dogs, chickens, rabbits and even horses. During the growing season, El-Mel sells bedding plants and a wide array of seeds. Local eggs and honey are also available year round, as are garden tools, animal traps (like for moles), and all kinds of lawn chemicals and organic soil amendments."[248]

Waldbart Nursery

Waldbart Nursery at 5517 North Hwy 67 is described on the Waldbart web site: "Shortly after the Civil War, when the western United States was struggling to build a frontier society, Alex Waldbart and his sons in 1872 began a fruit tree and flowering shrubs business in downtown Saint Louis. The family successfully grew that business, relocated several times, and eventually moved into the more suburban area of north St. Louis County.... The nursery has grown from a small, one-family operation to a three-location business in two states, in 1980 expanding to Illinois where they have 300 acre farm. In spite of the many changes that Missouri and Illinois have seen over those 140 years, the owners, managers, and employees have carried on the tradition started long ago: High quality plants, exemplary customer service, and friendly team-oriented employees…. The company employs designers with bachelor's degrees in horticulture with an emphasis on landscape design and supervisors who are certified nurserymen…."[249]

Baronwood Kennels

Baronwood Kennels, 17220 New Halls Ferry Road, offers boarding, grooming, and training services. Baronwood was founded in 1971. Brian and Terrie Bert took over ownership in 2007, live on the premises, and are very involved in the day-to-day operation of the kennel. Terrie started working at Baronwood Kennels in 1999 as a kennel worker, taking care of the dogs and cats. When the original owners decided to retire in 2007, she loved the place so much that she bought it to make sure the pets who stayed here would continue to receive the quality care Baronwood's customers had come to expect.[250]

Jamestown Mall

Jamestown Mall opened in 1973 offering regional commercial merchandise on the suburban fringe of St. Louis, in anticipation of residential development moving into the area [and expectations that nearby Illinois residents would provide about 50 percent of the sales.] The anticipated residential units never materialized and, unfortunately, in recent years, new regional shopping destinations [in Illinois] that are closer to larger populations of shoppers [and to interstates] degraded the effective trade area of Jamestown Mall, causing a decline in sales and foot traffic.[251]

As the mall declined and stores closed, in 2009 and 2011 St. Louis County contracted with consultants for a panel study in 2009 and plan creation in 2010. The 2010 effort involved a six-day design charrette that brought together community members, community leaders, elected officials, and the design team to work toward a common solution. The 2010 plan called for the demolition of the whole mall except the J.C. Penney and Macy's stores, with the rest of the complex to be re-developed as a mixed-use center.

The J.C. Penney outlet store, which was renamed J.C.'s 5 Start Outlet, closed in late 2013. Jamestown Mall closed completely in July 2014.

As reported in the ©St. Louis Post-Dispatch, May 2015: In 2015 St. Louis County took an ownership stake in a piece of the mall in hopes of sparking interest from developers. The county has no imminent plans for the property but pursued the acquisition to have a say in its future. "The former JCPenney building became available at an affordable price and St. Louis County Port Authority purchased it along with the accompanying parking spaces," St. Louis County Executive Steve Stenger said in an email in response to questions from the ©St. Louis Post-Dispatch. "The acquisition is part of my strategy to get the site ready for future use by a private-sector developer."[252]

Since then, St. Louis County was able to obtain the Macy's property for $1. As of February 10, 2017, the Port Authority controlled three of the five parcels of land that together form the former mall site. Negotiations were underway to buy a fourth property but the authority may turn to eminent domain to allow purchase of the fifth tract.[253]

Boeing Leadership Center

The impressive Boeing Leadership Center complex on the west side of New Halls Ferry Road at Shackelford is just outside Old Jamestown boundaries. But despite not being very noticeable from the road, it is a significant presence in the neighborhood. It was well described in these excerpts from "Winging it at Boeing's Leadership Center," Workforce, October 2000[254]

> "....On the 286- acre campus snuggled against a hillside that overlooks the confluence of the Missouri, Illinois, and Mississippi Rivers in northwest suburban St. Louis, the three lodge buildings that make up Boeing's Leadership Center provide just the right mix of a secluded, well-appointed, and well-equipped location for the task at hand. And that task is part academic and part social, providing a central location to help everyone from the company's chief executive down to newly minted managers hone their work and leadership skills within a custom-designed curriculum....
>
> "The facility, the former Desloge estate and gentleman's farm, came to the aerospace giant through its merger with McDonnell Douglas in 1997. The main building was originally an underground ballroom. Today it serves as a meeting room and dining area. The old carriage house has been renovated for seminar rooms.
>
> "The $60 million Boeing Leadership Center opened in March of 1999. ...Boeing's chief operating officer gave the opening address and...continues as a regular lecturer. The university-like facility has 120 private residence rooms, a workshop with a large lecture hall, three large classrooms, and 21 breakout rooms where students work in teams on collaborative projects. The dining room, with its panoramic view of the bluffs overlooking the Illinois River, seats 156. There is also a fitness center.
>
> "Since opening, the center has proven so popular that Boeing is preparing to add a seven-story residence hall, doubling the space provided by the current wings, Mercer said....
>
> "This bringing together of workers from diverse business units is a key to the center's success.... 'The classroom program I participated in...could very well have been done at my worksite but I realized as soon as I got here, a critical part of the program was the people I met,' said Milligan, the facilities manager from California.... 'The emphasis is on working out common processes together, whether you are working in Anaheim, Seattle, or Houston.'"

Since that article was written, the residential facility has been expanded and the Vouziers mansion on the property has been adapted for employee meetings, etc.

Churches

A testament to the faith of Old Jamestown residents are the many churches within its boundaries:

St. Andrew United Methodist Church

St. Andrew UMC, 3975 North Highway 67, was established in 1965. Five families from the neighboring St. Mark's and North Hills Methodist Churches were commissioned to serve in the new congregation. Between April and June 1965 many meetings were held at the parsonage in Cross Keys Apartments. During these meetings the name of the church was discussed. Suggestions included Shoveltown Methodist Church based on the location of the new church property – Shoveltown was the name of the small community surrounding the new church at Old Halls Ferry and Hwy 67. Finally, the name "St. Andrew" was chosen — in honor of the first Apostle to follow Christ. Twenty-four people attended the first service in Black Jack Elementary School, where services were held until the new building was completed. St. Andrew continues to be one of the most ethnically and culturally diverse congregations in the Missouri Conference of the United Methodist Church. Diversity of pastoral leaders, staff, and laity is at the core of the unique call of St. Andrew to "make disciples for the transformation of the world." Christ-centered blended worship, music, mission, service, interfaith, ecumenical, and community engagement with people of all races, ages, class, and support of women in pastoral ministry is the strength of St. Andrew United Methodist Church. [255]

Salem Baptist Church

Salem Baptist Church, 19715 Old Jamestown Road, has existed in Old Jamestown for over 200 years. See Chapter 7 for a history of the church and its origins in Cold Water Cemetery.

Shalom Church City of Peace

Shalom's journey began on Sunday, June 6, 1993 at the home of Pastor Freddy and Cheryl Clark where 15 people met for the sole purpose of finding a place to worship. The name "Shalom" (which means peace) was given to the church in hopes of embracing the vision of Shalom where preaching, teaching, and praying are exemplified. The first worship service was held June 13, 1993 at Holiday Inn (Woodson Rd.) where 250 persons united over a period of one year. Then a larger facility was needed. In June 1994, worship services were held in the gymnasium of Ascension Catholic School located on the north side of the city. While there, another 100 persons united. Again, space ran out! On June 11, 2006, Shalom Church had its inaugural worship at the Hwy 67 campus. Now, the one church operates in two locations, Hwy 67 and Berkeley. Shalom Church continued to grow by leaps and bounds. Over the years Shalom Church has strengthened their reach into the community with holiday food baskets, toy drives, health awareness programs, scholarship awards, prison ministry, practical living classes, financial seminars and college fairs. Shalom Church hosted community meetings, and Seminary classes and graduations.[256]

St. Angela Merici Catholic Church

Archbishop Joseph Ritter founded Saint Angela Merici Parish, 3860 North Hwy 67, in June 1962. Father Paul Kersgieter was appointed the first Pastor. The parish opened with about 200 families. The first Masses were held in the Rectory until the Church was completed and dedicated in June 1964. The first four rooms of the school were opened in 1965 with 163 students. Enrollment today is more than 200 students. In June 1980 the Buckley Montine Center was dedicated and the expansion continued with the opening of additional classrooms and library. In fall 1995, portable classrooms were added to house a Kindergarten. In July 2005 the vision for the St. Louis Archdiocesan North County Deanery was enacted and St. Angela Merici welcomed its newest members from the closed Transfiguration and St. Christopher parishes. St. Angela now consists of over 1200 households.[257]

St. Norbert Catholic Church

St. Norbert Parish is on the west side of New Halls Ferry. In April 1966 ground was broken for the new church and by September 1966, 559 families were registered. Mass was offered for the first time in the new church in September 1967. In 1969, land was purchased for the athletic fields and in 1974, there were 900 families registered. After the 800+ home Barrington Downs was developed, parishioners saw the need for a school and in 1988 St. Norbert School opened with kindergarten, first, second and third grades – one grade was added each year. In 1992, with 1400 families, the new church building was dedicated. The original church was renovated into a parish hall with additional classrooms in 1994 and in June 1995, St. Norbert School had its first graduating class. In 2010 the K-8 students from St. Sabina Parish joined the St. Norbert students at the New Halls Ferry facility. The preschools were combined and additional classes were added for each age level. The preschool is located at the St. Sabina facility on Swallow Rd.[258]

Residents

Old Jamestown enjoys a diversity of residents who live comfortably and productively in subdivisions or on individual lots, all near the beauty of its natural blessings. Here are some demographic statistics for recent years.

According to the St. Louis Business Journal's July 2016 list of 25 "Wealthiest St. Louis Area Zip codes" in 2016 Old Jamestown had approximately 18,000 residents in 6700 households. Homes had an average value of $218,639 and median household income was $77,345.[259]

Between census years (the last one was 2010), the U.S. Census Bureau updates some of its data in the American Community Survey. The 2010-2014 Survey reports that for the Old Jamestown CDP (Census Designated Place), 93.4 percent of persons 25 or older have a high school diploma or higher and 36.7 percent of persons 25 or older have a bachelor's degree or higher.

More statistical info about Old Jamestown is on the USA.com web site-- http://www.usa.com/old-jamestown-mo.htm This is a private organization and we do not know the source of their data. World Media Group, LLC, http://www.worldmediagroupllc.com/

Old Jamestown remains a beautiful, enticing location with a fascinating history and continues to be home to an abundance of good people. For ongoing information about Old Jamestown, check out:

    Old Jamestown Association web site, www.oldjamestownassn.org, and

    Old Jamestown Association on Facebook https://www.facebook.com/OldJamestownAssociation

Current and former residents have shared many, many stories and connections to Old Jamestown, its people and its land. They could not all be included in this book. Over time, some will be added to an 'outtakes' section under the history tab on the OJA web site.

Chapter 11 Photos and Maps

Photos 11-1 and 11-2 Old Jamestown Association presidents:
Ken Smith, 1987-2011, and Chan Mahanta, 2012-2015
Current president Ellen Lutzow presents OJA 2016 Citizen of the Year award to Trudy Williams, for the Jamestown Bluffs Branch of St. Louis County Library

Photo 11-3 Pallottine Renewal Center
Drone Photo by Chan Mahanta

Photo 11-4 Jamestown New Horizons
Photo by Bonnie Grueninger, Founder

Photo 11-5 Jamestown Bluffs Branch
of St. Louis County Library:
http://www.slcl.org/content/jamestown-bluff-branch

Photo 11-6 Early Days of Black
Jack Fire Protection District:
http://www.blackjackfire.org/aboutbjfpd.shtml

Appendices

Appendix 1 - Old Jamestown Association History and Activity

The Old Jamestown Association was incorporated in 1942 as a benevolent organization by the State of Missouri. The reasons for forming the Association then are essentially the same reasons for its existence today. However, some of the concerns of area residents were quite different then:

Evaluate the pros and cons of incorporating as a village...The feeding of garbage to the hogs by local farmers...Trash burning along Sinks Road...Building of snow fences and snowplowing the roads (the Association owned its own snowplow)...

The Association continued to operate during the 1950s, often responding to such issues as, the threat of "being gobbled up by Florissant," the proposal to install a marine transmitting station for riverboat communications, and the project by Laclede Gas to store all of the natural gas for the St. Louis metropolitan area in a porous rock formation 1200 feet below the ground surface in the Old Jamestown Area.

The Association became inactive in 1963 and remained so until 1987 when St. Louis County announced the formation of the "New Jamestown" Area Study committee, whose purpose was to "help draft a plan for developing one of the County's few areas that remain largely undeveloped." The concept of a comprehensive plan was generally supported by residents. However, the virtual omission of area residents from the citizens' study committee, among other concerns, was viewed as intentional.

Assisted by Gaynor and Jane Blake who had participated in forming the original Old Jamestown Association in 1942, Jack and Loretta Becker and Ken and Olga Smith reactivated the Association in October 1987. Ken Smith was the first president and served for 24 years.

The Association took a contributory role in the Area Study by providing information to the County and keeping residents advised of the progress. The Area Study was complete and submitted to the County Council in April 1988, six months later than originally planned. A copy of the plan can be seen at http://www.stlouisco.com/Portals/8/docs/Document Library/planning/community planning and revitalization/north county/Old Jamestown Community Area Study.pdf

---

The selections below from 1988 Old Jamestown Association Newsletter cover the many development projects that were going in on the late 1980s and the Association's efforts to maintain the integrity of the area.

J.L. Mason Group – 1700 homes/36 hole golf course – East of Hwy 367 on Hwy 67 extension. Status: Inactive due to geological problems and extensive road development costs. Purchase options returned to property owners.

Mobil Oil – Gas/carwash/convenience store – Southeast corner of Old Halls Ferry Road and Hwy 67. Status: Original proposal approved by Planning Commission (5-4). The County Council returned it to the Planning Commission for reconsideration because it did not comply with the Old Jamestown Study guidelines. Planning Commission denied approval by a 6-2 vote. The Association advised residents in the immediate area of the details of this proposal.

F.M. Kemp Group – Portland Lake Estates – Thirty-two acres/R-2 single family (Planned Environment Unit) – Northeast side of Old Halls Ferry Road, northwest of Vaile Ave. (Keeven sod farm). Status: Approved by County Council. Construction has started. Seven acres of this project were sold to the Hazelwood School District for a potential school site. This project was originally requested for R-3 density but was reduced to R-2 because of area study guidelines.

Donald Basford – Village of Fours – sixty-eight units on eighteen acres arranged in fourteen four family buildings at R-2 and R-3 density (PEU) – North side of Hwy 67 approximately one half mile west of Old Jamestown Road. Status: Construction underway last year but stopped last Fall. No activity since then due to apparent financial problems.

Inwood Corporation (George Mustermann) – Bay Pointe – Twenty-three acres of R-2 and R-3 single family (PEU) consisting of 69 units – North side of Hwy 67 immediately adjacent to the west of the Village of Fours. Status: Approved by County Council. Awaiting developer's start.

Behlmann Associates – Parc Argonne Forest – Forty-nine acres/R-1 single family (PEU) – Old Jamestown Road and Vaile Avenue. Status: Project under constructions. Sewage from this project will be pumped along Vaile Avenue to Old Halls Ferry Road.

Gary Mazander – Glen Eagles – Twenty-one single family units (three acre lots) on sixty-six acres in Non-Urban zoning. Southeast side of Vaile Avenue, northeast of Old Halls Ferry Road. Status: Site development underway. This project was approved in 1985 for 106 single family units in R-1 and R-1A density. The developer subsequently became aware that the ruggedness of the karst topography made the site unsuitable for the density of development initially approved. The developer subsequently requested the zoning revert back to the non-urban development in three acre sites.

New Halls Ferry Landfill – New Halls Ferry Road and Douglas Road. Status: The landfill's construction permit has been upheld by the permit board. There appears to be no legal obstacles hindering the opening of the landfill at this point. The next move would be to appeal the air pollution permit to the state courts.

Chouteau Petroleum Co. – Service station and convenience store – Southwest corner of New Halls Ferry Road and Shackelford Road. Status: This project was being proposed on property owned by the Desloge family. Request denied by the Planning Commission.

Westlake Quarry – Fort Bellefontaine Road and New Jamestown Road. Status: Truck entrance and weigh station moved to Hwy 367. Expanding quarry operations on ninety-nine acres along the east side of New Jamestown Road south of existing quarry. The County began work on July 18 to the culvert on New Jamestown Road to alleviate water backup on adjacent property caused by quarry operations. The Association was involved with the County on this project.

Wallace and Rees – Jamestown Forest – Three acre density development on fifty-six acres (19 sites ranging from 2 to 5 acres) – South side of Old Jamestown Road, approximately one half mile north of

Fort Bellefontaine Road. Status: Site development underway. The density development procedure (where some lots are smaller but the overall average is three acres) was utilized because the ruggedness of the karst area topography was too severe to accommodate an adequate building site on uniform three acre tracts. St. Louis County water main will be extended from present terminal point at the American Legion Post to the project.

Bob Evans Restaurant – Southwest corner of Hwy 67 and Highway 367. Status: Site cleared, but no progress in several months.

Walters-Kroenke Development Co. – Jamestown Center – Thirty acres of commercial including a large retain store (originally a Wal-Mart), grocery store, banking facility, two fast food restaurants, small retail shops, and two medical/office buildings – Northwest corner of Hwy 67 and Old Jamestown Road. Status: This project was approved in 1985 but did not proceed after Wal-Mart withdrew their interest in the location. The karst topography to the North of this property causes a major problem in the disposal of storm water runoff. The County has tentatively approved an elaborate automated pumping system in the event the sinkholes back up. The developer submitted a revised site plan this spring so the project will apparently proceed in the near future.

Waldbart Nursery – Nine acres on the west side of Old Jamestown Road, just north of Hwy 67 (not their present location). Status: The Planning Commission approved a request for a conditional use permit on five acres of the nine acre site. Waldbart received the nine acres in exchange for relinquishing the lease at their present location on Hwy 67. The entire operation will relocate this fall into a new building on Old Jamestown Road. The Association provided details of the Waldbart proposal to residents in the immediate vicinity. The Association supported the move as being consistent with the Area Study by providing a suitable transition from commercial on Hwy 67 to large lot single family residences to the north.

The Waldbart relocation will be the key to the progress of Jamestown Center and to the development of the fifty-one-remaining acres of the original Walters-Kroenke property. The Inwood Corporation has development rights to that property in addition to ownership of fifty acres adjacent to the west with frontage on Hwy 67. Therefore, there will most likely be a major development of at least 100 acres consisting of single/multi-family/commercial within the year at that location.

Dalton Construction – Diane Marie Estates – Twenty-nine acres R-1 single family --- Old Jamestown Road opposite Shamblin Drive. Status: Site development underway. Sewage from this project will be pumped along Vaile Avenue to Old Halls Ferry Road.

DNR GEOLOGIST VISITS OLD JAMESTOWN AREA

Mr. Jim Vandike, staff geologist for the Division of Geology and Land Survey of the Department of Natural Resources, visited the Old Jamestown area for a one day field trip in February. His visit followed a meeting in Rolla of assistant state geologist, Jerry Vineyard, and Ken Smith, Association president. The Association had requested the state agency to provide information that would confirm the unique characteristics of the karst area in North County and how development would affect the area.

The field trip contingent of five persons included Mr. Ross Soper, staff planner for the County Department of Planning, who had expressed an interest in the DNR visit. The itinerary for the field trip included a one mile walk along the Missouri River and visits to known springs, caves, and major sinkhole formations in the area. Several springs and caves previously unrecorded were documented by Jim Vandike for state records. Water samples taken at several springs tested to be of drinking quality. That evening, after dinner at the Thurman residence, he met with the Association executive board.

The following excerpts are taken from the four page follow-up letter of the field trip. A copy of that letter is on record with the St. Louis County Planning Department as part of the area study and is therefore available to developers and their engineering consultants.

> "The Florissant Karst area is different from other regions of intense sinkhole development in eastern Missouri. It even differs from the karst in south St. Louis County, even though only a few miles separate the areas and they are developed in the same stratigraphic units."

> "One of the key differences between the type of sinkhole development in south St. Louis County and that of the Old Jamestown area is the size of the sinkholes. As you well know, urban development in the Oakville area has taken place in sinkhole plains. Some of the sinkholes were plugged and filled; drainage wells were installed in others. However, based on data from the Oakville 7 ½ minute topographic map, the sinkholes were mostly 10 to 20 feet deep, and relatively small diameter. Sinkholes in the Old Jamestown area, shown on the Florissant 7 ½ minute topographic map, are quite different. The sinkhole development is more intense here, sinkhole density is greater, and the sinkholes are deeper. Many shallow sinkholes are present, but there are also many that are 30, 40, and even 50 feet or more deep. Sinkhole diameters range from less than 100 feet to more than 1,000 feet."

> "It is difficult to imagine intense residential development in the sinkhole plain of the Old Jamestown area. Parts of the sinkhole plain in the area between sinkhole sub-basins, where sinkholes are shallower and fewer, could be selectively developed using techniques similar to those used in development in south St. Louis County. Much of the area, though, contains steep-sided, deep sinkholes and high sinkhole density. Where these conditions exist, I feel low-density residential development similar to that already existing in the Old Jamestown area is a far wiser and more environmentally sound choice. The karst area is so unique; preserving its natural state as much as possible would certainly be desirable."

There were a number of locations that were not visited due to shortage of time that day. Jim Vandike is coming back this fall or winter for further study of those and other features. Please advise the Association if you are aware of any unusual features on your property.

Appendix 2 - Old Jamestown Geographic Features

"The Florissant quadrangle is underlain by Paleozoic age limestone and shale. The majority of the quadrangle is underlain by the Burlington/Keokuk Formation and the Warsaw Formation. The bedrock in this area ranges from 290 feet msl to 450 feet msl. The bedrock is overlain by between 10 to 130 feet of surficial materials in the uplands and Missouri floodplain, respectively." Geological Overview on Missouri Department of Natural Resources 2010 Map.[260]

St. Louis County Department of Planning Map, December 2006:

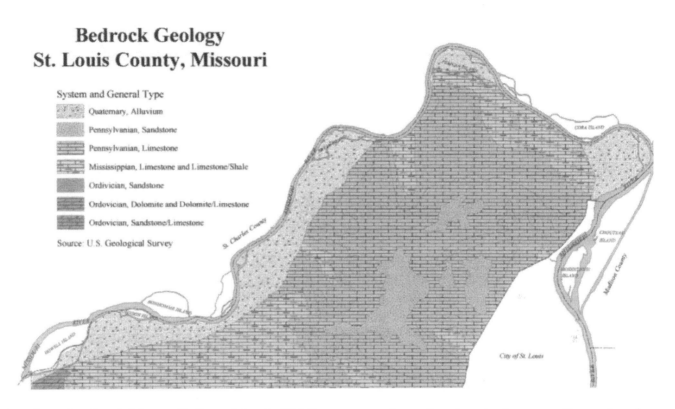

Other than the floodplain on Pelican Island, Old Jamestown along the river is shown as Pennsylvania, Limestone (green) and Mississippian, Limestone and Limestone/Shale (blue).

A bit of explanation about the Pennsylvanian and Mississippian periods, both part of the Paleozoic era, comes from these excerpts from "Missouri, The WPA Guide to the 'Show Me' State,":[261]

> "....Near the end of the Proterozoic era, about 500,000,000 years ago, the St. Francois Mountains gradually sank to their former level and were submerged by southern seas that swept over nearly a third of the continent."

"The arrival of the seas opened the long Paleozoic era, important in Missouri because most of the rock strata above the igneous rocks were deposited during this time. Beginning with the Cambrian period, the seas advanced again and again, some of them from the Gulf of Mexico, others from the Arctic regions, but each bringing great quantities of fine and coarse materials gleaned from adjacent lands...."

"Throughout the uniformly warm Paleozoic era the shallow seas teemed with life.... Crinoids, popularly known as "stone lilies," reached maximum abundance and variety during the subsequent Mississippian period. Growing in densely populated colonies of great extent, on flexible stalks at the bottom of the clear, shallow Mississippian sea, the crinoids probably looked much like fields of waving grain. Their remains form the major ingredient of Burlington limestone, the predominant surface rock that lies in a broad belt around the Ozark region, curving westward and southward from St. Louis to the vicinity of Springfield...."

"The last Paleozoic period of which there is a record in Missouri was the Pennsylvanian, which began perhaps 250,000,000 years ago. The Pennsylvanian is considered an important period because it was during this time that most of the coal of Missouri was formed and immense quantities of lead, zinc, and barite ores were deposited. The shales, sandstones, and limestones of the period cover more than a third of the State. The land was low and poorly drained at this time, permitting vegetation to accumulate on the swamp bottoms, layer upon layer, to be gradually converted into coal strata.

"At the same time, the subsoils of the swampy, tropical jungles, robbed of their minerals by the roots of coal-forming forests, were gradually altered to refractory, or fire, clays. These clays underlie much of St. Louis and are found in abundant deposits in central Missouri... During this time, also, the first insects appeared – giant cockroaches and dragonflies, many times the size of their modern descendants. ----- [OK, way more than you wanted to know.]...."

The formation of the Missouri River system from geography.about.com:

"The basin of the Jefferson-Mississippi-Missouri River system was first shaped after a period of major volcanic activity` and geologic stresses that formed the mountain systems of North America some two billion years ago. After significant erosion, several depressions in the ground were carved, including the valley in which the Mississippi River now flows. Much later the surrounding seas continuously flooded the area, further eroding the landscape and leaving a lot of water behind as they went away.

"More recently, about two million years ago, glaciers of 6,500 feet thick repeatedly encroached upon and retreated from the land. When the last ice age ended approximately 15,000 years ago, massive quantities of water were left behind to form the lakes and rivers of North America. The Jefferson-Mississippi-Missouri River system is just one of the many water features that fill the giant swatch of plain between the Appalachian Mounts of the east and the Rocky Mounts of the West." http://geography.about.com/od/specificplacesofinterest/a/mississippi.htm

Appendix 3 - Living with the Sinks – Missouri Resources Magazine

The text of this article and associated photos were graciously formatted and provided by the Missouri Department of Natural Resources

Living With the Sinks
Sinkholes in north St. Louis are cause for careful development by James Vandike
Fall 1995

When someone mentions St. Louis, any of several images may come to mind, from professional baseball to malls, restaurants, museums or rivers.

Bounded by the Missouri, Mississippi and Meramec rivers, about 84 percent of the St. Louis County and city borders are formed by water. Rivers are among the most prominent features of the St. Louis area, but there are other significant natural resources that receive less attention, yet play a role in the area's growth. These include karst features, such as sinkholes, losing streams, caves and springs, all of which are interrelated.

Although much of St. Louis County has been urbanized, there are many areas in which development has been limited because of terrain, geology, or water. One of these areas is at the northern tip of St. Louis County, in the community of Old Jamestown.

You won't find Old Jamestown on many maps, but the community is north of Coldwater Creek, west of U.S. Highway 67 (North Lindbergh Blvd.), and south of the Missouri River. Its western boundary generally follows Vaile Avenue and Old Halls Ferry Road.

A major reason why the Old Jamestown area has not been extensively developed is its karst geology – more than 56 percent of its landscape is drained by sinkholes.

Karst is a term that describes features formed by the disintegration of soluble rocks such as limestone and dolomite. These rocks can be "eaten away" by the carbon dioxide in rain water and groundwater, which reacts with the calcium carbonate in the rocks to form carbonic acid.

Sinkholes are bowl-shaped depressions on the surface that are formed by the removal of soil and rock beneath the surface. They indicate the presence of cavelike channels in the rock and well-established groundwater circulation.

Old Jamestown is mostly an upland area just south of the Missouri River. The bedrock is limestone overlain by a thick mantle of loess, unconsolidated silt deposited during the Pleistocene or Ice Ages. The loess generally is thickest close to the rivers and thins farther away. Its thickness in the Old Jamestown area varies from zero, where it has been removed by erosion, to more than 40 feet. The loess rests upon much older rock, the lower part of the Ste. Genevieve Limestone or the upper part of the St. Louis Limestone.

In the Ste. Genevieve and St. Louis limestones, sinkholes appear to form where the cave passages breach the bedrock surface along vertical fractures. Groundwater moving down through the soil causes the void to enlarge upward from the bedrock opening. The enlargement continues upward until the thin layer of loess bridging the surface cannot support its own weight and collapses, and a sinkhole is formed.

Sinkholes are constantly formed in karst areas. A dozen or more new sinkholes are reported in Missouri per year. Ken Smith, President of the Old Jamestown Association, said, "Long-time residents can point out sinkholes that cycle between being blocked and holding water, and then later going dry. New sinkholes can be seen forming throughout the area."

New sinkholes can be triggered by excessive soil moisture, overly dry soil, changes in surface drainage or other natural or man-made factors.

Although the area is called Old Jamestown, the karst has long been referred to as the "Florissant Karst Area." In the 3.3 square miles of the sinkhole plain, all water drains through sinkholes; there are no surface streams or valleys that channel water away after rainfall. All of the water that enters the sinkholes passes through underground cave systems before discharging into springs or rivers.

Within this sinkhole plain are hundreds of sinkholes ranging from a few feet to several hundred feet in diameter, and from a few feet to more than 70 feet deep. Small sinkholes may drain less than an acre. The largest sinkhole in the Old Jamestown Area contains a large pond that drains more than 200 acres. Many of the sinks are classic steep-sided, cone-shaped depressions.

The sinkhole plains can create problems for land use and urban development. Because sinkholes are an integral part of the surface water drainage system, modifying or filling them can cause problems for adjacent landowners. Where sinkholes are widely scattered, shallow, and have small diameters, development may not be seriously affected. But in the Old Jamestown, the sinkholes are large, deep and closely spaced. Even something as simple as a road can be difficult to build in the sinkhole plain.

Roads usually follow major compass directions, railroads or streams, or have some other rationale for their directional route. But, most roads in Old Jamestown are serpentine by necessity. Sinks and Old Jamestown roads, the major transportation arteries through the area, narrowly miss dozens of sinkholes as they snake through the pockmarked surface of the karst plain overlooking the Missouri River. Evidence of ground movement can be seen by the pavement deterioration on the inside of every curve adjoining a sinkhole along these two roads.

Road builders deal with minor problems compared to those encountered by home builders. The areas older homes generally are on large lots and are placed well away from sinkholes to avoid many problems inherent with development in karst settings. This is important because most older homes in the area have individual wastewater treatment systems and private domestic wells.

It takes careful engineering to fill a sinkhole to level a site for building. The fill must be well compacted to avoid settling. If a building is placed partly or completely on fill material, later settling can cause cracked foundations, basement leakage or other problems.

Changing the surface topography or routing water away from one sinkhole into another before it is injected into the underlying cave passage, alters the hydrology of the cave. In addition, the rate of surface-water runoff from undeveloped forest or grassland is considerably less than that of concrete, asphalt and rooftops. After development, the volume of direct surface-water runoff may increase as much as 35 percent.

The problems of developing subdivisions in karst areas have long been recognized in St. Louis County. Other karst areas of the city and county have received considerably more development than the karst area of Old Jamestown – but there are several important differences.

Most of the developed sinkhole areas are in the older part of the city or in the Jefferson Barracks-Oakville area of south St. Louis County. Here, the karst developed in the same rock unit as in north county, but there are fewer sinkholes. They also are generally smaller in diameter, more shallow, in some cases, drained by larger caves.

Developers in the other areas capped the bedrock openings of some sinkholes and back-filled them to a level grade. Other sinkholes that opened into the underlying cave system were equipped with inlet pipes before they were filled. The pipes channel stormwater runoff through the caves. As a precaution, the vertical stormwater inlet pipes were equipped with overflow pipes as a backup. These convey water to a nearby surface drainage if the vertical drain and cave fail to provide adequate drainage. Some large sinkholes were left undeveloped to serve as stormwater retention basins. Public water and sewer systems are also available in these areas.

Because of its geologic makeup, the sinkhole plain in the Old Jamestown area cannot safely support intense urbanization as other parts of the county can. Many of the individual sinkholes are too steep and too deep to allow development anywhere except on the rims between adjacent sinkholes. Many of the areas residents still rely on relatively shallow private water wells and private waste disposal systems.

Great care must be taken when septic systems, sinkholes and private wells are close together and share water in the same aquifer. Aquifers are partly recharged by rain water that drains into sinkholes. Newer waste disposal systems in this area often are complex and expensive, but necessary to protect water quality.

St. Louis County planners, engineers, and area residents recognized years ago that much of Old Jamestown could not safely support the level of urban development possible in other parts of the county. In 1987, Old Jamestown was recognized as an environmentally sensitive area by the St. Louis County Department of Planning. To cope with problems presented by the karst terrain, an area study was commissioned in 1988.

"The study was a natural outgrowth of the renewed interest in the area by residents and developers," says June Fowler, manager of the Comprehensive Planning Division in the county's Department of Planning. "It offered a great opportunity to be proactive in the land use process for this part of the county."

"The Community Area Study was undertaken to provide guidelines for future development decisions that would respect the environmental sensitivity and even protect it as a unique geological feature of the county," said D. Ross Soper, who coordinated the study for St. Louis County's Department of Planning.

The study recommended low-density residential development in the sinkhole plain with minimum lot sizes of three acres or larger. This level of development will not adversely alter the karst area or change sinkhole drainage patterns. Subsequent zoning requirements reflected these recommendations. Since then, there have been several requests for zoning changes that were denied because they would not have followed the recommendations contained in the 1988 study.

Geologists with the Missouri Department of Natural Resources' Division of Geology and Land Survey (DGLS) have studied the geologic and water resources of Old Jamestown. They have provided technical information and evaluations to homeowners and county officials. An effort has been made by DGLS, the Old Jamestown Association, and the St. Louis County Department of Planning to maintain the area's natural beauty while allowing a reasonable level of development.

The future of Old Jamestown appears bright. Through close cooperation with St. Louis County, area residents have been able to play an active role in deciding what development can take place safely.

Urban development in any karst area must take geologic and hydrologic factors and limitations into account. Without this awareness, the irreplaceable karst features so carefully sculpted by nature can be destroyed. It also can invite a host of environmental and economic problems that can be expensive to correct and difficult to live with.

"The lesson we must remember is that we are recent tenants of this delicate and slightly mysterious environment," said Soper. "There is a limit to how much we can alter what has taken ages to evolve in the earth beneath our feet. The hard thing for us to do is to remember just where and what those limits are. But if we forget, we will get a reminder; it's just a matter of time."

James Vandike is a Geologist and Acting Chief of the Groundwater Section in DNR's Division of Geology and Land Survey.

Appendix 3 Photos

All photos are from the article *Living with the Sinks*, provided by the Department of Natural Resources

Photo 1 One of the largest sinkholes in Old Jamestown forms a lake near a residential area

Photo 2 The Laclede Gas Co. stores natural gas in wells far beneath sinkholes and other karst features. A domelike rock formation prevents the gas from escaping.

Photo 3 The pavement on a road that winds through the Old Jamestown area starts to crumble because of the unstable ground around a sinkhole.

Appendix 4 - Newspaper Article – Early Days in Missouri

(Possibly from Watchman-Advocate) article is taken from St. Charles Cosmos. Unknown date – "St. Charles Cosmos" was published from 1869 to 1902. Other newspapers with St. Charles Cosmos in the name were published before and after that time.

Early Days in Missouri

Interesting Reminiscences of Pioneer Life in "Upper Louisiana."

Owen's Fort a Hundred Years Ago. The First American Settler in St. Louis County

About the year 1780, there resided in the western part of North Carolina, a Mr. John Patterson. The soil of that part of the State being thin, and distance from market too serious an obstacle to the transportation of farm products, the worldly condition of Mr. John Patterson was far from opulent. A large family of sons were growing up around him, and, if a desire to better his condition rose within him, the knowledge of the way to do so was unrevealed and unknown to him.

One evening two travelers rode up to the Patterson homestead, asked for a night's lodging and were kindly bidden to stay. The next morning one of the travelers mounted his horse and rode off, leaving his companion still domiciled at the house. Acquaintance, fellowship and friendship soon sprung up between the guest, Mr. James Richardson, and Mr. John Patterson. Richardson told Patterson that he and his friend were from Missouri, then called Upper Louisiana; that it was the country for poor men like Patterson, and that the Spanish Alcalde gave large tracts of land to actual settlers; and ended by advising his new friend to pack up and go back with him to Upper Louisiana, promising him all the assistance in his power.

Richardson's companion was gone about three weeks, when one evening he returned in company with a beautiful and accomplished lady. A minister was sent for, and a wedding took place between the lady and Mr. Richardson. Old Mr. John Patterson used to say, long years after, that Mrs. Richardson was the finest dressed lady he ever saw, and the silk dress she wore was the first that ever came into his section of North Carolina. After spending a day or so with Mr. Patterson, Richardson and wife and companion started for their far-off Western home.

It seems that some few years previous to the time we are speaking of, Mr. Richardson had had some kind of difficulty with a neighbor, and prudence counseled flight on his part. He fled, came to Missouri and settled at Owen's Station and Owen's Fort, now Bridgeton, in St. Louis County. But he had left behind him a sweetheart, the only woman dear to him, --- for whom he resolved to risk much to gain. Thinking it would not be safe for himself to venture into the immediate neighborhood of his old difficulty, where dwelt his inamorata, he took with him a trusty Western friend, journeyed on until he reached Mr. Patterson's, and from there sent his friend to bring his future wife to him.

This Mr. James Richardson was a man of warm, generous impulses, and many were the poor immigrants that he befriended, helped and supported, not only those around him but to all passing through Owen's Fort, on their way to join Daniel Boone in his home in Northern Missouri. Richardson was a saddler by trade. Learning that the wife of the Spanish Alcalde was fond of equestrian exercise, but was denied the pleasure through want of a saddle, he made her one, gaining thereby not only her gratitude, but the old Alcalde's, who gave him 1000 arpens of land in the Florissant Valley, and which is known to this day as United survey No. 405, including in its boundaries the present large farm of James, Stanton and George Hume, and the Tunstall and John Hyatt places.

From all the information I can obtain I feel warranted in asserting that James Richardson was the first American or English-speaking citizen that settled in this section. A few years afterward came Daniel Boone, who moved to and settled in the northern part of the State. Richardson was the chief man or captain at Owen's Fort, and was, even in those days, a man of considerable property, which he used and generously shared with all deserving immigrants. It seemed to be the desire of Richardson to induce as many Americans as he could to move and settle here. Every Kentuckian that came here in those times wished to get as near to Daniel Boone as he could. The journey was long and dangerous, and generally on entering Missouri at St. Louis, they would start for Owen's Fort, where Richardson would rest them, supply them with what was most needed, and then forward them by guide to Pond's Fort, on the Boonville road in St. Charles County, and sometimes as far as Loutre's Fort, on Loutre Island, above St. Charles.

We believe that Richardson lies in the old Fee Fee Church-yard, and, if a splendid monument is not erected over his grave, it should be, for if ever a man loved his fellowman that man was James Richardson. One thing is sure, his good and generous acts are still remembered by the grandchildren of many old pioneers in this valley, who speak in warmest praise of him who was such a stanch friend of their grandfathers and grandmothers.

Every place in olden times that was settled by Americans was called a fort. Opposite Boonville are salt springs or "licks," and here was built Fort Cooper. These salt springs, or licks, were, for thirty or forty years, the only place from which salt could be procured. Said an old pioneer lady: "In early days we had two things to trouble us—to get salt and pay taxes." This same lady was married in August, and she quaintly remarked that the wedding guests ate a whole bullock, to keep it from being spoiled by the weather.

The year after Richardson's visit to North Carolina, Mr. John Patterson started to move to Missouri. The whole wealth of the family was packed on the backs of four horses. There were no roads, no bridges and no ferries, so that it was impossible to travel by wagons. With plenty of powder and balls, a few axes, a small amount of clothing, and a gun for every one capable of handling the same, even to the mother, they began their journey of over 1,200 miles.

That was a memorable migration. Arriving on the banks of a stream, search was made up and down its banks for a ford, and should none be discovered, constructing a rude raft and floating thereon the mother and children. At night they lay down without fire, for fear of lurking savages, whilst by turns they stood guard over the sleepers. Their food was the wild game that came in their way, cooked and eaten without salt or bread. Sometimes a few wild herbs, a scant supply of berries or some forest fruit provided them with a change of diet.

Thus they journeyed through Kentucky and Illinois, until they arrived at Kaskaskia, where they were warned to stop and take shelter in the fort, as the Indians were on the war-path, and even threatened that stronghold. For eighteen months they rested here, starved here, fought the Indians and tried to raise corn, but always had it destroyed by the savages before maturity.

This is known to all the Pattersons as the "starving time," and to this day, Mrs. Acena Patterson, now very old, declares she dislikes to see even the smallest bit of bread wasted.

Again taking up the westward march, Mr. John Patterson and family entered the Territory of Upper Louisiana in the year 1784. The country was under Spanish rule, Zenou Trudeau being the Alcalde or Governor. St. Louis had but ten or twelve dwellings, besides a fort. To Owen's Fort went Mr. John Patterson and family, where they were graciously received by their old friend Richardson.

The Spanish Alcalde refused them a grant of land, but lion-hearted and generous Richardson soon found a farm for sale suited to them, and with his assistance they were soon settled in their Western home. There was a log cabin, fifteen by twenty, on the farm; a few acres were already cleared and broke, and, with nothing but an ax, Mr. Patterson set to work to make himself furniture, plows and farm utensils.

An inside view of one of those old pioneer cabins would be a subject for the pencil of an artist—the table, benches, bedsteads, stools and other furniture being hewed and shaped in form by the ax only. The beds were leaves, straw, and in some few instances wool. Many an infant's cradle was only a hollow log, cut off at either end, and easily made to rock. Plates were either wood or tin, chinaware being too brittle for transportation, whilst the cups were gourds or wooden vessels. Wolves being plentiful, everything they could destroy had to be housed. Sheep were never far from the watchful eyes of a keeper during the day, and at night were securely fastened up.

Corn, cotton, flax and wheat were the principal crops. The women did the cooking, carding, spinning and weaving of the cotton, wool and flax. They also helped their husbands in the fields, wielding alongside of them the short, old-time sickle, binding, shocking and even threshing the grain…and clearing it of chaff with a hand-fan! Those were happy times, when modern inventions were not even dreamed of, and the slow laborious process of garnering, threshing and cleaning the grain was labor indeed.

There was not a mill of any kind in the land. The grain was put in a hollow stump or log, and pounded or broken with a heavy pestle, attached to a swoop, similar to those used for drawing water from wells. The flour was sifted, and, though coarse, was made into good, palatable bread. The manner of baking bread was novel. It is to be remembered there were no stoves, no "Dutch overs," in fact, no iron vessels whatever. A board was made perfectly smooth, greased and set before the fire of live coals on an incline of 45 degrees; the cake or bread was put on this, and, by constant turning, was done brown through and through.

With the rude implements of farming used in those days, no great area of land could be cultivated. Sometimes a man's crop became almost worthless before his turn came for borrowing a sickle of his neighbor, for it was not everyone that was smithy enough to manufacture and sharpen a rude one for himself. There was not a blacksmith in all the land. Thus it was that the real scarcity, if not want, often boded near the pioneer's dwelling, and though wild game was plentiful, yet man, civilized man, craves bread and salt, and must have them.

In those early times there was no market, no demand, for agricultural products. Each raised enough for himself and family, and may occasionally have had a little to spare; but to whom should he make sale? In St. Louis? Ah! Many times, even so late as 1820, has the farmer offered to give away his load of potatoes, corn or other farm products in St. Louis, in order not to waste or carry it back with him in the country, and been informed that was not wanted! Once as late as 1825, a farmer went to St. Louis with a load of corn meal, for which he tried to get almost any price the purchaser might be pleased to give. He could not make sale of a bushel of it. At last he drove up to a house, knocked at the door, and, on the landlady's appearance, offered to present her with all the corn meal she wished as a free gift. She asked him if it was sifted. On being informed that it was not, she declined taking any of it, even as a present!

Here at the old homestead, died the wife of John Patterson, she who had journeyed with him from North Carolina. The old gentleman remained a widower for a year or so and then married a widow Jamison; their united families, his and hers, made thirty children under one roof!

Notwithstanding John Patterson was born and raised in a slave State, he was, undoubtedly, the first Free Soiler in the West. He was bitterly opposed to slavery; believed it a sin and demoralizing in its effects on both slave and master. When it came to the question of freedom or slavery on the admission of the State of Missouri in the Union, he boldly spoke and used all his influence in favor of freedom. None of his children have ever owned slaves by purchase; some, it is true, came in their possession by inheritance, but they were so humanely treated that today they are employed by their former unwilling owners.

Virtues may not be hereditary, but they seem to cling to certain families from generation to generation, and so it is with the present race of Pattersons. They are noted for many sterling qualities of heart and mind that lift them above the mass, among which are veneration and respect for ancestors and their moral teachings, allied to a certain independence of right action, let the consequences be what they may.

Appendix 5 - Congressional Testimony – Election Judge at Musick's Ferry

Documents, House of Representatives, First Session of the Forth-Seventh Congress, 1981-1982, Washington, Government Printing Office, 1882. *Pages 970 to 973 have testimony about possible denial of voting opportunities to people who live in St. Louis City. The following transcript is from pages 1052 to 1054 about possible voting by nonresidents or other problems at Musick's Ferry.*

109 GUSTAVUS WITTICH, produced, sworn, and examined on the part of the contestant, deposeth and saith:

By Mr. POLLARD:

Question. What is your full name? – Answer. Gustavus Wittich.

Q. Where do you live? – A. Saint Ferdinand Township

Q. You were a judge at the election up there on that day? – A. Yes, sir.

Q. What is the number of your precinct of which you were a judge, sir? – A. Number 11, on Music's Ferry.

Q. What do you know, Mr. Wittich, about any ballots that were received and counted for Mr. Frost for Congress, which had been mutilated – torn in two? – A. I objected against one vote there for counting of that vote, but I was overruled by the majority, and it was counted.

Q. Why did you object? – A. I objected because it was half Republican and half Democratic. It was torn right through the middle and stuck together.

Q. Were there on that ticket the names for duplicate offices; I mean, were there any names for Republican officers and Democrats for the same offices? – A. Yes, sir; there are one there, anyhow. I don't know exactly which name it was on that ticket. I think it was for Wickham and Thompson, if I am not mistaken; but I cannot tell for certain. I think that both of those names were on that ticket.

Q. They were both running for the same offices, weren't they? – A. Yes, sir.

Q. One was a Democrat and one a Republican? – A. Yes, sir; one was a Democrat and one was a Republican.

Q. That ticket remained in and was counted for Frost? – A. I was counted out myself on that proposition.

Q. I mean that ticket was counted? – A. It was counted, yes, sir.

Q. And it was returned as counted for Mr. Frost? – A. Yes, sir.

Cross-examination by MR. DONOVAN, counsel for contestee:

Q. Is that the only ticket that you know of? – A. That is the only ticket.

Q. That is all the trouble that you had that day? -- A. That is the only trouble we got, and that was no trouble.

Q. How many votes were cast at your poll for Frost and how many for Sessinghaus? – A. Well, it was close to 75 for Frost and 25 for Sessinghaus.

Q. You are giving your best recollection of the returns, are you? – A. I am giving my best recollection; yes, sir. It was close on 100; and it was three-fourth for Frost and one-fourth for Sessinghaus.

Q. Are there any colored men in that polling district? – A. Not very many, so far as I can collected – six or seven.

Q. Do you know whether they live in the vicinity of Musick's Ferry? -- A. Yes, sir.

Q. Farm hands there? – A. Well, some farm hands.

Q. Do you know whether any came from Illinois to vote at that poll? – A. Now, sir; not one; the vote was honest and fair.

Q. How far is Black Jack from Musick's Ferry? – A. About six miles.

Q. You were not down at Black Jack that day? – A. No, sir; I was not down there.

Q. Do you know of colored men being brought over from Illinois to vote at Black Jack? – A. No, I guess I never heard of it.

Q. How long have you lived, Mr. Wittich, in Saint Ferdinand Township? – A. I have lived there for about twenty-five years.

Q. Have you ever been at the poll at Black Jack? – A. I was there a good many times.

Q. Do you know whether it is a habit of Republican managers to bring negroes from Illinois to vote them on every election? – A. I never heard of this. There is no registration there; I know that.

Q. The registration law does not apply to the county? – A. Nobody is registered there. Everybody can vote where he likes to vote.

Q. Do you know whether or not, from your experience at Black Jack, if that is not the habit of Republican managers to dose that poll with colored voters from Illinois? – A. No, sir; I never saw one there. I was voting down there myself because I live within three miles of Black Jack, and a very little way from Musick's Ferry.

Q. It was done at Black Jack when Mr. Metcalfe was running? – A. Then I voted for Metcalfe at that time. I was clerk at that time, and I think I know all them colored men that lives in St. Ferdinand Township pretty near.

Q. I was not asking you as to gentlemen living in the township, but whether or not, it was the habit of Republican managers to bring colored men over from the State of Illinois and vote them at Black Jack, and whether or not that has not been so at all elections? – A. No, sir.

Q. That is, not to your knowledge? – A. No, sir; not to my knowledges; because I know there is too much honesty there to do such things.

Q. Who are the honest men there? – A. Well, I expect everybody there is honest, without any exception.

Q. All the white and black together? – A. Yes, sir; altogether.

Q. All are honest men at Black Jack? – A. Yes, sir; yes, sir.

Q. They may not be saints though? – A. Well, I hardly think you can make any objections to that.

MR. POLLARD. A man cannot be a saint until he has been dead one hundred years; I believe that is the law of your church, Mr. DONOVAN.

By Mr. DONOVAN:

Q. Now, how many judges and clerks were there at your poll at Musick's Ferry? – A. Musick's Ferry there were four.

Q. Two judges and two clerks? – A. Four clerks.

Q. Four judges and two clerks? – A. Four judges and four clerks.

Q. Half of them were Republican and half were Democrats? – A. Half of them were Republicans and half were Democrats.

Q. Your Republican brother judge did not agree with you in regard to this ticket; he thought it ought to be counted? -- A. Certainly thought so.

Q. You were the only one of the four that raised any question in regard to it? – A. Well, I objected against it. We took a vote, and all of the judges ------

Q. And they were three to one? – A. Three against one. Somebody that voted took a Republican ticket; then he took a Democratic ticket; voted for Garfield for President and for the Democratic State officers.

Q. Just cut the tickets in two, didn't he? – A. Not for State officers as far as I can recollect; it was a whole Republican ticket, till the county officers and Congress.

Q. Just about where did he split off the Republican ticket? – A. If I am not mistaken the ticket was number 180.

Mr. POLLARD. Between what names was it cut is Mr. Donovan's question. – A. I say it was made of two tickets of both sides of politics.

By Mr. DONOVAN:

Q. Just about where did he divide his ticket? – A. Well, I say it was right below; the head was from the Republican ticket and the bottom was a Democratic ticket; there was no two tickets, but there was two half tickets, half Republican and half Democratic; and where these tickets joined two men ran for the same office on different tickets. If am not mistaken those names were Wickham and Thompson. It may be, it was one more, or another name; I can't recollect now.

Q. But three of the judges thought it was proper to count the ticket that the man had made use of that way, and they so received his vote? – A. Yes, sir.

Signature waived.

Appendix 6 - Occasional Crime at Musick's Ferry

Over the years, Musick's Ferry occasionally appeared in newspaper stories about crime or violence. Here are some snippets…

1885 – A Stone-Thrower "Downs" a Man Who Relied Upon a Hoe. Last Sunday night at Musick's Ferry, John Smiley, an old resident, engaged in a rough and tumble fight, free-for-all rules, with an itinerant preacher named Brown, in which both of them were very severely injured. Brown, or rather the Rev. Mr. Brown as he is better known, has been dispensing the gospel according to the Methodist belief to the inhabitants of the French villages of Cross Keys, Florissant and Musick's Ferry for over a year past; sometimes exhorting his flock from under the shady recesses of a haystack or a spreading chestnut tree, then again in a barn or school-house, and on rare occasions in a church, as the opportunity and place afforded. He has no particular following and his congregations were slow to help the hand that guides them when the collection hat was passed around. Brown has been forced to "board around" and put in his odd hours in work as a hired hand to the neighboring farmers. Last week he stayed at the house of Mr. Smiley…. [During a dispute between the two about money owed, Smiley picked up] an old fashioned blacksmith-made hoe and slashed in Brown's direction, striking the reverend gentleman on the left arm, …nearly severing that member from his body. Brown yelled with pain and … let fly a stone at the old man which caught him just at aft the ear, knocking him down and leaving him insensible. Brown came to this city this morning to have his wounded arm dressed. Smiley's wound is not so severe as at first supposed. This morning he had recovered sufficiently to be able to ride over to Florissant to secure legal advice about prosecuting Brown and he expressed his intention of dealing out the full penalty of the law to the reference gentleman. The old French settlers around Cross Keys and Musick's Ferry are very much wrought up over the affair on account of the prominence of Smiley,, who is one of the oldest residents of the county, and has borne an excellent reputation.

1895 – Horrible and Probably Fatal Assault Upon Young Louis Hardy. The villagers at Musick's Ferry … are anxious to catch George Knappitz and have him punished for his cowardly and brutal attack with a club upon Louis Hardy, a 17-year-old boy. Officers of St. Louis and St. Charles Counties are searching for the fugitive. ….   Knappitz, his son George and Hardy have been working for a Musick's Ferry quarryman named [John B.]Warren with whom they boarded. Last Sunday young Knappitz and Hardy went swimming in the Missouri River at the Ferry and indulged in the usual frolics. After a time they quarreled and …they threw river mud at each other but did not come to blows. Last Monday morning Hardy was engaged in loading a wagon with stone in the quarry. … [as soon as they were alone the elder] Knappitz stepped up behind Hardy and struck him on the back of the head. The boy fell unconscious, his head in front of the wagon wheel and near the heels of one of the mules. It is believed that Knappitz then plied the club on Hardy's head three times and inflicted the scalp wounds. … A few minutes later the elder Warren returned and saw Hardy lying in a pool of blood. … As soon as Hardy was made comfortable in Warren's house the alarm was given and a search was made for Knappitz. He was discovered rowing a skiff down the Missouri toward the Mississippi, and had too great a lead to be overtaken. A messenger was sent post haste to Florissant, five miles distant, for Dr. Jensen. He labored for three days to restore Hardy to consciousness and succeeded Thursday.

1915 – Boys Overturn Stolen Auto. Robert Walsh, 18 years old, of Montgomery street, and George Turner, 17 of Cass avenue, and three other youths, were in an automobile which ran into a fence and was overturned and wrecked at Musick's Ferry on the Hall's Ferry road, at 1:30 o'clock this morning. The other three ran away. Walsh and Turner were detained by persons residing near the scene of the wreck until Constable John Mueller arrived. He arrested them on the charge of reckless driving, and locked them up in Clayton. The automobile bore the license number 12,143 issued to O. K. Grammer of Semple place. The machine was stolen from in front of his home last night.

1916 – Man Held for Grand Jury on Arson Charge. Frederick Fischer, 36 years old, a carpenter of Musick's Ferry, was bound over to the grand jury under a bond of $2000 at his preliminary hearing today at Florissant on a charge of arson. Floyd W. Brooks, Assistant Prosecuting Attorney, said Fischer admitted having set fire to the home of Edward Teason, near Musick's Ferry, September 21, because Teason objected to Fischer courting his 16-year-old daughter.

1974 – Alton Telegraph. "Todd Friedman's body found; murder apparent. The bodies of an Alton clerk and his boss were found shot to death in dense woods in northwest St. Louis County, ending one of the biggest missing person hunts in St. Louis County police history. The mysterious disappearance of Todd Friedman, 22, of Alton and Fred Gent, 21, from the Radio Shack in Florissant reached its end when their badly decomposed bodies were discovered in deep undergrowth only 4-6 miles from the scene of the kidnapping. Friedman, son of prominent Alton businessman Julian Friedman, and Gent, the Radio Shack manager, each died of a single bullet fired into the back of the head.... Off-duty St. Louis Police Homicide detective Edwin Kaelin and his daughter, Peggy, 13, were tramping through the woods, looking for a Christmas tree, when they found the bodies…. [No arrests were made for the Radio Shack abduction and murders but the crime was similar to an earlier abduction and murder of a pharmacist and clerk near Hampton and Goodfellow in St. Louis. Suspects were arrested for those murders and they pled guilty.] [Peggy Kaelin later became a Bellefontaine Neighbors Police officer and died when struck by a car while on her way to work in 2015. She attributed her interest in police work to being with her father when they found the bodies.]

Appendix 7 - Vincent Family – New Coldwater Burying Ground

Mystery of Little Cemetery Is Solved, Florissant Valley Reporter, February 26, 1959

By JoAnn Bender

The sole trustee today of the "Coldwater Burial Ground" is Frazier Vincent, Sr., who looks 20 years younger than his 77 years as proved by his birth certificate.

Both of his parents were slaves. Both are buried in the little cemetery.

Mr. Vincent's father, Henry Vincent, died and was buried in 1900 in this little one-half acre cemetery. He helped collected $50 from area residents for which to buy the land on Sept. 27, 1886.

The site for it was chosen on which the African Church and school was already located.

"We had a preacher, mostly every Sunday," told Mr. Vincent. And then with his eyes dancing, he began to tell about the good old days when, right after church, good ol' basket dinners would be spread out under the shade of some big trees which once were nearby the church. That's the only way some older people have their enjoyment now, said Mr. Vincent, by recalling the days when they had such easy, good times. "Nobody is going their way today," he explained, "They're only going the other way."

Delia (Hayes) Vincent died and was buried in 1909. She was such a stout woman, said her son, that the frame had to be taken out of the window so they could get her casket out. She weighed over 300 pounds but just how much more was never known because the scale she was weighed on only went to 300 pounds.

He told how his mother was sold at the age of 16 for $800. "She was a fine looking woman," he said. His father, he said, was a slave in Bridgeton. Later the family lived for 14 years on New Halls Ferry Road near Shackelford on property which they rented to farm. He thought his parents had met at a church function.

Delia and Henry Vincent had five children, two of whom are buried in the little cemetery: Mannie, who died at the age of 78; and Eddie died in 1949 at the age of 75. Fred, who died at 76, is buried in Washington Park, and his sister Emma Bragg, who was born in 1859, died in 1918 and is buried in Troy, Missouri. His mother's brother William B. Hays, who died in January 1930, is also buried there. He also was a slave.

Speaking of his parents' slavehood, Mr. Vincent said that "Some had good homes and some had bad homes," but his parents had "good homes."

Mr. Vincent went to school in the little combination school and church which he estimated burned about 30 years ago [1929]. Miss Mary Keen was the teacher. He estimated that he went to school off and on quitting to help on the farm, with what was a fourth grade education. He also told of going to another school in the area called "Sink" which was held in a two-room home, one room of which was carried on a basket weaving trade, and in the other the school.

Mr. Vincent and his wife Franzitter (Johnson) moved to Robertson when they lost everything when their house on five acres of ground burned to the ground. Their two oldest children, Josephine Allen,

Robertson, and James H. Vincent, 36, O'Fallon, then went to stay with their grandparents in Webster Groves so they could go to school. Later their two younger children, Frazier S., Jr., 34, Robertson, and Bettie V. Britts, 30, West Alton, went to stay with their uncle in Overland so they could go to Elm Wood School.

Eddie Vincent was married to Daisy Campbell of Black Jack. There are two sons surviving them. They are Sylvester Vincent of St. Louis and Armond Vincent of Prospect Hills, Missouri. Mr. Vincent's sister, Emma Bragg, had two children Vincent Bragg of St. Louis and Cyril Borner of Detroit, Michigan. Theodore Vincent married Beaulah Todd of Randoph County near Huntsville, Missouri, who at the age of 76 is now living in Robertson.

Mr. Vincent figured that a couple hundred persons must have been interred in the small cemetery over the years without charge. "Some are strangers. Not plum strangers but were not known to all the family," related Mr. Vincent.

In the deed it states that permission must come from the trustees for burial there and the order in which they will be buried.

"I've done something of everything" said Mr. Vincent of his former jobs. Primarily he was a farmer, now retired. He spoke with pride of his son James who was in the Navy during WW II and of his son Frazier who was in the Army and stationed in Germany in WW II.

"To get people to tell the truth is a very hard thing," he felt today. That is why he brought with him a copy of the hand-written deed to the cemetery, the methodical and aging list of the people who had given money for the cemetery, and his birth certificate.

"All this won't interest people who don't know anything about it, but they will learn by reading about it. It will be interesting to all those people who used to know us who don't know if we're living or not," he continued. "Folks like Mr. Paul Wehmer who wrote that letter. (Ed. Note: See Mr. Wehmer's letter, submitted to our Black Jack columnist Joe Hagedorn and which appears in an adjoining column) it brings their thoughts back to the old times. And it brought me back to tell what I knew," he concluded.

As for future plans for the cemetery he said, "I'm going to take care of it. I'm going to do the biggest part myself to get it in shape."

Joe Desloge, Jr., wrote about [Frazier Vincent] in his 1995 book, Passport to Manhood:[262]

> "In September, 1992, I wrote the ©St. Louis Post-Dispatch that [Frazier Vincent's] name leapt out at me from the August 24, 1992 article concerning an overgrown abandoned cemetery in Black Jack and Vincent's lack of a headstone. It instantly carried me back 60 years to when I was 7 years old. Could this be the old gentleman who worked for Papa in the early 1930s Depression? Rapidly reading the article, I concluded it indeed was! Papa mentioned how Frazier had been buried in an old small cemetery in Black Jack especially for colored folk.
>
> "Frazier, a hard worker who didn't want to take a chance losing his precious $2.00/day job, faithfully brought his wages home to his wife, Mattie, and his children. When

Frazier's little frame house mysteriously burned down, Papa helped him rebuild--this time of brick. Frazier always smoked his 10-cent corncob pipe, wore a faded sweat-stained corduroy hunting cap over his gray hair and carried a dollar pocket watch. I wondered why it only had an hour hand. He explained that it had been given to him and besides the hour hand was all he needed to tell dinner time which was noon. I asked why he never ate his sandwich with Papa's other employees. He explained they didn't want to eat with a Negro but that was all right with him. Being 7 years old, I tried to convince him he was imagining the discrimination. All he said was, 'God bless you, when you get older you will change.'…."

Appendix 8 - Baptist Friends to Humanity

From the National Register of Historic Places Application for Cold Water Cemetery:

Although often called "Emancipators" by others, according to Peck the Baptist churches that began calling themselves "Friends to Humanity" around 1807, "differed widely from modern abolitionists of the Northern States and England, at least in the following particulars":

> 1. They never adopted the dogma that slaveholding is a "sin per se," -- a sin in itself, irrespective of all the circumstances in which the parties might be providentially placed. Hence they could consistently buy slaves and prepare them for freedom; or contribute funds to enable slaves to purchase themselves, with a clear conscience.
> 2. They never aided fugitive slaves to escape from their masters, or secreted them, in violation of the constitution and laws of the land.
> 3. They never interfered in any objectionable way with the legal and political rights of slaveholders. They preached the gospel in an acceptable manner among slaveholders.
> 4. They aimed to do good both to master and servant, in a quiet, lawful and peaceable mode.
> 5. They endeavored to consult the true interests of all parties concerned.
> 6. They ever upheld the constitution and laws of the country in a peaceful way.

Although the movement had arisen in Kentucky ca. 1807, already in 1813 a New England Baptist noted that the "Friends to Humanity" had been making themselves felt in the western territories as well. He wrote of an association of Baptist churches on both sides of the Mississippi between the Ohio and Missouri rivers that had been formed about 1807 but "disputes about slavery were introduced in [the association]. And effected its division in 1809. Three churches maintained the holding of slaves, and the rest opposed it. Disputes rose so high, that they could no longer travel in fellowship."

Appendix 9 – Slavery and Civil War

Written by Cindy Winkler for her Civil War Presentation to the Old Jamestown Association, May 2012, http://cindywinkler.com/civil-war-presentation-to-the-old-jamestown-association/

For more than 150 years, we Americans have been fascinated by the Civil War/War Between the States/The War of Northern Aggression, etc. The war's prevalence in popular culture tends to go in and out of vogue in movies, books, and TV shows.

And of course, Missouri did secede from the Union....or maybe it would be better to say that we were admitted into the Confederate States of America in November of 1861. Only the Confederate-sympathizing portion of the Missouri government seceded. The loyal Union portion of the state remained a part of the United States of America. It must have been a very confusing time to be a Missouri resident – and politician.

I know out in Western Missouri there are historical markers reminding daily of losses sustained during the Civil War. Jayhawking this or Bushwacking that….. But we don't have so many around here. The only one I know of off the top of my head is in Portage Des Sioux. It would be easy for us Missourians to forget – or not to know at all – that Missouri saw more battles and skirmishes during the Civil War than any other states except Virginia and Tennessee.

Of course the two major issues that precipitated the war were Slavery and State's rights. And of course we all know that Missouri was admitted to the union in 1821 as a slave state.

Tonight I'm going to share with you a few things I've found with respect to both State's rights and Slavery, during the time of the Civil War, right here in the Old Jamestown Area. Make no mistake: This is not a scholarly presentation. Think of it as, "History on Ice," akin to "Disney on Ice," in that it is for entertainment and basic information only. I do not pretend to be an expert on the Civil War. I enjoy reading about it. Like many others, I am fascinated by it. But quite frankly, for me, looking at Xs on battlefields and memorizing general's names and dates has always been tedious and … um… not what I want to know.

I want to know how historical events affected regular people who lived through them. Something like looking into the history of mankind rather than the history of civilization.

Anyway. I like to do genealogy, and I feel like I've done a little genealogy for the Old Jamestown area, that I'll share with you tonight.

So. I'll get on with it then. I'm going to begin with State's rights.

Let me start by asking you if you know what Presidents Lincoln, G.W. Bush and Obama have in common? And that is not a setup for a bad joke. Each of these presidents has signed laws allowing the suspension of the protection of habeas corpus, or of the right to be charged if you are arrested.

Abraham Lincoln suspended habeas corpus nationally in September 1862, but he suspended that constitutional right a year and a half earlier, at the outbreak of the war, for 'some Midwestern states' and Maryland. This was done in conjunction with Lincoln's enactment of martial law – or military rule.

In response to 9/11, the second President George Bush signed into law the Military Commission Act, which contains suspensions of writs of habeas corpus for suspected terrorists, among other things. Obama recently renewed that law. So clearly, some of the issues struggled with a century and a half ago are still relevant today.

But back to 1861-ish. Here's a refresher for us all:

If you would, please set your clocks back to August 1861. The war has begun just four months earlier. Lincoln has called for 75,000 volunteers to serve for 90 days, and Missouri was to raise four regiments toward that 75,000 troop number. Does anyone know how many soldiers four regiments might involve? I do not. Our southern-leaning Governor Jackson, says uh-uh to raising regiments, and that Missouri is neutral, which makes the Union nervous because of the large number of arms at the St. Louis Arsenal. The arms are then removed from St. Louis to Illinois, with a plan by Jeff Davis to intercept them (which didn't work). We have had two battles in Western Missouri. We've opened the Gratiot Street Prison in St. Louis. Martial Law – Military Rule -- is declared in St. Louis on August 14th, 1861. (http://www.civilwarstlouis.com/timeline/index.htm)

And we now have a Provost Marshal in charge of the military rule of our area.

And the Provost Marshal is hearing from the local citizens. And they are investigating and arresting people on the suspicion of being secessionists. Can you imagine the opportunity this must have created for feuding neighbors? It must have been a time of great paranoia, and I am sure it brought out the worst in a lot of people.

The Provost Marshal records are available on the Missouri Secretary of State website. They are fantastic. They are voluminous, and they seem to run the gamut from seemingly ridiculous, such as this:

| Evans, David H. | Saint Louis | St. Louis | Statement that while in his restaurant, he heard J. Stewart tell A. Nesbit that he'd insulted Mr. Lyon, a merchant, and that Nesbit should apologize to him | 01-29-1862 | F1204 | | |

To the far more serious, such as this list of 'disloyal persons':

| Patterson, P.; Patterson, Joe; Harris, Solon; Harris, Jim; Myers, Montgomery; Hyatt, Joe; Tunstall, Bob; Hurnes, James; Evans, Watt; Patterson, Ed; Douglass, Nic; Ferguson, James; Ferguson, Charles; Lewis, [unknown] | Saint Louis | St. Louis | List of disloyal persons. | 08-25-1862 | F1587 | 0206 | 1894 |

Some of these folks lived in the Old Jamestown area. We will see their names again soon. Here is the actual report that supports this indexed Provost Marshal entry:

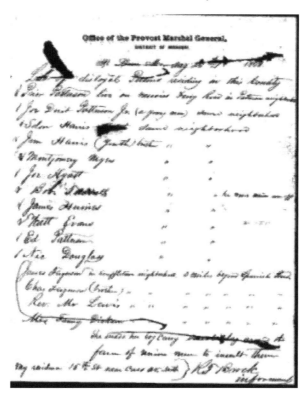

Hmmm. Looks like James Ferguson lives in the "Scuffletown" neighborhood. Maybe that was the former name of Shoveltown?

Here's a good example of families being at complete odds during this war.

Durrett Patterson was a slaveholder in the Old Jamestown Area. His land looks to be not far from the Desloge property/Boeing facility, abutting the Missouri River. He is a son of Elisha and Lucy Patterson, and a grandson of John Patterson, Sr., who settled much of what we call the Old Jamestown area. And Durrett's got a rap sheet with the Provost Marshal. He's about 50-55 years old:

Durrett's brother, Lewis Patterson, on the other hand, gives a statement against a Reuben Carrico, alleging Reuben is a 'notorious rebel.' Carrico is a recognizable name around here; although, this Reuben appears to have lived in a log cabin in Columbia Bottoms. Reuben had to pay $1,000 bond and swear an oath of loyalty to be released from prison.

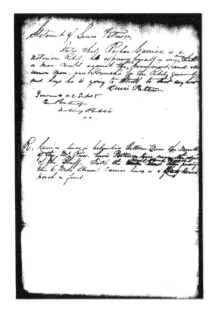 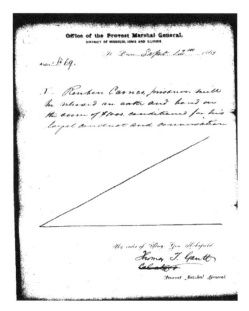

So Lewis Patterson has "informed on" Mr. Carrico, while Lewis's brother Durrett is out 'violating laws of war and oath.'

That issue must have divided the Patterson family greatly. I wonder how their mother, Lucy Patterson, dealt with it all, with her family so divided – I would assume bitterly divided. Those are the stories in all of this.

And some of these Provost Marshal records set the stage for how it might have been in the early days of the war here in the "St. Ferdinand Township."

So let's say the date is August 28, 1861. St. Louis has been under martial law for two weeks, and what I'm about to read to you transpired two DAYS before the whole state is put under Martial Law. Imagine being awakened by the noise of 50 men on horseback riding by. They are led by Captain Karcher of the 12th Missouri Volunteers, Rifles Division. He's looking for a cache of arms secreted somewhere around here. Please let me read Captain Karcher's report to his superior, Col. Osterhaus, who reports to Major General Fremont. Fremont is in charge of the Army's Department of the West (West of MS River to California). He's in charge of a lot here in August 1861.

Here it is:

Pursuant to an order from headquarters, I with 50 men proceeded to within one and a half miles from Florissant for the purpose of seizing a lot of arms secreted there. I arrived there at one o'clock a.., August 28th. I was then informed that the arms above mentioned were secreted at a place called Sinks Grocery, about four miles south of the above-mentioned place. I proceeded tither, surrounded the place, and held a general search, but without success. At Sinks Grocery, I arrested three men, named J. Grow, Warren and Thompson, who were pointed out to me as secessionists. J. Grow is a justice of the peace, and reported to be the leader of a company of 40 secessionists. I was then informed that arms were secreted at the residence of Dr. Gibson on the Bellefontaine Road, 8 miles' distance from St. Louis. I searched his house, but not finding any arms, I started for St. Louis, where I arrived at 8:00 p.m., August 28th, 1861.

Again, this is two weeks after Martial Law is declared in St. Louis, and the citizens are now subject to the control of the provost marshal. I can't imagine the stress and dis-ease people of this area must have been experiencing. Someone turned these guys in – Dr. Gibson, Warren, Grow, Thompson. Maybe they were rebels with arms, maybe not.

I've done a little research on Dr. Gibson, and his place was "Tanglewood," which must be near Chambers and Bellefontaine Road. It's now a park, I believe. I don't know if the Warren referenced in this report is from the family of Warrens who are near Douglas and New Halls Ferry. I really wanted the Sinks Grocery referred to above to be on Sinks Road, but I think it refers to the owner, Powell Sinks. I am trying to determine if he lived on or had access to one of the Missouri/Mississippi River islands near us here.

I want to say that the Missouri Secretary of State website is where I have obtained a lot of this information. If you like this sort of thing, you should definitely check out the Historian/Genealogist link on the page. It's fantastic.

Now on to Slavery in the Old Jamestown Area.

Again, Missouri was a slave state. The Old Jamestown area is to some extent semi-rural, even now, and must have been the flat-out 'the country' in the 1860s. I've read the inventory records of a few wills of local citizens in that era, and I believe that then, too, they grew a lot of corn and wheat. There were a lot of farms here.

The 1860 Census Slave Schedules list the names of the slave owners, not the names of the slaves. They do include some helpful information from a genealogy standpoint, in that they list the slaves' ages, sex, whether black or mulatto, whether there were any slaves 'fugitive from the state,' the number manumitted (freed), and the number of slave houses.

I printed the entire schedule for the St. Ferdinand Census district. The best I can tell, of the 11 pages of the Slave Schedules from 1860, St. Ferdinand Township, two pages can be attributed to the Old Jamestown Area: Pages 3 and 4. There are a total of 148 people listed as slaves on those two pages, and a total of 31 Slave Owners. There were 37 listed slave houses.

The Dr. Gibson that we talked about earlier as a potential arms trader appears on the list, albeit out of the "Old Jamestown area" range.

Reuben Musick, who owned a lot of land in our area, particularly near the Douglas/New Halls Ferry area, owned 12 slaves, and had three slave houses. At the last meeting, I brought in some old prints of photos made in the area in the early 1900s. Many are of small 'river' houses down near Musick's Ferry. Could these be remnants of those slave houses? I wonder…..

I looked at a few of the 1870 census records for those who owned slaves in 1860. Living in the home next to the Valles/Veals (John Veale owned a 37-year-old slave in 1860), I found Harris Hyatt, 40-year-old Black Male, whose age fits that of one of Elizabeth Hyatt's slaves per the 1860 Slave Schedules. By the way, do you suppose "Veale," when spoken by an Englishman, might sound a little like "Vail"?

John Ferguson died in 1864. He owned a 7-year-old child per the 1860 Slave Census. The 1870 Census shows Mrs. Mary Ferguson as head of a household that includes one Jasper Evans. His age is consistent with a slave owned by W.W. Evans on the 1860 slave census. Jasper's wife also lives in the home, and the census shows they were married in November of 1869. That's a bit of a guess on my part, but it sure looks like Jasper stayed on in the area.

Michael Cerre died in 1859. The 1860 slave census shows one male slave, 60 years old, owned by Cerre's estate. Mr. Cerre's will also includes reference to "A Negro man named Frank, around 60 years old." Cerre's family members were Creoles, and probably had been in the middle Mississippi River valley area since the 1750s. He had a paternal aunt married to Auguste Chouteau, and another married to Antoine Soulard. Soulard surveyed a large portion of St. Louis in its early settlement days, including the Old Jamestown area.

It would be interesting to know what happened to the 148 Old Jamestown Area enslaved residents after they were freed. Of course the Emancipation Proclamation did not free the slaves of states that did not officially secede. Freedom from bondage came with the 13th Amendment to the Constitution, which took effect in December 1865.

In closing, we most certainly had all of the elements that tore this country apart right here in 63034. We had families on both sides of the issues of the day, and we had a lot of slaves here. I plan to continue researching what became of the freed slaves, and I would be grateful to hear of anything you all may know about those historical dark times as they may pertain to Old Jamestown. Thank you!
Cindy Winkler

Appendix 10 - Ralph Wehmer's Stories and Photos

Ralph Wehmer lived his whole life in Old Jamestown (1916 to 2007). See Chapter 8 for information about the Wehmer family's deep roots in Old Jamestown. Ralph's very interesting stories were told shortly before his death to Olga Smith who was a BJC Hospice Lumina Project Volunteer.

==

I have so many stories to tell you. Where do I begin? Well, I was born in a log cabin, one mile down from this house. Back then, our street was called Accommodation Road, and it was a dirt road. Now, the street is called Old Jamestown Road. [Photo 1]

Growing up, my brothers and I would ride a corn grinder and it would go round and round like a merry-go-round. One afternoon, my brother and I were riding on it and Ed came out of the house and yelled at us: "Do not put your hands in there! Next thing I knew, I put my hand in the grinder and I lost part of my finger. [Holds up his hand] Boy, did I cry -- for hours. Because the nearest doctor was in Florissant, we drove our Model-T car. Because the road was dirt, we hitched it to a team of mules and we headed down the street to Salem Baptist Church with the reins through the windshield opening. We left the mules at the church and drove on into Florissant to the doctor's office. Every time we went to the doctor's, this is how we traveled. I can even remember my doctor's name, Dr. Milmann.

When I think of my father, I will tell you one thing: he was a smart guy. My father gave my three brothers, Louis, Jim, Bob and I a proposition. The proposition was: if we did not drink or smoke before the age of 21, he would give us a gold watch and $100. Well, a $100 was a lot of money back then, so we all made it and he had to pay us. I think that was a pretty smart idea. [Photo 2]

While growing up, our neighbor's house, down the road, caught on fire. One night my dad caught me building a fire in our family room and asked, "What are you doing?" I responded, "I want a new house." I was around 4 or 5 years old.

One foggy morning, around 8:30, while outside, at school, we heard a noise that caught our attention. That was Brown School, which is now a residence right downs the road here, near Carrico Road, across from the church. We saw a plane coming down low in front of our school. The plane was really low, probably 50 feet in the air. The plane would come down low and go back up again. As the plane came down low, he cut the engine and hollered, "Where's the nearest airport?" We pointed in the direction of the airport, which was then Anglum, Missouri [now Robertson]. We kids made a 'human arrow'. The oldest kid, Bill Brinker, organized us. He circled back around and yelled down, "Thank you!" The person in the plane happened to be Charles Lindbergh! [At the time, there were spotlights every 10 miles from Alton, over Vaile to Florissant and on to the airport for pilots to find their way. It was so foggy that morning, that he couldn't see them.] [Photo 3]

…I graduated from the eighth grade at the age of 13. One afternoon, in August, my mother took me to Ferguson (and I drove the car) to enroll in high school. I asked, "How am going to get to school?" She said, "Son, you are going to drive to school." Even though I was only 13, I drove myself to school every day.

That is, until, one day I saw a very good-looking girl and she asked for a ride. On the way home, her father (Ferguson's only police man) stopped us. [Florissant had only one police officer, and he was the town drunk!] He looked at me and said, "How old are you, young man?" "I'm 16", I said. He nailed me. "I'll bet you're not a day over 13". Then, he went on to say, "If I ever see you driving again, I will inform the Ferguson law enforcement about your age and you will go to jail!" So, I quickly came home and told my dad that I could not go to high school anymore. He would not allow that, so he had me drive the car to C.J. Lumber Co. and park the car and told me: "Forget that girl."

After I parked the car, I walked the rest of the way to school, crossing over the railroad tracks. Whenever a snowstorm was coming I went straight to the principal to inform her of my situation and she would let me go home. She was real good like that. After four years, I graduated from Ferguson High School.

At the age of 19, I earned a job at the Florissant Post Office, as a postal clerk and worked at that for 11 years. [Al Pondrom] was the Post Master. After that, I was a Rural Mail Carrier for 25 years. I truly enjoyed that job, because of all of the people that I met. I once received Missouri's Outstanding Rural Letter Carrier Award.

While working at the Post Office, we received a letter addressed to "Grandma", sent from someone in Potosi. Everyone in the office thought that there was no way that we would find "Grandma". After I gave it a little thought, I knew who that "Grandma" might be. I told the guys that I would deliver it. I headed down to Lindsey Lane. Every day, outside the Bauer's house on Lindsey Lane, a little boy would greet me and I always gave him a piece of candy. And, the Bauer's received a lot of mail from the Potosi area. So, I blew the horn and I asked Mrs. Bauer if she was missing a letter. Well, she could not believe it.

Since I usually ended my routes around 1:30 p.m., I took a job as a bus- driver for the Hazelwood School District. I worked for the Hazelwood District for 25 years. There was one incident that I will never forget. If you can imagine, things have changed since I was a bus-driver. One day, while driving, one of my third graders called me a 'son of a bitch'. I told the principal of the situation and the principal suspended him. The next day, the principal, the parents and I had a meeting. The principal would not allow him to ride the bus until he apologized to me and he finally did. Can you believe that a third grader said that?

Another story that I like to tell is when I was traveling down Halls Ferry Road. I looked to the back of the bus in my rear view mirror and noticed food and garbage flying out of the bus window. So, I took Old Halls Ferry Road and headed back to the high school. I had two girls go get the principal, who was my brother- in-law Larry Fuqua. Larry came out and we discussed the situation, and I decided to just sit there. The bad kids left the bus. The kids started hollering at me about leaving those kids. I told the kids, "We're going to sit here until everyone is quiet. I'm paid by the hour, so I don't care." Boy, did they get quiet.

One more story about my bus-driving days. Well, I decided to take the route with the African-American kids. I always got a kick out of them, because they were always so much fun. They would rub my head and say, "We like our bus- driver!' It always made me feel really good.

I will tell you that my brother Jim was a really honest person. He worked for Riverview Stone and Material for years. While working, his boss asked him, "What are you paying those African-American drivers? Jim told him that he was paying them the same as the white men. And, his boss went on to say that he should dock the African-American's pay. Well, Jim disagreed and said, "No" and quit. He walked out of the office (and he had 12 kids!), but he disagreed with things like that. The Lord works in mysterious ways, because shortly after he quit, Jim found a job at Westlake Quarry with a better salary.

Here's another story about Jim. One of Jim's kids went to feed the dog in their big barn. Well, while feeding the dog, his son was playing with a match and ended up lighting the barn on fire. At the time of the fire, Jim was all the way in Anglum [now Robertson] and he could see the smoke from there, but he had no idea it was coming from his barn. When Jim got home and realized the damage, he said we should all stick around. "We're going to make something of this fire" and he went to the store to get hot dogs and buns so that we could have a "Wiener Roast."

SHEARING SHEEP - THE RIGHTEOUS RAM ISAIAH 53:7

My dad had 40 head of sheep. We had no telephone. He would drive 40 miles to Wentzville to get a sheep shearer. Ed Love sent one of his workers to Columbia, Missouri to learn how to shear sheep. So, I said, "When he learns how, tell him to come shear my Dad's sheep." A week passed and I said, "Well, Ed, how's the boy making out with the sheep?" He said, "He didn't learn nothin'". So, he loaned me his clippers. The Post Master gave me the day off to go shear my Dad's sheep. When I got there, the old sheep shearer came on. The Merino had a wrinkled neck. He gave me the Shropshire and he took the Merinos. Well, I sat that thing down on its rump and sheared him.

It's in Isaiah 53:7: He was like a sheep before the shearer. (By the end of the day- we were able to keep up with the old sheep shearer.) I even took some sheep downtown to the Famous Barr store when they had a Folk Fair right on the street. I could shear a sheep in two minutes and 55 seconds- the fastest sheep shearer in town.

I asked if I could bring some school kids to watch the shearing and got permission to do that. One year, 76 busloads of kids came in one week. There's 10 pounds of wool on a sheep. It sold for 40 cents a pound down at the Fur Exchange. [Photo 4]

I went to Defiance, New Melle, Wentzville, Wright City, and Troy to shear sheep. I had the contract with Monsanto to shear sheep at their test farm. One time, I had 400 sheep to shear by the end of the month. Another time, they gave me seven lambs. I took them to the stockyards and sold them for $725. They also gave me 200 chickens. I put them in my mother's barn. We dressed about 20 of them that night. That was enough. I found the Boschert Turkey Farm in St. Charles and they dressed and froze them for 35 cents a head.

One of the rams wandered off to the Salem Church grounds and caught sight of himself in the church windows. He thought it was another ram and charged "him" (his reflection). He made a real mess in that church. [The ram's head is stuffed and hanging on the wall of the living room fireplace]

June 29, 2007, Florissant, Missouri

Documented by Olga S. Smith

RALPH WEHMER'S STORIES II – July 2007
MORE SHEARING SHEEP STORIES and OTHERS as told to his daughters Susan and Ginny

When I would take school kids to the farms around here, one of them was the Twillman Farm on Old Halls Ferry Road near what is Parc Argonne Subdivision, now. Mr. Twillman just loved those kids. He'd laugh so, and his belly would just shake. He really enjoyed having those kids on his farm.

There was another farmer on Vaile whose sheep I used to shear: [Jane and John Doe]. He was a really good farmer and a hard worker. But, when it rained, he liked to drink. He'd go over to the…Tavern at Shoveltown on Hwy 67 and Old Halls Ferry. He had about 40 sheep and I went over there to shear them one day. It was raining and [Jane] said that [John] couldn't help me (because he was drunk). She also said that they were penned up. I said that I thought if they were penned up, that I could do it myself. Pretty soon [John] came along. He was a bit tipsy. He picked up a bale of straw (thinking it was a sheep) and wrestled that bale, telling it, "You can't get away from me. Now you sit down." He was really a hardworking man and a good farmer.

That ram that destroyed the church was a mean one. When my mother would be working in the garden, he would butt her. It turned out, we found out later, that his horns were growing back into its head and making him crazy.

My cousin, Ed Hume, owned a Star brand car. I had a brand new Mackinaw coat. I wore it to church on a rainy day. Mom invited the Hume's to come over for dinner. I rode home on Nosey the horse. I had to climb a fence or stand on a box to get on him. [He was named Nosey because he could open gates and doors with his nose. He had to have a halter on when he was in the barn at night.]

Ed drove up behind me and honked the horn. The horse jumped and I fell off in the mud. My new coat got all muddy and I cried and cried and Mom and Ed tried to comfort me. I was about 5 years old then.

When Nosey did get out, Dad loaded up a shotgun with rock salt and shot him in the rump, and Nosey would run for the barn.

My Mom, Aurelia, [her maiden name was Thompson] walked out of the kitchen door one day to throw out some dishwater. We had to buy water for the cistern and we used all of it (dishwater, bathwater, etc.) to water the flowers. She stood on the wooden lid of the cistern and it gave way and she fell into the cistern. She threw out her arms and held on, somehow. She prayed to God for help. One of her prayers was "Dear Lord, get me out of here. I don't want people to think that Aurelia was despondent and tried to commit suicide!" She managed, somehow, to pull herself out of that place. When I had my own cistern, put a concrete lid on it.

When my Mom and Dad were going to get married, old Mr. Thompson [his portrait is in a frame above his bed] didn't like the idea. They lived in a very nice house (still in existence) on Carrico Road. He said, "That Louie Wehmer is going to take my daughter over on that hill in a log cabin and starve her to death." It didn't turn out that way. They were determined to make a go of it and they did.

My Dad went to the 1904 World's Fair in St. Louis, and bought an Avery steam engine Threshing Machine. We would go from farm to farm during the threshing season and have a party. Can you imagine what that would be worth now?

[Photo 5] [Photo 6]

July 12, 2007, Florissant, Missouri
Documented by Olga Smith

All photos shared by Susan Wehmer Kagy

Log cabin where Ralph Wehmer was born in 1916, photo about 1930.

Ralph Wehmer and his brothers about 1940, from left: Jim, Bob, Ralph, Louis

Ralph Wehmer in front of Brown School students 1922-23

Ralph Wehmer showing St. Louis City School students in mid 1970s how he shears sheep on the Twillman Farm

Threshing machine purchased at the World's Fair by Ralph's father, Louis Wehmer, in 1904.

Ralph Wehmer with his wife, Rosemary, about 1939.

Appendix 11 – Desloge Family & Vouziers Mansion

Two articles: First From the ©St. Louis Post-Dispatch 1992, Second from St. Louis Magazine, 2015

Vouziers - Some people build their castles in the air. Joseph Desloge built his in Florissant Valley

St. Louis ©St. Louis Post-Dispatch - Sunday, June 21, 1992, Renee Stovsky

"I BELIEVE a great home is more than a magnificent structure. It has a spirit about it," says Hal Kroeger, current master of Vouziers, the French country chateau built by Joseph Desloge in 1926 amid the rolling farmlands of Florissant Valley.

As he tours his estate with Taj, his white standard poodle - pointing out vistas of the Missouri River, downtown St. Louis and the Gateway Arch, the agricultural delta of St. Charles County, the distant bluffs of the Mississippi River - he adds quietly, "The spirit of **Vouziers** is one of people coming together."

Indeed, historical evidence suggests that this has been a gathering place since ancient times. Archaeologists believe that at least 11,000 years ago, Indian tribes came to this high point near the confluence of the Missouri, Mississippi and Illinois rivers each summer for potlach - to trade, to socialize, to compete at games, to arrange marriages. To this day, farmers turn up magnificent arrowheads and other artifacts in spring plowing.

"The Desloge family was very generous, holding magnificent parties here for all sorts of causes and hosting a myriad of international guests," says Kroeger, 52. He and his wife, Carole Ferris Kroeger, have owned the mansion and the 250 acres that surround it since 1977.

(The Desloge family still owns another 750 acres or so there; three of Desloge's four children - Joseph Desloge Jr., Anne Desloge Bates and Zoe Desloge Lippman - and their families continue to maintain homes on the property. Joseph Desloge's other son, Bernard Desloge, is deceased.)

"We have tried to continue the tradition as well, with fund-raisers for everything from the Alliance Francaise to the St. Louis Science Museum. And I will be very sad if that spirit ceases to be maintained in the future."

At the moment, however, the future of **Vouziers** is up for grabs, with an $8 million price tag on it. The estate has been on the market since late 1990, soon after Kroeger spun off his wholesale paper distribution company, Distribix, to Alco Standard of Valley Forge, Pa. Distribix had been housed in the estate's 6,000-square-foot carriage house.

"This was my home-office combination," says Kroeger. "In the East, where I grew up, lots of old estates in the Westchester, N.Y., area are preserved by such a mixed-use concept."

But now that the Kroegers' two sons are in college and "the business next door" has been sold, maintaining the estate has become an issue "not of money, but of time and lifestyle," he explains.

"I love this house; I sincerely believed I would be carried out of it," says Kroeger. "When I bought Vouziers, it was a dream come true.

"St. Louisans are spoiled; so many of them think of this location as remote. But where else can you find a country estate within a 20-minute drive of the city?

"The impulse was not a pretentious one - the opportunity to raise my children on a farm, with horses and go-carts and fishing, was too good to pass up."

Today, however, with homes in Aspen, Colo., and Ladue, the Kroegers spend precious little time at Vouziers.

"This home has been a labor of love," says Kroeger. "But I believe the worst thing that can happen to a property is for it to go unused. A house needs plenty of life around it to be a home. How else can its spirit be nourished? And life can sometimes change in unexpected ways."

World War I changed the life of Joseph Desloge, a descendent of one of Missouri's pioneer families, unexpectedly. Born in 1889, he grew up accustomed to affluence. His father, Firmin Desloge, had amassed a fortune after founding the Desloge Lead Co. in St. Francois County in 1873. The company was later acquired by St. Joseph Lead Co. (The family gave $1 million to St. Louis University to build a hospital, which was named for Firmin Desloge. The hospital is now called St. Louis University Hospital.)

But during the war, he served as an ambulance driver in France with the American Field Service, and subsequently was an officer in the French artillery. He returned to St. Louis a hero, having earned the Croix de Guerre for defending the town of Vouziers.

He also came back with a dream - to re-create in Missouri the Gallic village he had helped to preserve. To that end, in 1919 he bought a large tract of land near the intersection of what is now New Halls Ferry and Shackelford roads in North County and commissioned New Orleans architect Dennis McDonald to design a Louis XVI-style chateau.

By 1926, the 10-bedroom, four-story manor had been completed, with no expense spared. The Bedford limestone, used for its exterior, was floated down river from Indiana; the hand-carved wood walls of the third-floor Gothic reading room were shipped overseas from an old English parsonage.

The home boasted an entrance hall and winding staircase of rose marble, beautiful oak walls and floors, soaring ceilings, and nine working fireplaces. Louis XVI carved wood furniture was imported from France, as were Beauvais and Gobelin tapestries. Precious Aubusson and Savonnerie carpets covered the floors; cabinets were filled with grisaille from Limoges. Two huge mastiff statues guarded the main entrance; the family logo, an oak tree, was carved over the door.

Desloge, who went on to found four firms - Killark Electric Manufacturing Co., Minerva Oil Co., Louisiana Manufacturing Co. and Atlas Manufacturing Co. - continued to build additions to the estate as well.

Perhaps the most unusual structure on the grounds is the 4,000-square-foot ballroom, tunnel and receiving hall complex built into a hillside. But the compound also grew to include a hunting lodge, a charming tea pavilion, a swimming pool flanked by pavilions, perennial and rose gardens, a log cabin, tennis court, riding trails, stables and farmhouse.

The mansion also continued to be modified; the most spectacular addition is probably the sous sol - a basement built after the house was finished (it had to be jacked up on steel girders), with elaborate limestone archways carved with fleurs de lis and "his and her powder rooms" complete with onyx sinks.

"Vouziers was a magical house in which to grow up," says Anne Bates, who lived there until her marriage in 1949, and now occupies a red brick Georgian house nearby. "We led such a rich, full, wonderful family life - almost a 'Little House on the Prairie' existence. Compared to the grand homes on Portland Place in the Central West End, Vouziers was very manageable - almost cozy.

"And it was very rural; we were surrounded by farmers, most with large families. Many of papa's staff were actually neighbors - loyal, wonderful people. At night, you couldn't see a single light. I can remember looking out the windows with my sister and brothers; if a car went down Shackelford Road, it was an enormous curiosity."

In fact, in the early 1900s, many wealthy St. Louisans looking to escape the heat in the city built summer homes along the river's banks in North County, and commuted to work by train from Ferguson.

"One of my early memories is that of my mother Anne Kennett Farrar Desloge, who died in 1934 sitting out in the teahouse in a Singapore rocker, trying to stay cool in July and August. We used the teahouse like a screened-in porch; with its marble floors, it stayed relatively comfortable."

Bates cherishes other childhood memories as well: roller-skating in the ballroom; playing billiards and ping-pong in the sous sol and watching movies in the private screening room there; learning to swim in the river; making the fourth floor into a children's theater; waking up on Christmas mornings to find new horses in the gallery room. Horses - yes, real horses - were not only a favorite gift but a mode of transportation; she and her siblings would "often ride our horses into Florissant, which was then a quiet farm community.

"We were fairly self-sufficient when it came to entertaining ourselves. We had to be - we were so isolated-" she says. "I didn't go to school until I was in second grade; we were taught at Calvert Home School. When I was 14, I used to drive Zoe and myself to Community School (located at what is now Wilson School in Clayton); the trip took an hour each way.

"And if we got seriously ill, it was a major calamity. The nearest doctor was in Normandy; we had to be bundled up into a pick-up truck and taken there."

Of course, there were also innumerable social gatherings: charitable benefits, society debuts, weddings. Desloge was very active in community affairs, particularly the Academy of Science, the Missouri Historical Society, the Lewis and Clark Trail Commission and the Jefferson National Expansion Memorial Association.

Both Bates - who reigned as Veiled Prophet Queen in 1946 - and her sister were married at **Vouziers** . The festivities were overseen by Marie Saalfrank, who was employed as the children's governess after their mother's death. Saalfrank also played hostess to everyone from Russian ballerinas and Shakespearean actors - all of whom performed at Vouziers - to visiting French ambassadors and foreign dignitaries like Archduke Otto van Hapsburg and Empress Zita of Austria, who briefly sought refuge there after the Nazis deposed them.

In 1953, Desloge married Saalfrank ("she was a much beloved stepmother," says Bates); the couple resided in La Jolla, Calif. and at Vouziers until his death in 1971 at age 82. When Marie Saalfrank Desloge's health declined in the 1970s, the Desloge family decided to seek a buyer for Vouziers - one who could maintain the integrity of the house.

It was not the first time portions of the estate had been divided, however. Desloge - an ardent conservationist who delighted in the abundant wildlife at Vouziers - had donated both Sunset Park and Pelican Island to St. Louis County before his death. [3/5 of Pelican Island was actually donated by three of Joseph's children, the other child, Bernard, sold his portion of the Island to St. Louis County.] (He also donated 2,400 acres of land he owned in Reynolds County, which eventually became Johnson's Shut-Ins State Park.) *

What the Desloge family found in Hal Kroeger - a private owner with the means and sensitivity to maintain Vouziers properly - is exactly what Kroeger is looking for now. So far, the right buyer has been elusive.

"Most parties who look at the property think of it in terms of amenities - a small residential development with a private golf course or a conference-center type of hotel complex," says Kroeger.

Is Vouziers worth its $8 million price tag? Though neither Kroeger nor Edward L. Bakewell Inc., which has the real estate listing, would reveal his purchase price, land value has increased substantially in North County since the 1970s, when most of the area around Vouziers was being used for agriculture. In recent years, several subdivisions - Lexington Farms, Barrington Downs, North Fork - have been built near the estate.

"I think the land alone is worth $8 million, not including the home," says Kroeger, who estimates it would take another $20 million or $30 million to develop the property.

"…."
==============================

St. Louis Magazine (stlmag.com)

The Desloge Family: Getting the Lead Out, Jeannette Cooperman
August 20, 2015 – https://www.stlmag.com/news/the-desloge-family/

Asked what his granddad, Joseph Desloge, was like, Wesley Fordyce offers a story: "He had a factory downtown, and they used clarified lard as the lubricant. This cutting oil smelled horrible, and one of the guys was saying it had to be bad for you. So my granddad took a cup and dipped it into this lard that was full of metal shavings and totally rancid... Somebody knocked the cup out of his hand—I don't know whether he would have drunk it or not. But he was pretty fearless.

"And that's how he brought up his children and grandchildren," Fordyce adds. "There was a lot of fearlessness encouraged." They all grew up swimming in the river, for example: "Logs, catfish big as people, eddies that will suck you down to the bottom and spit you out. Nothing terrible."

The second son of older parents, Joseph grew up in a hotel on Washington Avenue. After school, he fought as an officer in the French artillery during World War I and was awarded the Croix de Guerre for defending the town of Vouziers. Then he came home and recreated that French village in Florissant.

His Vouziers was a 10-bedroom chateau on the bluffs of the Missouri River. The hand-carved wood paneling of the Gothic reading room on the third floor was shipped overseas from an old English parsonage; the staircase was rose marble; the family emblem, an oak tree, was carved above the door; a 4,000-square-foot ballroom was built into a hillside.

Zoe, Joseph Jr., Bernard, and Anne Desloge all grew up at Vouziers. Anne might have been teasing, just a little, when she told a Post reporter that life there was "almost a *Little House on the Prairie* existence." But it was remote, and rustic, and the neighbors were farmers. The Desloge kids roller-skated in the ballroom, and sometimes on Christmas morning they found their present had been led inside to wait for them in the gallery room, whinnying and neighing.

An industrialist, philanthropist, conservationist, historic preservationist, and sportsman, Joseph took a sharp and far-ranging interest in science and history, nature and culture. "It seemed to us that Papa chaired everything," Joe Jr. wrote in a memoir. At Vouziers, the family entertained Russian ballerinas and Shakespearean actors, King Hussein of Jordan, and the archduke of Austria (giving him brief shelter after he was deposed by the Nazis).

Because Joseph lived in Florissant, "he was a little bit over the horizon for nice people in Ladue," Fordyce says. "They all thought, 'God, how can you live out there?' People still ask me that." But being surrounded by rural folks guarantees perspective: "There was very little snobbery involved. We were always 'those rich people on the hill' at first, but once they get to know that you're a nice person, they treat you normally."

The chateau, just west of New Halls Ferry and Shackelford roads, is now the Boeing Leadership Center, bought for a cool $7 million. But Fordyce still lives next door, with some of Missouri's last old-growth forest shading the land between his house and the river. "The county seal has a plow on it," he once told a reporter. "It should have a bulldozer."

He even farmed his land for a while. He'd earned an MBA thinking he'd be working at the family's Killark Electric Company—but by the time he finished school, they'd decided to sell it. The other electric company in the family, Watlow, is owned by his second cousins.

The Desloge family's American saga began in 1823, when Firmin René Desloge left France to work in his uncle Ferdinand Rozier's dry goods store in Ste. Genevieve. Elise Desloge Tegtmeyer has read the early letters Firmin René sent home to France. (He copied out each letter for his files; they now fill six volumes in the Missouri History Museum archives.) "There's an awful lot of 'I'll send six hogs' heads and butter down to New Orleans," she remarks dryly—the exception being a tender letter to his future bride, Cynthian McIlvaine, confiding that she'd captured his heart.

"I have a feeling Firmin was very careful, very methodical," Tegtmeyer says. "My mother used to say, 'Oh, you are being so Desloge deliberate!' I see a lot of that in the family."

In the New World, the Desloges traded furs, smelted lead, mined zinc and uranium, built railroads, made heat and light—and with the profits, supported just about every worthy cause in the region. Some folks just write checks; the Desloges also gave us Pelican Island; Johnson's Shut-Ins, a boulder-strewn natural water park; and Firmin Desloge (now St. Louis University) Hospital, which first specialized in industrial accidents. Its namesake, Joseph's father, died one of the wealthiest men in the world, but never lost his sympathy for the factory workers.

Back in 1991, the family had a reunion—400 Desloges descendants, some traveling all the way from Singapore. Steve Desloge and Ellen Desloge Gray acted the part of their ancestors, and they all took a river boat cruise to Ste. Genevieve, visited early family homes in southern Missouri. The first Firmin Desloge had settled in Potosi, where he hung out with John James Audubon, did some fur trading, began finding lead veins, and built a smelting furnace. His son Firmin Vincent "won a plot of land in a poker game and developed it into the Desloge Lead Company," as Fordyce puts it. Firmin Vincent expanded the family's mining operations in the Lead Belt around Bonne Terre and consolidated them into the Desloge Lead Company, which would grow into one of the largest lead mining companies in America. He had two sons, Firmin Vincent Jr. and Joseph.

Once you've counted the Firmins, you start on the surnames—all those families they married into, like the Clarks, Mullanphys, Stiths, Valles, Biddles, Bains, Farrars, Howards, Kennetts, Hugers (Lucie Huger wrote the history of the family in America) and Fuszes.

"I'm in the Jules Desloge branch," Tegtmeyer says, "and that's where all the Mullanphys are. *That's* a family! The Browns of Brown Shoe Company were Mullanphy descendants—and Buster Brown was a real person. Uncle Buster! And he really did have a dog named Tige. And a stupid haircut."

Josephine Desloge married Lou Fusz, and before the Fuszes started selling cars, they worked for the Desloges' lead company. Three Desloges have been Veiled Prophet queens, and Anne Kennet Farrar Desloge Werner Bates was fondly referred to as "the queen" long after the ball was over, because she was smart, stylish, funny, and irreverent. After her first husband was killed in a plane crash, she married William Maffitt Bates Jr. (yes, a Chouteau descendant, as well as a Maffitt and a Bates).

Zoe Desloge, Fordyce's mother, had the same charm. "My dad was mostly absent, but my mom was very down to earth, very kind, generous, tolerant, utterly without prejudice or class distinctions," Fordyce says. "She was an incredible athlete—a 12-letter girl in high school—and at a cocktail party, she could hold a broom in her hand and jump over it."

Rick Desloge took his family's affability into journalism, humanizing St. Louis' corporate world with his color pieces in the *St. Louis Business Journal*. (His son Rick is currently touring with *Wicked*.) Another Desloge owned the St. Louis Stars soccer team. Anne's cousin George Taylor Stith Desloge, known as Taylor, grew up in St. Louis Hills, not a chateau. He loved acting in community theater and was always the first out on the dance floor, but he also earned a law degree, raised seven children, and helped direct the Missouri History Museum's growth for 35 years. (He also served on many other boards, including the Independence Center, which his cousin, Richard Stith, helped found). Taylor's grandson and namesake, Taylor Desloge II, fell close to the family tree's roots—he's the Lynne Cooper Harvey Fellow in American culture studies at Washington University, with a focus on early-1900s American history and urban reform.

All those minerals in the first Firmin's land were pure luck. The Desloges don't forget that.

For Joseph Desloge, Jr.,'s remembrances of growing up in Old Jamestown, see "Passport to Manhood: Adventures of a WWII Front Line Ambulance Drive with the British and the French Foreign Legion." Florissant, MO, 1995: http://www.porter-az.com/misc/desloge/pp2mtoc.html

Appendix 12 – Timeline

Pleistocene Epoch (series of Ice Ages) from about 1.8 million years ago until about 11,700 years ago.

Prehistoric cultural traditions in eastern North America (from *Cahokia Mounds – America's First City*, 2010)[263] :

- 9500-8000 BC PaleoIndian
- 8000-600 BC Archaic
- 600BC-750 AD Woodland
- 750-1050 AD Emergent Mississippian/Terminal Late Woodland
- 1050-1400 AD Mississippian
- 1400-1673 AD Oneota

1492 Columbus arrives in The Bahamas.

1541 Hernando de Soto claims the Mississippi and all its tributaries for Spain.

1607 Jamestown, Virginia, founded.

1620 Mayflower arrives in Massachusetts

1673 Jesuit priest, Jacques Marquette and companion, Louis Joliet, pass the Missouri River as they explore the Mississippi.

1682 Robert Cavelier, Sieur de La Salle explores the Mississippi valley, claims it for France and names the area "Louisiana."

1699 Cahokia, Illinois, founded.

1703 Kaskaskia, Illinois, founded.

1762 France secretly cedes to Spain all territory west of Mississippi.

1763 Seven Year War ends. Territory east of the Mississippi ceded to Great Britain by France.

1764 St. Louis founded.

1767 Spain openly takes possession of Louisiana from France.

1768 St. Charles founded.

1768 Spanish Captain Francisco Rui takes military possession of Upper Louisiana at St. Louis. Fort Don Carlos is built on the south bank of the Missouri River at its mouth with the Mississippi (Columbia Bottoms area).

1769 St. Ferdinand (Florissant) founded (according to Chouteau testimony)

1775 American Revolution begins.

1776 Declaration of Independence signed.

1794 Bridgeton founded.

1790s Spanish provide generous land grants to new settlers.

1799 Portage des Sioux founded.

1800 Spain secretly returns Louisiana to France – Upper Louisiana remains administered by Spanish.

1803 United States purchases Louisiana Territory from France.

@1800 James Ferry begins across Missouri River to St. Charles County

@1800 Rev. John Clark leads Protestant services in homes

1804 Lewis and Clark expedition begins.

1805 Rev. Clark starts Methodist classes in Old Jamestown and other areas.

1818-1821 – Economic Downturn, falling land prices

1848 German Revolution, Beginning of large German emigration to U.S.

1849 Cholera epidemic.

1861-1865 Civil War.

1865 Thirteenth Amendment to Constitution abolishes slavery.

1914-1918 World War I.

1920-1933 Prohibition.

1920s and 1930s Wealthy families build homes on the Missouri River bluffs.

1939-1945 World War II.

1955 Laclede Gas begins operation of underground storage facility.

1973 Jamestown Mall opens.

1980s Residential development increases in Old Jamestown.

2009 St. Louis County enacts Karst Protection District zoning.

2014 Jamestown Mall closes completely - 2017 St. Louis County working toward redevelopment.

End Notes

[1] Phineas James' ad, Missouri Gazette, the St. Louis area's first newspaper, June 16, 1819, page 1 (as reprinted in the September 1975 Hazelwood School District Newsletter)

[2] Joe Harl, Archaeological Research Center of St. Louis Inc., e-mail to Peggy Kruse, April 2014

[3] Tim O'Neil, *Look Back 250 • Ancient sea, ice ages form landscape that attracts first St. Louisans*, ©St. Louis Post-Dispatch, February 8, 2014

[4] *Lakota Prayer*, Marquette University web site: http://www.marquette.edu/faith/prayers-lakota.php

[5] Louis E. Pondrom, *Historical Records of St. Ferdinand of Florissant and St. Charles*, 1989 (typed by Gretchen Crank).

[6] *Road to Musick Ferry, Mo., offers Historic as Well as Scenic Points of Interest* ©St. Louis Post-Dispatch, June 22, 1919

[7] Renee Stovsky, *Vouziers - Some people build their castles in the air. Joseph Desloge built his in Florissant Valley*, ©St. Louis Post-Dispatch article, June 21, 1992.

[8] Renee Stovsky, *Vouziers - Some people build their castles in the air. Joseph Desloge built his in Florissant Valley*, ©St. Louis Post-Dispatch article, June 21, 1992

[9] Joe Harl, Archaeological Research Center of St. Louis Inc., e-mail to Peggy Kruse, April 2014

[10] NiNi Harris and Esley Hamilton, *St. Louis Parks*, Reedy Press, 2012, p. 146

[11] Kevin W. McKenney and Jeanne C. Hunter, *Captain Edmund Hodges and His Descendants: including the Hodges Family of the Niagara District of Ontario, Canada*. Self Published, 2012, p. 31

[12] *Rock House Built in the [18] 50s, Once Musick's Inn, to Be Razed*, Watchman Advocate, February 20, 1931

[13] Michael Rosenkötter, *From Westphalia into the World: A Farmer's Family from Westphalia in Search of a Better Future in the U.S.A.*, 2d ed. Norderstedt: Books on Demand GmbH, 2003

[14] William L. Thomas, *The History of St. Louis County Vol 2*, 1909, pages 517 and 518

[15] Esley Hamilton, *St. Louis County North Inventory of Historic Buildings, Phase I*, 1988, St. Louis County Department of Parks and Recreation under a grant from the Missouri Department of Natural Resources

[16] Louis Pondrom, *Compiled 1846 Atlas of Edward Hutawa and 1837 Atlas of E. Dupre*, 1974

[17] *The Past in our Presence: Historic Buildings in St. Louis County*, St. Louis County Department of Parks and Recreation, 1996

[18] St. Louis County, Sioux Passage Park web site: http://www.stlouisco.com/ParksandRecreation/ParkPages/SiouxPassage

[19] Joe Harl and Robin Machiran, *Prehistoric cultures of the City of Wildwood St. Louis County, Missouri*: Research Report #688B, Prepared for the City of Wildwood. St. Louis: Archaeological Research Center of St. Louis Inc., 2013, page 7

[20] Joe Harl, Archaeological Research Center of St. Louis Inc., e-mail to Peggy Kruse, April 2014

[21] Joe Harl and Robin Machiran, *Prehistoric cultures of the City of Wildwood St. Louis County, Missouri:* Research Report #688B Prepared for the City of Wildwood. St. Louis: Archaeological Research Center of St. Louis Inc., 2013

[22] Sally Bell, *Indians' suburbia found in Sioux Passage Park*, St. Louis Globe-Democrat, July 26, 1974

[23] 1970s Sioux Passage Park application for the National Register of Historic Places, summary paragraph sent by e-mail from Missouri Department of Natural Resources to Peggy Kruse, March 2014

[24] Charbonier Bluffs Application for National Register of Historic Places, National Park Service

[25] Tim O'Neil, *Look Back 250 Osage Indians pushed out by arriving Americans in 1808*, ©St. Louis Post-Dispatch, March 30, 2014

[26] Louis Houck, *The Spanish Regime in Missouri: S Collection of Papers and Documents Relating to Upper Louisiana*, Chicago: R. R. Donnelley & Sons Company, 1909, pgs 141-148

[27] *Street Names* Encyclopedia of St. Louis, Vol 4, page 2157

[28] *Road to Musick Ferry, Mo., offers Historic as Well as Scenic Points of Interest* ©St. Louis Post-Dispatch, June 22, 1919

[29] WPA *Guide to the "Show Me" State*, 1940, page 344

[30] Phil E. Chappell, *A History of the Missouri River*, Paper read before the Kansas State Historical Society, at its twenty-ninth annual meeting, 12-6-1904

[31] *Mississippi River*, Wikipedia: http://en.wikipedia.org/wiki/Mississippi_River

[32] Phil E. Chappell, *A History of the Missouri River*, Paper read before the Kansas State Historical Society, at its twenty-ninth annual meeting, 12-6-1904

[33] *Visitors Guide to the Middle Mississippi River Valley*: http://www.greatriverroad.com/stlouis/fortbelle.htm

[34] *Lewis & Clark*, National Geographic: http://www.nationalgeographic.com/lewisandclark/index.html

[35] *Lewis and Clark State Historic Site,* Camp Dubois, Hartford, IL, http://www.campdubois.com/html/history.html

[36] Cathy Riggs Salter, *Lost Missouri*, National Geographic, April 2002: http://ngm.nationalgeographic.com/ngm/0204/feature5/fulltext.html

[37] *Lewis & Clark*, National Geographic web site: http://www.nationalgeographic.com/lewisandclark/index.html

[38] *Pike – The Real Pathfinder: Pike in Missouri*: http://zebulonpike.org/pike-in-missouri-2.htm

[39] *Pike – The Real Pathfinder: Pike in Missouri*: http://zebulonpike.org/pike-in-missouri-2.htm

[40] Tim O'Neil, *Look Back 250 Osage Indians pushed out by arriving Americans in 1808*, ©St. Louis Post-Dispatch, March 30, 2014

[41] Professor Michael Fuller, St. Louis Community College, http://users.stlcc.edu/mfuller/Musick.html

[42] *The Mounds – America's First Cities, A Feasibility Study*, Heartlands Conservancy, 2014
http://mediad.publicbroadcasting.net/p/kwmu/files/201403/The_Mounds_-_America's_First_Cities_EXEC_SUM_3_15_14_final_with_captions.pdf

[43] J. Thomas Scharf, *History of St. Louis City and County, from the Earliest Periods to the Present Day Volume 1.* Philadelphia: Louis H. Everts & Co., 1883, page 30   https://archive.org/details/cihm_13266

[44] James D. Harlan and James M. Denny, *Atlas of Lewis & Clark in Missouri*, University of Missouri Press, Columbia and London, 2003

[45] SlidePlayer website: http://images.slideplayer.com/24/7414857/slides/slide_12.jpg

[46] Kevin W. McKenney and Jeanne C. Hunter, *Captain Edmund Hodges and His Descendants: including the Hodges Family of the Niagara District of Ontario, Canada.* Self Published, 2012, p. 31

[47] Jim Martin, *Wildwood before Lewis & Clark: The Rest of the Story*, Wildwood Historical Society Newsletter, May 2009

[48] Louis E. Pondrom, *Historical Records of St. Ferdinand of Florissant and St. Charles,* 1989 (typed by Gretchen Crank)

[49] *Spanish Land Grants*, Arkansas Commissioner of State Lands web site: http://history.cosl.org/spanish.htm

[50] *Louisiana Purchase*, Wikipedia: http://en.wikipedia.org/wiki/Louisiana_Purchase

[51] *Louisiana (New Spain),* Wikipedia: https://en.wikipedia.org/wiki/Louisiana_(New_Spain)

[52] Survey information from Pitzman 1878 Atlas and other Maps – and 1846 Hutawa lists of confirmed Spanish grants

[53] Inhabitants of Coldwater, *Petition for opening road from "Sarah James Ferry" to division line of settlements of St. Louis and Coldwater and thence to town of St. Louis*, June 18, 1805, Missouri History Museum, Coldwater—Roads Envelope

[54] *The Wilkinson Memorial: A Roster of Men in the Missouri Territory*, 1805, St. Louis Genealogical Society web site: http://stlgs.org/research-2/government/census/1805-missouri-territory-census

[55] *History of Kentucky*, Wikipedia: https://en.wikipedia.org/wiki/History_of_Kentucky#Kentucky_becomes_15th_US_state

[56] *Early Days in Missouri, Interesting Reminiscences of Pioneer Life in "Upper Louisiana,"* St. Charles Cosmos, unknown date, approximately 1900, possibly also published in Watchman Advocate

[57] *Judge Joseph Lafayette Wyatt*, Cold Water Cemetery web site: http://www.rootsweb.ancestry.com/~modarcwc/i132.htm#i2570

[58] Nancy Shattuck, Seeley descendant researching Seeley and James genealogy, in e-Mail to Peggy Kruse, December 25, 2013

[59] Robert Swanson, *Historic Missouri Homes*, Missouri Historical Research Record, April 1968

[60] Raymond Martin Bell and Harriet Lane Cates Hardaway, *James Clemens of Washington County, Pennsylvania, 1734-1795, and his family*, by Raymond Martin Bell and Harriet Lane Cates Hardaway, 1907[60]

[61] Kevin W. McKenney and Jeanne C. Hunter, *Captain Edmund Hodges and His Descendants: including the Hodges Family of the Niagara District of Ontario, Canada*, Self Published, 2012, pages 68, 78.

[62] Mrs. Russell Kaiser (nee Clara Carrico), St. Louis Genealogical Society Quarterly Summer 1987, Vol. XX No. 2

[63] St. Louis Probate Court Records – Court Ordered Slave Hires – Book C (Feb 1828 – August 1830).

[64] Kevin W. McKenney and Jeanne C. Hunter, *Captain Edmund Hodges and His Descendants: including the Hodges Family of the Niagara District of Ontario, Canada*. Self Published, 2012, p. 31

[65] Louis E. Pondrom, *Historical Records of St. Ferdinand of Florissant and St. Charles.* 1989 (typed by Gretchen Crank).

[66] Kate L. Gregg, *Building First American Fort West of the Mississippi*, Missouri Historical Review, State Historical Society of Missouri, Vol 30 No. 4 (July 1936)

[67] Louis E. Pondrom, *Historical Records of St. Ferdinand of Florissant and St. Charles.* 1989 (typed by Gretchen Crank).

[68] Community Area Study, Old Jamestown Area, St. Louis County Planning Commission, page 5 http://www.stlouisco.com/Portals/8/docs/Document%20Library/planning/community%20planning%20and%20revitalization/north%20county/Old%20Jamestown%20Community%20Area%20Study.pdf

[69] Phineas James' ad, Missouri Gazette, the St. Louis area's first newspaper, June 16, 1819, page 1 (as reprinted in the September 1975 Hazelwood School District Newsletter)

[70] Louis E. Pondrom, *Historical Records of St. Ferdinand of Florissant and St. Charles.* 1989 (typed by Gretchen Crank).

[71] Gregory Franzwa, *It's Official – Jamestown Elementary School Is Named*, Hazelwood School District News, September 1975

[72] Nancy Shattuck, Seeley descendant researching Seeley and James genealogy, in e-Mail to Peggy Kruse, December 25, 2013

[73] Louis E. Pondrom, *Historical Records of St. Ferdinand of Florissant and St. Charles.* 1989 (typed by Gretchen Crank), pgs 113, 114.

[74] Missouri Postal History web site: http://www.missouripostalhistory.org/data/County/Saint%20Louis.htm

[75] Gregory Franzwa, *It's Official – Jamestown Elementary School Is Named*, Hazelwood School District News, September 1975

[76] *Meeting to Establish a Steam Ferry at Jamestown*, St. Louis Daily Globe-Democrat, July 19, 1876

[77] William L. Thomas, *Black Jack in 1877*, History of St. Louis County Missouri Volume 1, The S.J. Clarke Publishing Co., 1911, page 314 (republished in 2011 by Todd S. Abrams)

[78] Robert E. Parkin, *Ezekial Lard, November 1765-1799 in Spanish Louisiana,* St. Louis Genealogical Society Quarterly, Spring 2014

[79] Kevin W. McKenney and Jeanne C. Hunter, *Captain Edmund Hodges and His Descendants: including the Hodges Family of the Niagara District of Ontario, Canada*. Self Published, 2012, p. 31

[80] Kevin W. McKenney and Jeanne C. Hunter, *Captain Edmund Hodges and His Descendants: including the Hodges Family of the Niagara District of Ontario, Canada.* Self Published, 2012, p. 31

[81] Louis Houck, *A History of Missouri from the Earliest Explorations and Settlements until the Admission of the State into the Union. 3 Volumes.* Chicago: R. R. Donnelley & Sons Company, 1908

[82] Frederic L. Billon, *Annals of St. Louis in its Early Days under the French and Spanish Dominations*, 1886 (quoted in *Captain Edmund Hodges and His Descendants*)

[83] James T. Hair, *The Methodist Episcopal Church*, Gazetteer of Madison County, 1866, page 133, https://archive.org/details/gazetteerofmadis00hair

[84] *Patterson, Elisha and Lucy, Farmstead Historic District*, National Register of Historic Places Registration Form, National Park Service, 2004, https://dnr.mo.gov/shpo/nps-nr/04001242.pdf

[85] *Early Days in Missouri, Interesting Reminiscences of Pioneer Life in "Upper Louisiana,"* St. Charles Cosmos, unknown date, approximately 1900, possibly also published in Watchman Advocate

[86] *William Patterson, 1759-1847,* Pike County Genealogical Society web site, http://www.pcgenweb.com/pcgs/bios/william_patterson_1.htm

[87] *William Patterson, 1759-1847,* Pike County Genealogical Society web site, http://www.pcgenweb.com/pcgs/bios/william_patterson_1.htm

[88] *Patterson, Elisha and Lucy, Farmstead Historic District*, National Register of Historic Places Registration Form, National Park Service, 2004, https://dnr.mo.gov/shpo/nps-nr/04001242.pdf

[89] St. Louis Christian Advocate, November 15, 1876 (quoted in *Patterson, Elisha and Lucy, Farmstead Historic District*, National Register of Historic Places Registration Form, National Park Service, 2004, https://dnr.mo.gov/shpo/nps-nr/04001242.pdf)

[90] Bill Putman, *Genealogy Stuff, Patterson and Related Families*, web site: http://www.billputman.com/THE%20PATTERSON%20FAMILY.htm

[91] William L. Thomas, *The History of St. Louis County Missouri*, Volume 2 http://cdm.sos.mo.gov/cdm/ref/collection/mocohist/id/11452

[92] William L. Thomas, *The History of St. Louis County Missouri*, Volume 2 http://cdm.sos.mo.gov/cdm/ref/collection/mocohist/id/11452

[93] *Salem Baptist Church Lamplighter*, July 1977 newsletter

[94] Cold Water Cemetery web site: http://www.rootsweb.ancestry.com/~modarcwc/index.htm

[95] Esley Hamilton, *St. Louis County North Inventory of Historic Buildings, Phase I*, 1988, St. Louis County Department of Parks and Recreation under a grant from the Missouri Department of Natural Resources

[96] Esley Hamilton, *St. Louis County North Inventory of Historic Buildings, Phase I*, 1988, St. Louis County Department of Parks and Recreation under a grant from the Missouri Department of Natural Resources

[97] *Patterson, Elisha and Lucy, Farmstead Historic District*, National Register of Historic Places Registration Form, National Park Service, 2004, https://dnr.mo.gov/shpo/nps-nr/04001242.pdf

[98] Esley Hamilton, *St. Louis County North Inventory of Historic Buildings, Phase I*, 1988, St. Louis County Department of Parks and Recreation under a grant from the Missouri Department of Natural Resources

[99] Inhabitants of Coldwater, *Petition for opening road from "Sarah James Ferry" to division line of settlements of St. Louis and Coldwater and thence to town of St. Louis*, June 18, 1805: Mo History Museum, Coldwater—Roads Envelope

[100] Louis E. Pondrom, *Historical Records of St. Ferdinand of Florissant and St. Charles*, 1989 (typed by Gretchen Crank).

[101] Barbara Lindemann as heard from her mother Betty Warren Lindemann, e-mail to Peggy Kruse, June 2015

[102] *Road to Musick Ferry, Mo., offers Historic as Well as Scenic Points of Interest* ©St. Louis Post-Dispatch, June 22, 1919

[103] Louis E. Pondrom, *Historical Records of St. Ferdinand of Florissant and St. Charles*, 1989 (typed by Gretchen Crank).

[104] Louis E. Pondrom, *Historical Records of St. Ferdinand of Florissant and St. Charles*, 1989 (typed by Gretchen Crank).

[105] *The Old Musick Estate, Half a Dozen Suburban Places Cut Up and Sold*, St. Louis Dispatch, September 21, 1875

[106] The Helmholz Papers quoted in *Family Group Sheet for Reuben Musick*, Musick Family Association of America

[107] *Questions and Answers Column*, The St. Louis Star and Times, February 23, 1933

[108] *Rock House Built in the [18] 50s, Once Musick's Inn, to Be Razed*, Watchman Advocate, February 20, 1931

[109] *Old Musick's Ferry Inn Being Wrecked*, ©St. Louis Post-Dispatch, June 8, 1938, page 16

[110] *Road to Musick Ferry, Mo., offers Historic as Well as Scenic Points of Interest* ©St. Louis Post-Dispatch, June 22, 1919

[111] *Ferry Rates a Little Higher*, Daily St. Charles Cosmos-Monitor, August 26, 1924

[112] *Encyclopedia of Louisville, Kentucky*, page 669

[113] *Business on the Boom at Oldtime Showboat – 600-Seat Theater on Missouri River Filled Nearly Every Night*, ©Post-Dispatch, 9-15-1932, pg 21

[114] *Descendants of Reuben Musick*, Musick Family Association of America

[115] William L. Thomas, *The History of St. Louis County Missouri*, Volume 2
http://cdm.sos.mo.gov/cdm/ref/collection/mocohist/id/11452

[116] Barbara Lindemann, granddaughter of George A. Warren, conversations and e-mails with Peggy Kruse

[117] Robert Swanson, *Halls Ferry Road*, Florissant Valley Reporter

[118] *Underground Railroad*, Alton Museum web site: http://www.altonmuseum.com/html/underground_railroad.html

[119] *Index to the Miscellaneous Documents of the House of Representatives for the First Session of the Forty-Seventh Congress, 1881-1882*, Washington: Government Printing Office, 1882

[120] *This Day in St. Louis History, January 16, 1920: The last night before Prohibition dries America's lips–* Missouri History Museum Facebook Page, January 16, 2014: https://www.facebook.com/search/top/?q=missouri%20history%20museum%20this%20day%20in%20st.%20louis%20history%20january%2016%201920

[121] *Dillon got another Still and brewery*, Daily St. Charles Cosmos-Monitor, March 19, 1927

[122] *Fight across from Musick's Ferry*, St. Louis Post-Dispatch, May 30, 1888

[123] Phil E. Chappell, *A History of the Missouri River*, Transactions of the Kansas State Historical Society 1905-1906, IV. River Navigation, Twenty-ninth meeting, December 6, 1904.

[124] Christina Lieffring, *Steamboat Travel Was Dirty and Dangerous Especially on the Missouri River*, KCUR - Kansas City Public Radio web site, July 14, 2015 http://kcur.org/post/steamboat-travel-was-dirty-and-dangerous-especially-missouri-river

[125] H. G. Hertich, Watchman Advocate, *History of Old Roads, Pioneers and Early Communities and Early Communities of St. Louis County*, 1935

[126] H. G. Hertich, Watchman Advocate, *History of Old Roads, Pioneers and Early Communities and Early Communities of St. Louis County*, 1935

[127] Cold Water Cemetery web site: http://www.rootsweb.ancestry.com/~modarcwc/index.htm

[128] Cold Water Cemetery application for National Register of Historic Places Application, National Park Service: https://dnr.mo.gov/shpo/nps-nr/04000462.pdf

[129] *Reviving a dead cemetery*, North County Journal, June 18, 1995

[130] *Mystery of Little Cemetery Is Solved,* Florissant Valley Reporter, February 26, 1959

[131] Cold Water Cemetery web site: http://www.rootsweb.ancestry.com/~modarcwc/index.htm

[132] Elisha and Lucy Patterson Farmstead Historic District, National Register of Historic Places Application, Section 8: https://dnr.mo.gov/shpo/nps-nr/04001242.pdf

[133] Journal of the Coldwater Church /Union Meeting House (original at Historic Florissant, Inc.)

[134] National Register of Historic Places Application, Cold Water Cemetery, Section 8, page 11. Reference Duncan, Baptists in Missouri, p. 54.

[135] *Mystery of Little Cemetery Is Solved,* Florissant Valley Reporter, February 26, 1959

[136] Gregory Franzwa, *History of the Hazelwood School District,* Hazelwood School District, 1977, pdf file available at http://www.hazelwoodschools.org/Domain/360

[137] Gregory Franzwa, *History of the Hazelwood School District,* Hazelwood School District, 1977, pdf file available at http://www.hazelwoodschools.org/Domain/360

[138] Esley Hamilton, Historic Inventory Form, Office of Historic Preservation, Jefferson City, St. Louis County Parks, June 1988

[139] Gregory Franzwa, *History of the Hazelwood School District,* Hazelwood School District, 1977, pdf file available at http://www.hazelwoodschools.org/Domain/360

[140] Gregory Franzwa, *History of the Hazelwood School District,* Hazelwood School District, 1977, pdf file available at http://www.hazelwoodschools.org/Domain/360

[141] Gregory Franzwa, *History of the Hazelwood School District,* Hazelwood School District, 1977, Chapter 1, pdf file available at http://www.hazelwoodschools.org/Domain/360

[142] Ralph Wehmer memories as told to Olga Smith, volunteer with BJC Hospice Project

[143] Gregory Franzwa, *History of the Hazelwood School District,* Hazelwood School District, 1977, Chapter 2, pdf file available at http://www.hazelwoodschools.org/Domain/360

[144] Mary Stellhorn e-mail to Peggy Kruse

[145] James Barrett, *Reviving a Dead Cemetery – Black Jack set to rededicate old graveyard,* North County Journal, June 18, 1995

[146] Gregory Franzwa, *History of the Hazelwood School District,* Hazelwood School District, 1977, Chapter 1, pdf file available at http://www.hazelwoodschools.org/Domain/360

[147] Gregory Franzwa, *History of the Hazelwood School District,* Hazelwood School District, 1977, Chapter 2, pdf file available at http://www.hazelwoodschools.org/Domain/360

[148] Esley Hamilton, *St. Louis County North Inventory of Historic Buildings, Phase I,* 1988, St. Louis County Department of Parks and Recreation under a grant from the Missouri Department of Natural Resources

[149] Michael Rosenkötter, *From Westphalia into the World: A Farmer's Family from Westphalia in Search of a Better Future in the U.S.A.,* 2d ed. Norderstedt: Books on Demand GmbH, 2003

[150] Michael Rosenkötter, *From Westphalia into the World: A Farmer's Family from Westphalia in Search of a Better Future in the U.S.A.,* 2d ed. Norderstedt: Books on Demand GmbH, 2003, page 74

[151] Elisha and Lucy Patterson Farmstead Historic District, National Register of Historic Places Application, Section 8: https://dnr.mo.gov/shpo/nps-nr/04001242.pdf

[152] John Kohnen, *The Big Tree – Memoirs of the Kohnen Family*

[153] Michael Rosenkötter, *From Westphalia into the World: A Farmer's Family from Westphalia in Search of a Better Future in the U.S.A.,* 2d ed. Norderstedt: Books on Demand GmbH, 2003

[154] J. Thomas Scharf, Scharf, *History of St. Louis City and County, from the Earliest Periods to the Present Day Volume 2.* Philadelphia: Louis H. Everts & Co., 1883, pages 517-518 https://archive.org/details/historyofsaintlov2scha

[155] Missouri Postal History Society web site: http://www.missouripostalhistory.org/county/y1905.htm

[156] Clara Scott, *A Little Bit of History,* First Capitol News of St. Charles, Missouri, Archives Blog: http://firstcapitolnews.blogspot.com/2005/04/little-bit-of-history-by-clara-scott_09.html

[157] *Packet Boat,* Merriam-Webster https://www.merriam-webster.com/dictionary/packet%20boat

[158] Findagrave.com, Jacob E. Veale, https://www.findagrave.com/cgi-bin/fg.cgi?page=gr&GSln=Veale&GSfn=Jacob&GSbyrel=all&GSdyrel=all&GSob=n&GRid=24926713&df=all&

[159] Esley Hamilton, *William Buenger House,* Historic Inventory Form, Office of Historic Preservation, Jefferson City, St. Louis County Parks, June 1988

[160] Ron Buenger, letter to St. Louis County, November 15, 2011

[161] William L. Thomas, *The History of St. Louis County Missouri, Volume 2*
http://cdm.sos.mo.gov/cdm/ref/collection/mocohist/id/11452

[162] Esley Hamilton, *Meyer-Lindemann-Kahre House*, Historic Inventory Form, Office of Historic Preservation, Jefferson City, St. Louis County Parks, June 1988:

[163] William L. Thomas, *The History of St. Louis County Missouri, Volume 2,* 1911
http://cdm.sos.mo.gov/cdm/ref/collection/mocohist/id/11452

[164] William L. Thomas, *The History of St. Louis County Missouri, Volume 2,* 1911
http://cdm.sos.mo.gov/cdm/ref/collection/mocohist/id/11452

[165] *Checking Erosion,* ©Post-Dispatch, July 20, 1947, page 95

[166] Ralph Wehmer's Memories as told to BJC Lumina Project Volunteer Olga Smith

[167] William L. Thomas, *The History of St. Louis County Missouri, Volume 2,* 1911
http://cdm.sos.mo.gov/cdm/ref/collection/mocohist/id/11452

[168] Cathy Gerling, e-mail to Peggy Kruse, April 2014

[169] Lois Farley, e-mail to Peggy Kruse, September 2011

[170] Michael Rosenkötter, *From Westphalia into the World: A Farmer's Family from Westphalia in Search of a Better Future in the U.S.A.,* 2d ed. Norderstedt: Books on Demand GmbH, 2003, page 66

171 Lee Mercer [Rosemary Davison] "Calico Jam," Florissant Valley Reporter, about 1970, displayed in *From Westphalia into the World: A Farmer's Family from Westphalia in Search of a Better Future in the U.S.A.*, 2003, page 73

[172] Gene and Mary Stellhorn, Interview with Jim Leighninger and Peggy Kruse, August 2013

[173] Cindy Winkler, *Civil War Presentation to the Old Jamestown Association,* October 16, 2012
http://cindywinkler.com/civil-war-presentation-to-the-old-jamestown-association/

[174] D. H. Rule, *Civil War St. Louis Timeline*, http://www.civilwarstlouis.com/timeline/index.htm

[175] Frederick Essen and John J. Hartnett, *History of St. Louis County Missouri*, Watchman-Advocate, 1920, p. 101, quoted by Michael Rosenkötter in *From Westphalia into the World: A Farmer's Family from Westphalia in Search of a Better Future in the U.S.A.,* page 59

[176] Don Gerling's remembrance of his uncle's stories in an e-mail to Peggy Kruse, April 2014

[177] *Back to the Farm for the Farmer's Daughter,* ©St. Louis Post-Dispatch, July 20, 1941, photographer Jack Gould (Photo also printed in ©St. Louis Post-Dispatch on November 1, 1992, and March 7, 1998)

[178] Esley Hamilton, *St. Louis County North Inventory of Historic Buildings, Phase I,* 1988, St. Louis County Department of Parks and Recreation under a grant from the Missouri Department of Natural Resources

[179] Renee Stovsky, *Vouziers - Some people build their castles in the air. Joseph Desloge built his in Florissant Valley*, ©St. Louis Post-Dispatch, June 21, 1992

[180] Wesley Fordyce, grandson of Joseph Desloge, Sr., e-mail to Peggy Kruse, July 2014

[181] *Francis M. Curlee Obituary*, ©St. Louis Post-Dispatch, March 18, 1958

[182] Esley Hamilton, *Francis Mesker House, "Fercrest," St. Louis County North Inventory of Historic Buildings* Form, 1988, St. Louis County Department of Parks and Recreation under a grant from the Missouri Department of Natural Resources

[183] Esley Hamilton, *John B. G. Mesker House, St. Louis County North Inventory of Historic Buildings* Form, 1988, St. Louis County Department of Parks and Recreation under a grant from the Missouri Department of Natural Resources

[184] *New Mesker Residence in French Chateau Style*, ©St. Louis Post-Dispatch, May 28, 1939

[185] Esley Hamilton, *Evarts A. Graham House, St. Louis County North Inventory of Historic Buildings* Form, 1988, St. Louis County Department of Parks and Recreation under a grant from the Missouri Department of Natural Resources

[186] C. Barber Mueller, *Helen's Modern Home* in *Evarts A. Graham*, 2002, Publisher BC Decker, Hamilton, Ontario, pages 382 – 384

[187] Beth Miller, *Ferkol named Hartmann Professor of Pediatrics*, January 13, 2012
http://source.wustl.edu/2012/01/ferkol-named-hartmann-professor-of-pediatrics

[188] *The Department of Pediatrics celebrates its first 100 years*, March 30, 2010, Washington University in St. Louis Newsroom https://source.wustl.edu/2010/03/the-department-of-pediatrics-celebrates-its-first-100-years/

[189] Esley Hamilton, *Vilray P. Blair House, Historic Inventory* Form, 1988, St. Louis County Department of Parks and Recreation under a grant from the Missouri Department of Natural Resources

[190] Esley Hamilton, *Ellis Fischel Guest House, Historic Inventory* Form, 1988, St. Louis County Department of Parks and Recreation under a grant from the Missouri Department of Natural Resources

[191] William L. Thomas, *The History of St. Louis County Missouri, Volume 2,* 1911
http://cdm.sos.mo.gov/cdm/ref/collection/mocohist/id/11452

[192] Patricia Rice, *Starbird Tribute: Finding Role Model Award, Talk to Honor Late Columnist and College Dean,* ©St. Louis Post - Dispatch 06 Apr 1988

[193] *Velma Wood Hammer; Renovated Historic Home*, ©St. Louis Post-Dispatch, June 23, 1995, page 4B

[194] *Oscar Lawrence Hammer; Renovated Historic Home*, ©St. Louis Post – Dispatch,, March 26. 1997, page 12C.

[195] Heather Ratcliffe, *6-year wait is over for missing woman's family Body surfaced in 1999 in Gulf of Mexico* ©St. Louis Post-Dispatch, May 15, 2005, page D1

[196] John J. Archibald, *She Learned to Fly to Aid War Effort,* ©St. Louis Post-Dispatch, March 19, 1989

[197] Adela Riek Scharr, *Sisters in the Sky Volume I,* Patrice Press, page 375

[198] Michael D. Sorkin, *Paul Behlmann dies; grew his North County used tire store into a giant car dealership*, ©St. Louis Post-Dispatch, October 26, 2013

[199] Krause&Yocom of Florissant: *Information about Bernard L Behlmann Sr.* http://www.genealogy.com/ftm/k/r/a/Bernie-J-Krause/WEBSITE-0001/UHP-0019.html

[200] William L. Thomas, *The History of St. Louis County Missouri, Volume 2*, 1911 http://cdm.sos.mo.gov/cdm/ref/collection/mocohist/id/11452

[201] William L. Thomas, *The History of St. Louis County Missouri, Volume 2*, 1911 http://cdm.sos.mo.gov/cdm/ref/collection/mocohist/id/11452, page 383

[202] Christian Cudnik, responding to Peggy Kruse e-mail, October 2016

[203] *Our People – Ballet - Jennifer Welch-Cudnik*, COCA (Center of Creative Arts), http://www.cocastl.org/?post_type=employees&s=cudnik

[204] *Eddie Moss*, Wikipedia, https://en.wikipedia.org/wiki/Eddie_Moss

[205] Leah Greenbaum, *Five St. Louis Ghost Stories That Just Won't Die,* Riverfront Times, October 25, 2012

[206] Kyyung Song, *Boeing Shows $60 Million Training Center* ©St. Louis Post-Dispatch, February 26, 1999

[207] Adele Starbird, *The Dean Speaks Up – Summer 'em and Winter 'em* ©St. Louis Post-Dispatch, April 27, 1954

[208] Michael D. Sorkin, *Paul Behlmann dies; grew his North County used tire store into a giant car dealership*, ©St. Louis Post-Dispatch, October 26, 2013

[209] Ken Smith, *Old Jamestown Association Statement on Florissant Karst Preservation District*, St. Louis County Council Meeting, March 3, 2009, http://oldjamestownassn.org/yahoo_site_admin/assets/docs/OJA_Karst_Statement_to_St_Louis_County_Council.136111157.pdf

[210] James Vandike, *Living with the Sinks*, Missouri Resources Magazine, Fall 1995 - Vol. 12, No. 3

[211] *Old Jamestown Association 1988 Newsletter*, http://oldjamestownassn.org/yahoo_site_admin/assets/docs/oja_history_ken.87164058.pdf

[212] *Karst Preservation District Regulation*, St. Louis County http://www.stlouisco.com/Portals/8/docs/Document%20Library/planning/zoning%20ordinance/Zoning%20Districts/109.pdf

[213] James Vandike, *Living with the Sinks*, Missouri Resources Magazine, Fall 1995 - Vol. 12, No. 3

[214] James Vandike, *Living with the Sinks*, Missouri Resources Magazine, Fall 1995 - Vol. 12, No. 3

[215] *Discovering a steamboat relic of Missouri River trade, Posted 4/4/2013*, by Eileen Williamson, Public Affairs Specialist http://www.nwo.usace.army.mil/Media/NewsStories/tabid/1834/Article/487850/discovering-a-steamboat-relic-of-missouri-river-trade.aspx

[216] *Loss of Lands in our County Caused by the Washings of the Missouri and Mississippi Rivers*, St. Louis County Watchman, February 1, 1833 (as printed in the Wildwood Historical Society Newsletter May 2009)

[217] *Rock House Built in the [18] 50s, Once Musick's Inn, to Be Razed*, Watchman Advocate, February 20, 1931

[218] Lawsuit summary (dispute over sidetrack on east side that benefits west side owner), *Knox County Stone Co v. Bellefontaine Quarry Inc.*, Missouri Court of Appeals, Eastern District, Division Three, Nos. 73826, 73872, Decided: December 15, 1998

[219] Janet McNichols, *Quarry's Request for Rezoning for Expansion draws neighbors*, ©St. Louis Post-Dispatch, April 27, 1998

[220] Janet McNichols, *Bellefontaine Quarry zoning decision is delayed for further review*, ©St. Louis Post-Dispatch, December 13, 1999

[221] Repps Hudson, *County aquifer is perfect site for Laclede gas*, ©St. Louis Post-Dispatch, June 24, 2001

[222] NiNi Harris and Esley Hamilton, *St. Louis Parks*, Reedy Press, 2012, p. 146

[223] *Park Pages, Sioux Passage*, St. Louis County Parks and Recreation, http://www.stlouisco.com/ParksandRecreation/ParkPages/SiouxPassage and *Park Maps: Sioux Passage*, http://www.stlouisco.com/Portals/8/docs/Document%20Library/parks/PDFs/parkmaps/SiouxPassage.pdf

[224] Harry Jackson, *Black Buffalo Trail [Sioux Passage Park]*, @St. Louis Post-Dispatch, September 8, 2010

[225] NiNi Harris and Esley Hamilton, *St. Louis Parks*, Reedy Press, 2012, p.146

[226] *Park History Documents: Briscoe Park*, St. Louis County Parks and Recreation, http://www.stlouisco.com/Portals/8/docs/Document%20Library/parks/PDFs/ParkHistory/BriscoeHistory.pdf

[227] NiNi Harris and Esley Hamilton, *St. Louis Parks*, Reedy Press, 2012, p.153

[228] Harry Jackson, *Trail of the week*, ©St. Louis Post-Dispatch, December 7, 2013

[229] *Park History Documents: Norman B. Champ Park*, St. Louis County Parks and Recreation, https://www.stlouisco.com/Portals/8/docs/Document%20Library/parks/PDFs/ParkHistory/ChampHistory.pdf

[230] *Car of Commerce Chute*, Rome of the West, http://www.romeofthewest.com/search?q=pelican

[231] Tim Renken, ©St. Louis Post-Dispatch articles, *County Will Keep Pelican Island Wild*, November 30, 1975, *Pelican Island New Part of Park System*, July 1, 1976, and *Pelican Island Is Destined to Become User Friendly*, August 18, 1991

[232] *Pelican Island*, Missouri Department of Conservation, https://nature.mdc.mo.gov/discover-nature/places/pelican-island

[233] Blythe Bernhard, *New reports of cancers near Coldwater Creek in North County*, ©St. Louis Post-Dispatch, January 16, 2014

[234] *Checking Erosion*, ©St. Louis Post-Dispatch Pictures Section, July 20, 1947, Photographer Jack Gould

[235] Shannon Howard, *The Gardens of NoCo: Chan Mahanta*, NOCOSTL (Former online magazine web site no longer active), Jul 27, 2010

[236] Mark Waier e-mail to Peggy Kruse, April 2016

[237] *Geothermal: How does it work?*, WaterFurnace, http://www.waterfurnace.com/how-it-works.aspx

[238] Jack Gould, Photographer, *Checking Erosion*, ©St. Louis Post-Dispatch Pictures Section, July 20, 1947

[239] Pallottine Renewal Center web site: http://pallottinerenewal.org/

[240] Jamestown New Horizons web site: http://www.jnh-goneriding.org

[241] Paul Artspace web site: www.paulartspace.org

[242] Florissant American Legion web site: http://www.florissantlegion.org/

[243] St. Louis County web site: http://stlouisco.com/

[244] U.S. Census Bureau web site: https://www.census.gov/geo/reference/gtc/gtc_place.html

[245] Old Jamestown Association web site: http://www.oldjamestownassn.org/

[246] St. Louis County Library web site: http://www.slcl.org/content/jamestown-bluffs-branch

[247] Black Jack Fire Protection District web site: http://www.blackjackfire.org/

[248] Shannon Howard, *El-Mel 48 years in Noco*, NOCOSTL (Former online magazine web site no longer active), July 27, 2010

[249] Waldbart Nursery web site: http://www.waldbartnursery.com/about.htm

[250] Baronwood Kennels web site: http://www.baronwood.com/About-Baronwood-Kennels.html

[251] *Jamestown Mall Area Plan Executive Summary*, St. Louis County, May 2011, https://main.stlpartnership.com/cmss_files/attachmentlibrary/Executive%20Summary%20-%20sm.pdf

[252] Lisa Brown, *St. Louis County invests in shuttered Jamestown Mall,* ©St. Louis Post-Dispatch, May 23, 2015

[253] Steve Geigerich, *Bypassing County Council, Stenger turns to Port Authority for Jamestown Mall redevelopment,* ©St. Louis Post-Dispatch, February 10, 2017

[254] Caroline Louis Cole, *Winging it at Boeing's Leadership Center*, Workforce Magazine, September 29, 2000 http://www.workforce.com/2000/09/29/winging-it-at-boeings-leadership-center/

[255] St. Andrew UMC web site: http://www.saintandrewsumc.net/about/our-history/

[256] Shalom Church web site: http://www.shalomccop.org/shalom-church-history

[257] St. Angela Merici web site: http://www.saintangelamerici.org/parish/history.html

[258] St. Norbert web site: http://www.saintnorbert.com/history.html and http://www.saintnorbert.com/school-history.html

[259] St. Louis Business Journal, *Top 25 Wealthiest Zip Codes* – July 8, 2016

[260] Geological Overview on Missouri Department of Natural Resources Map, *Surficial Material Geologic Map of the Florissant 7.5' Quadrangle, St. Charles County, Missouri*, Geology and Digital Compilation by David A. Gaunt and Travis Carr, 2010 https://dnr.mo.gov/geology/statemap/stLouis/OFM-10-560-GS.htm and http://earthquake.usgs.gov/research/external/reports/G09AP00113.pdf

[261] *Missouri, The WPA Guide to the "Show Me" State*, 1940, pages 12-14

[262] Joseph Desloge, Jr., *Passport to Manhood: Adventures of a WWII Front Line Ambulance Drive with the British and the French Foreign Legion*. Florissant, MO, 1995 http://www.porter-az.com/misc/desloge/dpressn.html

[263] William, Iseminger, *Cahokia Mounds – America's First City*, 2010

Bibliography

Family Histories

Desloge, Jr., Joseph. *Passport to Manhood: Adventures of a WWII Front Line Ambulance Drive with the British and the French Foreign Legion.* Florissant, MO, 1995

McKenney, Kevin W., and Hunter, Jeanne C. *Captain Edmund Hodges and His Descendants: including the Hodges Family of the Niagara District of Ontario, Canada.* Self Published

Meyer, Melvin C. *The Patterson Settlement: First Successful English Speaking Settlement in Spanish Territory, St. Louis CO. Mo.* 1797

Rosenkötter, Michael. *From Westphalia into the World: A Farmer's Family from Westphalia in Search of a Better Future in the U.S.A., 2d ed.* Norderstedt: Books on Demand GmbH, 2003.

Kohnen, John, and Goldkamp, Patricia Kohnen. *The Big Tree – Memoirs of the Kohnen Family.* Florissant: Kohnen Family

Putnam, Bill, web pages about members of Patterson and related families:
http://www.billputman.com/THE%20PATTERSON%20FAMILY.htm
Patterson Family: www.billputman.com/Johnpat1.pdf
Hume Family: http://www.billputman.com/Hume.pdf

Pike County Genealogical Society: Patterson and Related Families: William Patterson, 1759-1847 – History http://www.pcgenweb.com/pcgs/bios/william_patterson_1.htm

Wehmer, Ralph -- Personal stories on growing up and living near Old Jamestown and Carrico -- http://oldjamestownassn.org/yahoo_site_admin/assets/docs/Ralph_Wehmer_Memories_-_Adapted_for_web_site.32080253.pdf

Old Jamestown Area History

Crank, Gretchen. *Reflections of the Florissant Valley.* Dallas: Curtis Media Corporation, 1990.

Davison, Rosemary. *Florissant.* Virginia Beach: The Donning Company Publishers, 2002.

Franzwa, Gregory M. *History of the Hazelwood School District.* Florissant, MO: Hazelwood School District, 1969 (published 1977)
Digitized version on Hazelwood School District web site:
http://www.hazelwoodschools.org/ABOUTUS/HISTORYOFTHEDISTRICT/Documents/111036%20Hazelwood%20bookscan%202.pdf

Garraghan, Gilbert Joseph, S.J. Saint Ferdinand de Florissant: The Story of an Ancient Parish. Chicago: Loyola University Press, 1923. https://babel.hathitrust.org/cgi/pt?id=wu.89063852776;view=1up;seq=1

Gass, William. *The Past in Our Presence: Historic Buildings in St. Louis County.* St. Louis: St. Louis County Parks and Recreation, 1996

Handwritten journal: Minutes, contributions, disbursements – Coldwater Church and Union Meeting House, 1830s. Located at Historic Florissant, Inc.

Hertich, H. G. *History of Old Roads, Pioneers and Early Communities of St. Louis County*. St. Louis County: Watchman Advocate, 1935

Mueller, C. Barber, MD, FACS. *Evarts A. Graham: The Life, Lives, and Times of the Surgical Spirit of St. Louis*. Hamilton, Ontario: BC Decker, Inc., 2002.

Pondrom, Louis E. *Historical Records of St. Ferdinand of Florissant and St. Charles*. 1989 (typed by Gretchen Crank).

Scharr, Adela Riek. *Sisters in the Sky: Volume I – The WAFS*. St. Louis: The Patrice Press, 1986/1987/1991.

Scharr, Adela Riek. *Sisters in the Sky: Volume II – The WASP*. St. Louis: The Patrice Press, 1988

Wright, John A., Sr. *Florissant (Images of America)*. Charleston, etc.: Arcadia Publishing, 2004.

A History of Castlereagh Estates 1956 to 2006. Castlereagh Estates Subdivision

St. Louis Area History

Andre, R. Miriam. *The Moving Forces in the History of Old Bonhomme: The Manchester Missouri Area*. Charles E. Biggs and R. Miriam Andre, 1982.

Ehlmann, Steve. *Crossroads: A History of St. Charles County, Missouri*. St. Charles, MO: Lindenwood University Press, 2004

Faherty, William Barnaby, S.J. *Centuries of St. Louis*. St. Louis: Reedy Press, 2007.

Foley, William E., and Rice, C. David. The First Chouteaus: River Barons of Early St. Louis. Chicago, etc.: University of Illinois Press, 1983.

Harris, NiNi, and Hamilton, Esley. *St. Louis Parks*. St. Louis: Reedy Press, 2012.

Iseminger, William. *Cahokia Mounds: America's First City*. Charleston: The History Press, 2010

Leach, Mark W. *Chesterfield's Ancient Past*, 2013

Primm, James Neal. Lion of the Valley: St. Louis, Missouri, 1764-1980. St. Louis: Missouri Historical Society Press, 1981/1990/1998.

Starbird, Adele Chomeau. *Many Strings to My Lute*. Chicago: R. R. Donnelley & Sons Company, 1977.

Thomas, William L. *The History of St. Louis County Missouri, Vol I: The Story Told 100 Years Ago of the People, Towns and Events that made "The County" as we know it today*. St. Louis: Todd S. Abrams, 2011 (re-publication of 1911 book published by The S. J. Clarke Publishing Co.) Digitized version of Vol II, 1911 Click here: History of St. Louis County, Missouri Volume 2 :: Missouri County Histories
http://cdm.sos.mo.gov/cdm/ref/collection/mocohist/id/11452

Hyde, William, and Conard, Howard Louis. *Encyclopedia of the History of St. Louis* 4 Volumes. New York, Louisville, St. Louis: The Southern History Co., 1899
Digitized versions available on Missouri History Museum web site:
http://collections.mohistory.org/search/?text=encyclopedia%20of%20st%20louis&q=custom_search

Wolferman, Kristie C., The Indomitable Mary Easton Sibley: Pioneer of Women's Education in Missouri. Columbia and London: University of Missouri Press, 2008.

Missouri History

Goebel, Gert. *Longer than a Man's Lifetime in Missouri*. Columbia, MO: The State Historical Society of Missouri, 2013.

Houck, Louis. *A History of Missouri from the Earliest Explorations and Settlements until the Admission of the State into the Union. 3 Volumes*. Chicago: R. R. Donnelley & Sons Company, 1908.

Digitized versions online:

http://www.archive.org/details/historyofmissour01houc

http://books.google.com/books?id=3ZB5AAAAMAAJ&dq=A+history+of+Missouri+from+the+earliest+explorations

http://books.google.com/books?id=nmcOAAAAIAAJ&printsec=frontcover&dq=inauthor:"Louis+Houck"&hl=en&ei=ODq4TuGCBMXq0gHkZy_BA&sa=X&oi=book_result&ct=result&resnum=1&ved=0CDgQ6AEwAA#v=onepage&q&f=false

Houck, Louis. The Spanish Regime in Missouri: S Collection of Papers and Documents Relating to Upper Louisiana....2 Volumes. Chicago: R. R. Donnelley & Sons Company, 1909. (A collection of papers and documents relating to upper Louisiana principally within the present limits of Missouri during the dominion of Spain, from the Archives of the Indies at Seville, etc., translated from the original Spanish into English)

Digitized versions on line – Volumes 1 and 2:

http://www.archive.org/details/spanishregimeinm01houc

http://www.archive.org/details/spanishregimeinm02houc

Jones, Randell. *In the Footsteps of Daniel Boone*. Winston-Salem, NC: John F. Blair, Publisher, 2005.

Missouri, The WPA Guide to the "Show Me" State," 1940, pages 12-14:

Smith, Jeffrey E. (ed.). *Seeking a Newer World: The Fort Osage Journals and Letters of George Sibley 1808-1811*. St. Charles, MO: Lindenwood University Press, 2003.

Digitized Book:

A History of the Missouri River -- Talk given by Phil Chappell at the Kansas State Historical Society in 1904. The link below is to the whole report of the Historical Society. The Missouri River portion begins on page 237, His list of about 700 steamboats begins on page 295.
http://openlibrary.org/books/OL14045930M/Transactions_of_the_Kansas_State_Historical_Society.

Harlan, James D., and Denny, James M. Atlas of Lewis & Clark in Missouri, Columbia and London, University of Missouri Press, 2003

Magazines

Gateway -- Missouri History Museum

Missouri Conservationist – Missouri Department of Conservation. http://mdc.mo.gov/conmag

Missouri Historical Review – The State Historical Society of Missouri

Missouri Resources – Missouri Department of Natural Resources. Marceline, MO: Walsworth Publishing Co. http://dnr.mo.gov/magazine/index.html

St. Charles County Heritage – St. Charles County Historical Society

St. Louis Genealogical Society Quarterly Journal

Newspapers

Alton Telegraph (other names)

St. Charles Cosmos (other names)

St. Louis Globe-Democrat

St. Louis Post-Dispatch

Watchman Advocate

St. Louis Magazine

Riverfront Times

Government Documents

Community Area Study – Old Jamestown Area: An evaluation of a part of unincorporated St. Louis County for the St. Louis County Planning Commission, with the participation of the Old Jamestown Area Advisory Committee. Prepared by the St. Louis County Department of Planning. Adopted by the Planning Commission on April 4, 1988.
http://www.stlouisco.com/Portals/8/docs/Document%20Library/planning/community%20planning%20and%20revitalization/north%20county/Old%20Jamestown%20Community%20Area%20Study.pdf

Hamilton, Esley, St. Louis County North Inventory of Historic Buildings Phase I. St. Louis: St. Louis County Department of Parks and Recreation, 1988.

Hamilton, Esley, St. Louis County North Inventory of Historic Buildings Phase Two: Black Jack. St. Louis: St. Louis County Department of Parks and Recreation, 1989.

Harl, Joe, and Machiran, Robin. Prehistoric cultures of the City of Wildwood St. Louis County, Missouri: Research Report #688B Prepared for the City of Wildwood. St. Louis: Archaeological Research Center of St. Louis Inc., 2013

National Register of Historic Places – Applications for St. Louis County:
http://dnr.mo.gov/shpo/stlouis.htm

National Register of Historic Places – Cold Water Cemetery: http://dnr.mo.gov/shpo/nps-nr/04000462.pdf

Pitzman, Julius. Pitzman's New Atlas of the City and County of Saint Louis Missouri. Philadelphia: A. B. Holcombe and Co., 1878

Pitzman, Julius. Pitzman's Map of the County of Saint Louis Missouri. St. Louis, 1868

Scharf, J. Thomas. *History of St. Louis City and County, from the Earliest Periods to the Present Day Volume 1*. Philadelphia: Louis H. Everts & Co., 1883 https://archive.org/details/cihm_13266

Scharf, J. Thomas. *History of St. Louis City and County, from the Earliest Periods to the Present Day Volume 2*. Philadelphia: Louis H. Everts & Co., 1883 https://archive.org/details/historyofsaintlov2scha

Web sites

Cahokia Mounds State Historic Site: http://cahokiamounds.org/

Other Mounds in St. Louis area: http://mediad.publicbroadcasting.net/p/kwmu/files/201403/14-1-28_Mounds_ProjectArea.jpg (Map is very large, need to move around to see everything.)

Missouri Historical Society Research Library:

> http://www.mohistory.org/lrc-home/
> Digital Content: http://contentdm.mohistory.org/
> Books -- http://contentdm.mohistory.org/cdm4/browse.php?CISOROOT=/lib

St. Louis County Library Online Research

> Newspaper archives: http://www.slcl.org/research/subject/670
> Research Guidelines: http://www.slcl.org/research/guidelines

State Historical Society of Missouri, Columbia, MO -- online
General research fee $20.00 Some information on web site can be searched
http://shs.umsystem.edu

www.ancestry.com

www.newspapers.com

Sioux Passage Park -- history
http://ww5.stlouisco.com/parks/parkhistory/SiouxPassageHistory.pdf

Steamboat "Far West" -- ties to Custer's last stand -- eventually sunk near Musick's Ferry
http://www.americanhistory.si.edu/onthewater/collection/TR_335811.html

Pallottine Renewal Center - 15270 Old Halls Ferry Road
http://www.pallottinerenewal.org/bit_of_history_--_photos

Brief History of St. Louis County -- by Esley Hamilton
http://ww5.stlouisco.com/parks/History1.html

Laclede Gas Storage Area - ©St. Louis Post-Dispatch article
http://oldjamestownassn.org/yahoo_site_admin/assets/docs/OJA_-_Laclede_Gas_Storage.136121557.pdf

Fort Belle Fontaine (at northern end of Bellefontaine Road)
http://www.usgennet.org/usa/mo/county/stlouis/bellefontaine/fort.htm

Fort Bellefontaine - The Ghost on the Stairs
http://www.militaryghosts.com/fortbelle.html

St. Stanislaus Seminary (on Howdershell):
http://www.romeofthewest.com/2005/09/photos-of-old-saint-stanislaus.html

Historic Florissant
http://www.historicflorissant.com/about.shtml

Taille de Noyer Florissant Valley Historical Society
http://florissantoldtown.com/tailledenoyer.shtml

Old St. Ferdinand Shrine
http://florissantoldtown.com/stferdinandshrine.shtml

Frederick Hyatt Mansion - photos and history
http://www.usgennet.org/usa/mo/county/stlouis/hyatt_house

Rolling along the River in NoCo - Photos and remembrances of Toby Weiss
http://www.beltstl.com/2011/03/rolling-along-the-river-in-noco/

Cold Water Cemetery -- Pattersons - Rev. John Clark -- Others
Official site: http://www.rootsweb.ancestry.com/~modarcwc/
With Links to History and Names of those buried there

Artifacts found at Musick's Ferry area
http://users.stlcc.edu/mfuller/Musick.html

Car of Commerce Chute
http://www.romeofthewest.com/2010/06/car-of-commerce-chute.html

Pelican Island brief information:
http://mdc.mo.gov/discover-nature/places-go/natural-areas/pelican-island

Genealogy in St. Louis, web site by Dave Lossos (page has links to a variety of subjects related to St. Louis history): http://stlouis.genealogyvillage.com/

Surnames appearing in the index to the Pitzman's 1878 St. Louis Atlas by Dave Lossos
http://stlouis.genealogyvillage.com/atlasidx.htm

Library of Congress – Geography and Map Reading Room http://www.loc.gov/rr/geogmap/gmpage.html

Bridgeton History – Videos of residents sharing memories -- https://vimeo.com/bridgetonmohistory

Prologue Magazine -- Articles from National Archives -- http://www.archives.gov/publications/prologue/

Online St. Louis, Missouri Death Records, Indexes & Obituaries
A Genealogy Directory for Finding Death Certificates, Obituaries & Other Records

http://www.deathindexes.com/missouri/st-louis.html

Click here: Search For Soldiers - The Civil War (U.S. National Park Service) Results for search of "Carrico." Can search for other names. https://www.nps.gov/civilwar/search-soldiers.htm?submitted=1&firstName=&lastName=Carrico&stateCode=MO&multiselect=MO&warSideCode=C&battleUnitName=#results

The Missouri Stone Industry – Variety of Facts
http://quarriesandbeyond.org/states/mo/mo-stone_industry/mo-stone_indus_2.html

Missouri State Archives – Secretary of State web site --
Links to Collections: http://www.sos.mo.gov/archives/resources/ordb.asp

St. Louis County Web Site

    Real Estate Parcel information, includes more
    recent ownership transfers.http://revenue.stlouisco.com/IAS/

    Interactive Property Maps: http://maps.stlouisco.com/propertyview/

    Downloadable Maps: Choose "Maps and GIS" from list
    http://stlouisco.com/PropertyandRoads/MapsandGIS/DownloadMaps.aspx

Lewis & Clark Trail:
Home page: http://www.lewisandclarktrail.com/index.html
Lewis & Clark 101: http://www.lewisandclarktrail.com/101.htm

Acknowledgements

I am very, very grateful to the many historians who plowed the ground, providing a great deal of information for this book, which is a compilation of Old Jamestown history.

Bev Girardier, Ken and Olga Smith, and Mary Stellhorn shared many documents and articles they had collected over the years and shared stories about the area from their experiences. Bev collected many snippets of history in books and newspapers and has compiled historical articles for the Old Jamestown Association newsletter. Special thanks to Chan Mahanta who provided descriptive words for the OJ area and took great drone photos used for the cover and book.

Cindy Winkler researched and shared the area's Civil War history and was very supportive in my occasional searches for other area information. Cindy and Mary Stellhorn were frequent 'go-to' people for questions that arose. If they didn't know the answer, they often checked with their sources.

OJA History Committee members Don Zykan and Patty Murray shared connections and bits of information as questions arose. Barbara Lindemann shared Warren family history. Wesley Fordyce shared Desloge family history. Gene and Mary Stellhorn, Lois Hoffman, Carlene Randolph, and Bill Lichtenberg shared their memories and photos.

Mark Waier invited us to visit his beautiful home on Portage Road. Jim Hume's comprehensive Cold Water Cemetery web site was very helpful and Jim was generous in responding to e-mail questions. From California, Nancy Shattuck's James and Seeley family research provided hints for further discoveries.

Esley Hamilton and Danny Gonzales, St. Louis County historians, and Joe Harl, Archaeological Research Center of St. Louis, Inc., were very supportive and helpful.

Gregory Franzwa's 1977 "History of Hazelwood School District" and 1975 HSD newsletter article on the naming of Jamestown School provided much interesting and useful information. The St. Louis Post-Dispatch, St. Louis Magazine, Riverfront Times, nocostl.org, Missouri Resources Magazine, and St. Louis Genealogical Society graciously provided permission to use their articles.

Alone and with others, I have visited and been assisted by many at museums – Missouri History Museum Research Library (Dennis Northcott, Jaime Bourassa), Historic Florissant (Gretchen Crank and Carol Kane). Phil Skroska of the Washington U. Becker Medical Library shared photos Dr. Graham. St. Louis County Library sent copies of newspaper articles before they became available on newspapers.com.

I was also greatly aided by the abundance of online searchable information, web sites with stories of history, digitized books, and newspaper articles. I am grateful to all the individuals and organizations who continue to add content to those sites. And I love Google!!!!

Jim Leighninger, my husband Ray, son Kevin, and grandson Brian provided much appreciated feedback on early drafts. Mary Stellhorn and Jim reviewed ongoing drafts several times. Brent Furrow, Jeff Ackerman, Dolores Fitzgerald, and Chan Mahanta helped with the final reviews and provided great feedback.

And I am continuously grateful to God whose power, working in us, can do infinitely more than we can ask or imagine. (Ref. Eph. 3:14-21)

Acknowledgements Page Photos

Photo 1 OJA History Committee
First Meeting September 2011 at Bev Girardier's home:
L-R Don Zykan, Olga Smith, Peggy Kruse, Patty Murray, Bev Girardier, Ken Smith
Photo by Member Chan Mahanta.
Mary Stellhorn and Jim Leighninger joined the committee after the first meeting.

Photo 2 Bill Lichtenberg, Lois Hoffman, and Carlene Randolph sharing photos, maps and stories at Jamestown Bluffs Library Photo by Peggy Kruse

Photo 3 Gene and Mary Lange Stellhorn at November 2016 Old Jamestown Association meeting
Photo by Peggy Kruse

Photo 4 Wesley Fordyce meets with Bev Girardier and Jim Leighninger at Bev's home, 2012. – Photo by Peggy Kruse

Photo 5 Chan Mahanta and Peggy Kruse with Mark Waier at his Portage Road home (Mesker) – Photo by Bev Girardier

Index

A

Accommodation Road, 39, 40, 107, 139, 190
Ackerman, 226
Adair, 141, 142
Adams, 53
African Americans, 36, 59, 73, 75, 85, 86, 89, 108, 112, 175, 182, 191, 192
Afshari, 108
Afshari Estates, 108
Ahlfeldt, 76, 77
Albers, 9, 109, 111, 115, 206
Allen, 33, 76, 77, 180
Alton, 10, 26, 35, 37, 39, 53, 67, 68, 73, 74, 75, 93, 113, 140, 179, 181, 190
Alton Telegraph, 179, 222
American Indians, 10, 11, 12, 13, 17, 19, 20, 22, 23, 26, 27, 35, 58, 118, 138, 142, 147
American Legion, 152, 153, 162
American Revolution, 204
Anabaptist, 37, 51
Anderson, 48, 53
Andrae, 93
Andre, 220
Anglum, 190, 192
Archaeological Research Center, 19, 205, 206, 222
Archaic, 203
Arctic, 165
Arkansas, 27, 31, 130
Armstrong, 16, 122
Art's Lawn Mower, 110
Atkinson, 25
atlas, 60, 110, 222, 224
Atlas Manufacturing, 197
Aubuchon, 126
Aunt Betsy, 43, 69

B

Baden, 12, 50, 99, 103, 154
Ballet, 130
Ballet Initiative, 130
Baptist, 62, 74, 84, 86, 88, 89, 127, 157, 183, 209
Barnes Hospital, 121
Baronwood Kennels, 155, 217
Barrington Downs, 158
Barrington Elementary School, 153
Barton County, 104
Basford, 161
Bates, 39, 67, 68, 74, 87, 196, 198, 201
Bauer, 191
Bay Pointe, 161
Becker, 160
bedrock, 20, 164, 166, 167
Behlmann, 105, 128, 129, 161
Bellefontaine Cemetery, 68
Bellefontaine Quarry, 140
Bellefontaine Road, 23, 35, 223
Bender, 180
Bernhard, 216
Bert, 155
BFI, 130, 139
Bibliography, 219
Bielefeld, 64, 99
Birkemeier, 64, 99
Bishop, 16, 37, 51, 52, 53, 125, 129
Black Jack, 10, 41, 74, 75, 86, 95, 99, 100, 101, 102, 110, 127, 175, 176, 181, 222
Black Jack Fire Protection District, 111, 154
black tongue disease, 104
Black Walnut, 70, 103
Blackburn, 42, 43, 69, 89
Blacklock, 17
Blair, 16, 68, 117, 120, 122, 123, 124
Blake, 160
Blick, 20, 21
Blossom, 120, 124
bluff, 11, 12, 15, 20, 21, 22, 39, 41, 62, 73, 118, 119, 121, 122, 124, 139, 151, 153, 156, 196, 200, 217
boat ramp, 142
Bob Evans, 162
Boeing, 73, 109, 118, 156, 217
Boeing Leadership Center, 73, 83, 151, 156, 200
Bonne Terre, 201
Boone, 11, 15, 33, 34, 54, 55, 119, 170, 171, 221
Boone County, 49, 54
Borgman, 102
Bourassa, 226
Bragg, 181
Breckenridge, 61, 63
Bremen, 15, 79, 99, 100
Bridgeton, 34, 51, 58, 86, 170, 180, 204, 224
Brier, 93
Brinker, 93, 190
Briscoe Park, 53, 142, 143
Britain, 203
British, 13, 25, 27, 31, 87, 202, 218, 219
Britts, 181
Brooks, 85, 179
Brown, 17, 32, 33, 36, 37, 43, 51, 53, 69, 71, 72, 84, 89, 90, 92, 93, 101, 107, 178, 217
Brown School, 14, 17, 43, 72, 89, 90, 92, 93, 97, 107, 125, 190
Bubblehead, 131
Buenger, 104, 105, 114, 115, 213
Buhrmeister, 107
Burlington/Keokuk, 164
Burr, 33, 67

C

Cahokia, 203
Cahokia Mounds, 10, 11, 13, 19, 20, 21, 29, 220, 223
Calico Jam, 110, 213
California, 106, 147, 156
Cambrian, 164
Campbell, 181
Canada, 13, 22, 24, 31, 35, 36, 48, 49, 50, 52, 208, 209
cancer, 111, 121, 122, 123, 124, 144, 145
Captain Edmund Hodges, 48, 49, 54, 55, 207, 208, 209
Car of Commerce, 15, 43, 48, 77, 119, 142, 143, 144, 149, 224
Carolina, 34, 37, 42, 53, 57, 58, 60, 170, 171, 173
Carrico, 14, 33, 36, 37, 68, 71, 92, 93, 107, 109, 113, 119, 131, 187, 190, 193, 208, 219, 225
Carrico Road, 107, 109, 131
Castlereagh, 15, 119, 220
Catholic, 37, 43, 51, 57, 64, 72, 86, 87, 157, 158
Cavelier, 203
Census Designated Place, 10, 153, 158
Central Stone, 120, 140
Cerre, 112, 189
Chambers Road, 69
Champ County Park, 143
Chappell, 24, 77, 221
Charbonier, 22, 139, 206
Chase Hotel, 125
chateau, 15, 73, 118, 120, 196, 197, 200, 202
chert, 20
Children's, 16, 123
Chitwood, 52
Cholera, 53, 204
Chomeau, 17, 90, 98, 125, 126, 220
Choteau, 112
Chouteau, 23, 27, 71, 161, 201
Christ Church Cathedral, 125
Christian Hospital, 129
Circuit Court, 53
Citizens Bank, 129

Civil War, 10, 15, 62, 68, 72, 89, 99, 101, 110, 112, 113, 154, 184, 204, 225, 226
Clark, 14, 23, 61, 84, 86, 87, 88, 97, 104, 138, 157, 204, 224
Clark River, 70
Clayton, 17, 77, 78, 93, 126, 179, 198
Clemens, 35, 47, 105, 207
Clifford, 120
coal, 76, 91, 94
COCA, 130
Cold War, 145
Cold Water Cemetery, 14, 17, 35, 59, 61, 62, 63, 84, 85, 86, 87, 88, 90, 97, 126, 157, 207, 209, 211, 222, 224, 226
Coldwater, 10, 33, 37, 38, 55, 84, 87, 91, 207, 210
Coldwater Cemetery, 211
Coldwater Church, 60, 62, 88, 90, 98, 211, 219
Coldwater Creek, 10, 14, 19, 26, 31, 32, 35, 37, 41, 57, 85, 86, 87, 94, 117, 127, 144, 145, 166, 216
Coldwater Hall, 94
Coldwater School, 14, 62, 64, 89, 90, 93, 94, 95, 111, 154
Columbia, 70, 71, 124, 192, 221, 223
Columbia Bottoms, 71, 203
Columbus, 203
Community Area Study, 222
Confederate, 15, 62, 101, 112, 184
Congress, 31, 74, 144, 174, 176, 224
Conroy, 69
Cooper, 34, 85, 171, 202
Cooperman, 199
Corps of Engineers, 41, 72, 73, 138, 139
Costello, 76
County Council, 123, 160, 161
Crank, 205, 208, 219, 226
Creole, 112, 189
Creve Coeur, 147
Crigler, 61
Cross Keys, 15, 42, 62, 94, 99, 101, 109, 157, 178
Cuba, 32, 87
Cudnik, 108, 130
Curlee, 15, 62, 118, 119
Curtiss Wright, 17, 126

D

Dale, 93, 98
Dalton Construction, 162
Daughters of the American Revolution, 85
Davis, 33, 54

Davison, 219
de Soto, 23, 203
Dearborn, 38
Defiance, 119, 192
Delassus, 50
Democratic, 174, 176, 177
Denny, 221
Department of Conservation, 119, 144, 221
Department of Natural Resources, 136, 162, 205, 209, 210, 212, 214
Depression, 124, 181
Desjarlais, 32, 33, 36, 37, 39, 42, 48, 49, 51, 54
Desloge, 9, 13, 15, 73, 75, 86, 118, 119, 144, 156, 161, 181, 196, 197, 199, 200, 201, 205, 214, 218, 219, 226
Detroit, 181
Diane Marie Estates, 162
Dillon, 75, 76
Distribix, 196
dolomite, 137, 141, 166
Donovan, 174, 176
Douglas, 14, 90, 113
Douglas Road, 14, 38, 40, 67, 75, 79, 107, 110, 139, 144, 161
Douglas School, 89
Douglass, 17, 63, 84, 90, 125, 126
Downs, 109, 153, 199
Dubois, 25, 26, 206
Duncan, 119
Dunn Road, 110
Dupre, 205
DuQuoin, 121
Durrett, 33, 59
dysentery, 101

E

Eagles Lodge, 88, 94
Easton, 14, 39, 53, 54, 67, 68, 74, 220
Ebbesmeyer, 129
Edwards, 23
Eggert, 112
El Mel, 154
Eldon, 126
Elks, 153
Ellis, 33, 124
Ellis Fischel State Cancer Hospital, 124
Elm Grove School District, 90
Emancipation Proclamation, 113
England, 23, 104, 183
English, 10
Episcopal Church, 125
Episcopal Theological Seminary, 125
Estates at Behlmann Farm, 129
Evans, 189
explorers, 11, 13

F

Faherty, 220
Fallis, 50, 51
Farley, 115, 213
farm, 15, 17, 34, 38, 40, 51, 57, 58, 59, 60, 62, 63, 64, 67, 72, 74, 86, 89, 91, 93, 94, 95, 99, 100, 101, 102, 105, 106, 107, 108, 109, 110, 111, 113, 117, 127, 129, 154, 156, 170, 171, 172, 173, 175, 180, 192, 193, 194, 197, 198
farmers, 10, 11, 14, 17, 68, 69, 72, 86, 99, 100, 101, 104, 105, 113, 129, 141, 144, 160, 178, 196, 198, 200
Farrar, 198, 201
Ferguson, 61, 62, 63, 93, 94, 130, 190, 191, 198
Ferguson Baptist Church, 127
First Capitol News, 103, 212
Fischel, 120, 124, 125
Fischer, 62, 64, 99, 179
Fitzgerald, 226
Florissant, 10, 11, 12, 13, 23, 31, 38, 40, 41, 43, 57, 60, 61, 64, 76, 77, 93, 94, 100, 104, 107, 129, 130, 145, 151, 153, 160, 178, 179, 190, 191, 198, 203, 219, 220
Florissant Chamber of Commerce, 130
Florissant Post Office, 107, 191
Florissant Tire Center, 129
Florissant Valley Reporter, 73, 86, 89, 180, 210, 211, 213
Foley, 220
Fordyce, 144, 199, 200, 201, 214, 226
Fort Bellefontaine, 35
Fort Belle Fontaine, 13, 25, 26, 223
Fort Bellefontaine, 26, 224
Fort Bellefontaine Road, 161, 162
Fort Don Carlos, 203
Fountainbleu, 108
France, 24, 25, 32, 50, 72, 118, 125, 126, 197, 200, 203
Francis, 15, 41, 48, 85, 119, 120
Frankfurter, 125
Franklin County, 48, 54
Franzwa, 91, 92, 95, 97, 98, 107, 219, 226
French, 12, 13, 23, 24, 31, 49, 51, 57, 60, 84, 118, 120, 126, 178, 196, 197, 200, 202, 209, 219
Friedman, 179
Friends to Humanity, 88, 183
From Westphalia Into the World, 100
Frost, 74, 174, 175
Fugate, 71
Fuller, 28
Fuqua, 191

Furrow, 226
Fusz, 201

G

Garraghan, 219
Garrett, 76, 77
Garth, 110
Gass, 219
Gassaway, 85, 89
Gateway Arch, 118, 196
Gazetteer, 23, 53
Gellhorn, 125
Gent, 179
Geological, 217
Georgia, 87
Geothermal Heating/Cooling, 147
Gerbers, 129
Gerbes, 112
Gerling, 75, 101, 109, 110, 112, 113, 115, 213
German, 10, 11, 17, 64, 75, 93, 94, 99, 110
German Revolution, 204
Germany, 15, 86, 91, 99, 100, 101, 102, 105, 106, 109, 110, 112, 129, 181
Gettemier, 100
Gibson, 188
Girardier, 226
glaciers, 19, 165
Glen Eagles, 161
Globe-Democrat, 20, 41, 206, 208, 222
Godfrey, 48
Goebel, 221
Goerken, 77
Goessmann, 131
Goodwin, 64
Graham, 16, 121, 122, 123, 141, 145, 214, 220
Grammer, 179
granite, 12, 141
Gray, 201
Greene County, 36, 37, 48, 49, 53, 54, 55
Grey, 14, 69
Griffin, 52
Griffith, 33, 37
Groegan, 77
Grow, 187
Grueninger, 112, 152
Gulf Coast, 141
Gulf of Mexico, 24, 164

H

Hagedorn, 181
Hall, 38, 49, 73, 89
Halls Ferry, 39, 85

Halls Ferry and Transfer Company, 70
Halls Ferry Road, 12, 23, 62, 67, 68, 69, 70, 73, 78, 79, 191, 223
Haltmann, 106
Hamilton, 63, 104, 106, 120, 121, 142, 212, 214, 216, 220, 222, 223, 226
Hammer, 17, 89, 126, 127
Hammersen, 89
Hanson, 121
Harder, 109
Hardy, 178
Harl, 205, 222
Harl, Joe, 13, 19, 205
Harlan, 221
Harrington, 37
Harris, 142, 216, 220
Harrison, 38
Hart, 33, 37
Hartmann, 16, 123, 214
Hartwig, 102, 116, 154
Harvard, 124, 125
Hayes, 86, 180
Hays, 180
Hazelwood, 61, 91, 129
Hazelwood Central High School, 90, 154
Hazelwood Engineering, 121
Hazelwood North Middle School, 153
Hazelwood School District, 14, 62, 89, 90, 91, 93, 107, 154, 161, 191, 205, 208, 211, 212, 219
Hecht, 122
Heins, 69, 139
Hellman, 76
Helmholz Papers, 68, 210
Hemingway, 125
Henley, 89
Hepperman, 100
Herculaneum, 87
Heritage Foundation, 91
Herrington, 33, 37
Hertich, 220
Hill, 62, 64
Historic Florissant, 98, 219, 224, 226
Historic Inventory, 63, 124, 211, 213, 214
History of Hazelwood School District, 90, 91, 92, 95, 97, 107, 211, 212, 226
History of Missouri, 50, 221
History of St. Louis City and County,, 222
History of St. Louis County, 71, 102, 105, 106, 108, 113, 125, 220
Hodges, 13, 32, 33, 35, 36, 37, 42, 43, 48, 49, 50, 51, 52, 53, 54, 55, 67, 205, 207, 208, 209, 219
Hoffman, 81, 116, 226, 227

Hoffmeister, 64, 91, 99, 110
Hollywood Showboat, 70, 75
Homburg, 101, 110
Hornaday, 59
Houck, 50, 209, 221
Hubbard, 33, 36, 39, 47, 53, 59, 60, 61, 84, 87, 88
Hughes, 63, 143
Huhs, 102
Hume, 34, 61, 62, 63, 64, 69, 84, 89, 109, 119, 171, 193, 219, 226
Hund, 77
Hunt, 40
Hutawa, 205
Hwy 66, 110
Hwy 67, 10, 14, 15, 40, 90, 91, 99, 101, 103, 106, 109, 110, 111, 128, 129, 130, 140, 154, 157, 160, 161, 162, 166, 193
Hyatt, 34, 35, 61, 62, 63, 64, 72, 171, 224
Hyde, 220
hydrocephalus, 131

I

Ice Age, 19
Illinois, 10, 11, 13, 19, 22, 23, 24, 25, 26, 36, 37, 39, 48, 49, 53, 54, 55, 58, 67, 68, 71, 73, 74, 75, 87, 101, 107, 113, 121, 140, 145, 154, 155, 156, 171, 175, 220
Illinois River, 12, 13, 156
India, 147
Indiana, 197
Interstate 270, 129
Inventory of Historic Buildings, 121, 205, 209, 210, 212, 214, 222
Inwood, 161, 162
Iowa, 121, 122, 139
Iseminger, 218, 220

J

Jackson, 185, 216
Jacobsmeyer, 112
James, 11, 14, 15, 29, 32, 33, 35, 36, 37, 38, 39, 40, 41, 42, 43, 46, 47, 48, 51, 52, 53, 54, 64, 67, 68, 69, 89, 90, 92, 102, 104, 105, 118, 204, 207, 210
James School, 89, 92
James' Town, 11, 39
Jamestown Acres, 16, 121, 123, 129
Jamestown Bluffs Library, 153
Jamestown Center, 162
Jamestown Farms, 35, 105, 119
Jamestown Forest, 161

Jamestown Landing, 39, 41
Jamestown Mall, 91, 111, 155, 204, 217
Jamestown New Horizons, 152
Jamison, 17, 33, 36, 39, 47, 53, 59, 60, 173
Jefferson County, 23, 87
Jensen, 178
Jesuit, 203
Joachim Creek, 87
Johnson's Shut-Ins, 199
Joliet, 24, 29, 203
Jones, 221
Julius, 72, 101, 109

K

Kaelin, 179
Kahre, 106, 213
Kamp, 93, 112
Kane, 226
Kansas City, 22, 27, 78, 211
karst, 16, 17, 20, 64, 136, 137, 140, 161, 162, 163, 166, 167, 168
Karst Protection District, 151, 204
Kaskaskia, 22, 58, 171, 203
Kaufman, 125
Keeven, 161
Kemp, 161
Kennett, 198
Kentucky, 11, 13, 31, 35, 36, 49, 58, 60, 61, 70, 87, 171, 183, 210
Kersgieter, 157
Killark Electric, 197
Kingsbury, 38, 146
Kingshighway, 23, 123
Kitty's Corner, 101
Knappitz, 178
Koester, 64
Kohnen, 100, 219
Korte, 109
Kroeger, 13, 118, 196, 199
Krueger, 63, 101
Kuhn, 77, 109
Kunz, 76, 77

L

La Salle, 24, 203
Laclede, 22, 124, 140, 141, 142
Laclede Gas, 16, 17, 111, 122, 140, 148, 149, 151, 160, 204, 223
Lambert Field, 127, 128
Lampe, 116
Land Commissioners, 42, 54
land grant, 10, 31, 32, 34, 36, 37, 38, 42, 43, 48, 58, 59, 60, 61, 67, 71, 84, 90, 105

Lange, 94, 110, 111, 116, 117, 141
Lard, 33, 42, 208
LaSalle, 13, 23
Latimer, 61
Leach, 220
Leber, 91, 110, 116
Leighninger, 226
Levick, 141
Lewis, 204
Lewis & Clark, 13, 24, 25, 26, 27, 29, 206, 225
Lexington Farms, 109, 199
Lichtenberg, 226
limestone, 12, 16, 21, 26, 39, 72, 73, 119, 122, 136, 137, 164, 165, 166, 197
Limestone, 164, 166
Lincoln, 67, 113
Lindbergh, 93, 190
Lindemann, 62, 72, 101, 106, 112, 210, 213, 226
Lippman, 196
Little, 22, 33, 35, 41, 120
Logston, 127
London, 87
Long, 22, 25, 142
Lord, 108
Louisiana, 13, 23, 25, 27, 31, 32, 34, 35, 50, 57, 58, 67, 87, 170, 172, 204, 206, 207, 208
Louisiana Manufacturing, 197
Louisiana Purchase, 13, 27, 31, 57
Louisiana territory, 13
Loutre, 34, 171
Love, 192
Lovejoy, 73, 74
Lueke, 139
Lumina Project, 107, 190, 213
Lusson, 51, 52
Lutzow, 159

M

Machiran, 19, 205, 206, 222
Madison County, 53, 61
Mahanta, 146, 149, 226
Mallinckrodt, 145
Marais des Liards, 34
Mark Twain, 35, 105
Marquette, 13, 23, 24, 29, 203
Martial Law, 112, 188
Marty, 64
Mason, 160
Massachusetts, 36, 48, 49
Mayflower, 48, 203
Mazander, 161
McBride High School, 129
McClurg, 145

McDonald, 15, 73, 118, 197
McDonnell Douglas, 17, 118, 126, 129, 156
McDonnell Douglas Boulevard, 128, 129
McDowns, 42
McIlvaine, 201
McKensie, 32, 37
McNair, 121, 146
Meigs, 38
Mellon, 61
Memorial Day, 85
Menke, 70, 71
Mesker, 15, 118, 120, 124, 125, 146, 147, 228
Mesker Brothers Iron Company, 120
Metcalfe, 175
Methodist, 14, 37, 53, 61, 84, 86, 87, 88, 157, 178
Meyer, 64, 101, 105, 106, 111, 113, 139, 213, 219
Mill Creek, 19, 26, 41, 53, 111
Mills, 92, 119
Milmann, 107, 190
Minerva Oil, 197
Minnesota., 108
Mirly, 141, 142
Mississippi, 119
Mississippi River, 10, 11, 12, 13, 14, 15, 20, 21, 23, 24, 25, 26, 32, 38, 39, 40, 42, 50, 53, 70, 73, 75, 84, 88, 99, 100, 106, 112, 118, 124, 138, 139, 140, 141, 156, 165, 178, 183, 196, 206, 208
Mississippian, 13, 19, 21, 22, 142, 164, 165, 203
Missouri, 11, 12, 15, 20, 21, 22, 23, 25, 26, 27, 34, 35, 36, 41, 42, 49, 50, 52, 53, 54, 55, 57, 58, 59, 60, 61, 62, 63, 67, 68, 71, 85, 93, 99, 102, 104, 108, 111, 112, 113, 119, 121, 123, 124, 127, 136, 143, 153, 160, 164, 165, 170, 171, 173, 181, 206, 207, 218, 220, 221
Missouri Cavalry, 113
Missouri Death Records, 224
Missouri Department of Conservation, 144
Missouri Department of Natural Resources, 21, 168, 221
Missouri Episcopal Diocese, 16, 125
Missouri Gazette, 11, 39, 205, 208
Missouri Historical Review, 38, 208, 221
Missouri Historical Society, 223
Missouri History Museum, 73, 75, 81, 82, 114, 115, 201, 202, 220, 221, 226

Missouri History Museum of St. Louis, 65, 66
Missouri Resources Magazine, 136, 137, 166, 215
Missouri River, 10, 11, 12, 13, 14, 15, 19, 20, 21, 22, 23, 24, 25, 26, 27, 35, 36, 38, 39, 41, 42, 43, 48, 50, 52, 53, 62, 63, 67, 68, 69, 70, 72, 75, 76, 77, 78, 103, 109, 118, 119, 120, 121, 122, 124, 128, 131, 136, 137, 138, 139, 140, 141, 142, 143, 144, 145, 146, 147, 148, 149, 151, 153, 156, 163, 165, 166, 167, 178, 183, 196, 200, 206, 210, 211, 215, 221
Missouri State Archives, 225
Missouri State University, 130
Missouri Supreme Court, 16, 141
Missouri Territory, 23, 33, 67, 207
MKT railroad, 75
MO-367, 10, 15, 140
Mobil Oil, 160
Model-T, 190
Monahan, 76, 77
Monroe, 87, 89
Monroe County, 87
Monsanto, 192
Morgan, 111
Moss, 130
Mudd, 41, 77
Mueller, 102, 179, 214, 220
Mullanphy, 35, 105, 201
Municipal Free Bridge, 70
Murphysboro, 121
Musick, 14, 36, 37, 38, 52, 60, 61, 68, 69, 71, 76, 112, 139, 210
Musick Ferry Plank Road, 79
Musick's Ferry, 9, 10, 12, 14, 23, 29, 36, 39, 43, 46, 62, 67, 68, 69, 70, 71, 72, 73, 74, 75, 76, 77, 81, 103, 110, 112, 113, 118, 139, 140, 144, 174, 175, 176, 178, 179, 223, 224
Mustermann, 161

N

National Council of Churches, 125
National Register of Historic Places, 84, 88, 99, 142, 209, 211, 212, 222
Native plants, 146, 147
Nazis, 199, 200
Neal, 42, 220
Nevada, 126
New Bielefeld, 99
New Coldwater Burying Ground, 85, 86, 89, 96, 180, 211
New Halls Ferry, 161
New Halls Ferry Road, 9, 10, 13, 14, 15, 23, 32, 38, 55, 60, 62, 64, 67, 68, 73, 75, 86, 90, 93, 94, 99, 101, 104, 109, 111, 118, 153, 154, 155, 156, 158, 161, 180, 197, 200
New Jamestown Road, 106, 161
New Melle, 192
New Orleans, 15, 73, 99, 100, 101, 106, 118, 127, 197, 201
New York, 76, 125, 130, 220
Newcombe, 111
NFL, 130
Nicholson, 41
Niehaus, 109, 112, 116
Niemeyer, 106
nocostl.com, 146, 154
Nolte, 92, 108, 112
Normandy, 93, 125, 198
North County Journal, 85, 211
North Fork, 199
Northcott, 226

O

O'Neil, 12, 22, 27, 206
Oak Grove Cemetery, 103
Oakville, 136, 163, 167
Oetker, 63
Ohio River, 183
Old Halls Ferry Road, 14, 15, 17, 41, 63, 84, 85, 90, 99, 101, 109, 110, 111, 125, 126, 128, 139, 151, 153, 154, 157, 160, 161, 162, 166, 193
Old Halls Ferry Stables, 17, 126
Old Jamestown Association, 9, 16, 112, 136, 137, 139, 146, 147, 151, 153, 160, 166, 168, 184
Old Jamestown Estates, 108
Old Jamestown Lane, 121
Old Jamestown Road, 9, 14, 15, 40, 88, 89, 103, 104, 105, 107, 111, 119, 121, 122, 129, 140, 143, 152, 153, 154, 157, 161, 162, 190
Old Jamestown Study, 160
Oneota, 203
Orrick, 103
Osage, 22, 25, 26, 27, 206
Osage Gas Company, 123
Overland, 181
Owen's Fort, 34, 58, 170, 171, 172
Owen's Station, 51, 170

P

Pacific Ocean, 25, 27
PaleoIndian, 203
Paleozoic, 164, 165
Pallottine Renewal Center, 129, 151, 223
Parc Argonne, 100, 128, 129, 193
Parc Argonne Estates, 105, 128
Parc Argonne Forest, 161
paresis, 126
Parker Road, 40, 95, 154
Patterson, 14, 17, 32, 33, 34, 35, 36, 37, 39, 49, 53, 54, 57, 58, 59, 60, 61, 62, 63, 64, 69, 84, 86, 87, 88, 89, 90, 99, 100, 101, 104, 106, 109, 113, 125, 136, 170, 171, 172, 173, 186, 219
Patterson Settlement, 10, 14, 57, 219
Paul Artspace, 151, 152
PBS, 130
Pea Ridge School, 102
Pelican Island, 67, 75, 76, 77, 119, 142, 143, 144, 148, 149, 164, 199, 201, 224
Pennsylvania, 57, 130, 164, 207
Perryville, 70
Philadelphia, 64, 130, 222
Phinehas James, 36, 39, 40, 41, 67, 118
Phoenix, 125
Piggott, 84, 89, 104
Pike, 13, 24, 25, 26, 59, 142
Pike County, 59, 104
Pike County Genealogical Society, 59, 209
Pitzman, 110, 207, 222, 224
Planning Commission, 160, 161, 162, 222
Pleistocene, 19, 166, 203
Pollard, 174, 176
Pond's Fort, 34, 171
Pondrom, 12, 41, 68, 107, 112, 126, 191, 205, 208, 220
Portage des Sioux, 10, 12, 23, 78, 204
Portage Des Sioux, 184
Portage Road, 15, 16, 23, 35, 39, 40, 46, 117, 120, 123, 124, 125, 147, 154, 226, 228
Portland Cement, 15, 72, 95, 102, 109, 140
Portland Lake, 161
Possum Hollow, 62, 119
Post – Dispatch,, 214
Post-Dispatch, 12, 22, 27, 67, 70, 76, 77, 118, 120, 122, 125, 126, 140, 142, 143, 144, 146, 155, 181, 196, 205, 206, 210, 211, 214, 215, 216, 217, 222, 223
Potosi, 191, 201
Precambrian, 141
Presbyterian, 51, 86
Pritchard, 109
Prohibition, 10, 75, 100, 204
Prologue Magazine, 224
Proterozoic, 164

Protestant, 14, 51, 57, 60, 61, 84, 85, 86, 87, 88
Provost Marshal, 112, 113, 185
Prussia, 64, 106
Pulltight, 42
Purcelle, 42

Q

quarry, 15, 67, 69, 71, 72, 102, 120, 139, 140, 161, 178

R

railroads, 75, 78, 140, 167, 191, 201
Randolph, 103, 110, 116, 226, 227
Randoph County, 181
Rau, 111
Renken, 216
Republican, 75, 174, 175, 176
Revolutionary War, 10, 31, 48, 49, 57, 59, 84, 87, 103
Reynolds County, 199
Rhodes, 89
Rice, 126, 214, 220
Richardson, 32, 34, 35, 37, 38, 57, 58, 63, 170, 171, 172
Rickers, 106
Riverfront Times, 131
Riverview Boulevard, 140
Riverview Quarry, 139
Riverview Stone, 108, 192
Roads End Tavern, 75
Robbins, 103
Robbins Mill, 14, 40, 91, 102, 103, 106, 109, 110, 116
Robertson, 93, 180, 181, 190, 192
Romine, 53
Rosenkoetter, 15, 17, 63, 91, 99, 100, 101, 109, 110, 113, 193
Rosenkötter, 205, 212, 213, 219
Rozier, 200
Rubsam, 111
Ruegg, 15, 102, 140
Ruegg Post Office, 15, 102
Rui, 203
Russel, 89
Russell, 53, 64, 208
Ryan, 121

S

Saalfrank, 199
Sacred Heart Church, 64
Salem Baptist Church, 9, 14, 62, 88, 89, 90, 107, 109, 127, 157, 190, 209
Salem Lutheran Church, 99, 101
Saucier, 23
Scarlett, 16, 122, 125, 129
Scharf, 222
Scharr, 127, 128, 214, 220
Schnatzmeyer, 111
Schnitker, 101
School of American Ballet, 130
Schuler, 63
Schutte, 106, 112
Scotch Irish, 57
Scotland, 92, 108
Scottish, 10, 87
Seaver, 129
Seeley, 32, 33, 35, 37, 40, 41, 43, 47, 48, 52, 53, 105
Sessinghaus, 74, 175
settlers, 11, 12, 13, 14, 19, 23, 27, 31, 33, 49, 52, 53, 57, 84, 87, 89, 90, 99, 102, 118, 170, 178
Seven Year War, 203
Shackelford, 15, 55, 62, 63, 67, 73, 86, 90, 109, 118, 156, 161, 180, 200
Shackelford Road, 13, 197
shale, 164
Shalom Church City of Peace, 157
Shamblin, 108
Shamblin Drive, 162
Shattuck, 226
sheep, 60, 64, 192, 193
Shoveltown, 15, 99, 101, 110, 111, 157, 193
Showboats, 70, 75
Shuttuck, 208
Sibley, 220, 221
Sidney Street, 70
Sink, 180
sinkholes, 11, 16, 20, 136, 137, 140, 162, 163, 166, 167, 168
Sinks, 16, 17, 62, 64, 95, 100, 110, 111, 112, 122, 136, 137, 140, 141, 142, 148, 152, 160, 166, 167, 169, 215
Sinks Road, 111
Sioux Passage Park, 11, 13, 19, 20, 21, 26, 29, 52, 53, 111, 118, 136, 142, 144, 146, 148, 149, 154, 205, 206, 223
Sisters in the Sky, 128, 214, 220
Slack's Division, 62
slavery, 10, 11, 17, 36, 58, 59, 73, 74, 85, 86, 88, 90, 112, 113, 173, 180, 183, 184, 204
Smiley, 93, 98, 178
Smith, 76, 107, 130, 142, 159, 160, 162, 166, 190, 193, 194, 212, 213, 221, 226
Soper, 163, 168
Soulard, 112
Spain, 13, 25, 27, 31, 32, 50, 84, 203, 221
Spanish, 13, 17, 22, 23, 25, 26, 31, 32, 34, 50, 51, 57, 58, 63, 84, 86, 87, 105, 170, 172, 206, 207, 208, 209
Spanish Lake, 10, 100, 101, 102
Spanish Pond, 42
Spanish Regime in Missouri, 221
Spring Ferry, 39, 68
Springfield, 102, 165
St. Andrew UMC, 156, 157
St. Angela Merici, 157
St. Ann, 145
St. Charles, 23, 26, 38, 51, 52, 67, 68, 69, 73, 77, 103, 192, 203
St. Charles Borromeo, 51
St. Charles Cosmos, 34, 57, 70, 170, 222
St. Charles Cosmos-Monitor, 75, 210, 211
St. Charles County, 10, 12, 14, 23, 28, 34, 38, 41, 50, 67, 69, 70, 75, 76, 77, 78, 103, 118, 141, 171, 196, 220
St. Charles County Heritage, 222
St. Ferdinand, 11, 37, 40, 50, 51, 52, 54, 55, 101, 105, 203, 224
St. Ferdinand de Florissant, 36, 42, 48, 49, 51, 219
St. Ferdinand Township, 10, 54, 74, 75, 105, 106, 174, 175
St. Francois County, 197
St. Louis, 9, 10, 12, 13, 21, 22, 23, 26, 27, 31, 33, 34, 35, 37, 39, 50, 55, 57, 58, 67, 68, 69, 70, 71, 72, 75, 77, 87, 102, 103, 105, 108, 112, 118, 119, 122, 125, 127, 140, 142, 151, 160, 165, 166, 174, 194, 205, 206, 207, 208, 209, 210, 220, 223, 224
St. Louis Board of Education, 127
St. Louis Business Journal, 158, 201
St. Louis Christian Advocate, 60
St. Louis Cold Drawn, 121
St. Louis Community College, 28
St. Louis County, 10, 11, 12, 16, 31, 41, 49, 55, 57, 59, 60, 61, 63, 64, 68, 69, 71, 73, 78, 82, 84, 91, 99, 100, 101, 102, 105, 106, 112, 115, 119, 125, 126, 131, 136, 137, 138, 139, 140, 142, 144, 145, 146, 151, 152, 153, 154, 155, 160, 162, 163, 164, 166, 167, 168, 170, 179, 199, 204, 205, 208, 209, 210, 211, 212, 213, 214, 215, 216, 217, 219, 220, 222, 223, 225, 226
St. Louis County Land Title Company, 125
St. Louis County Library, 226
St. Louis Football Cardinals, 130
St. Louis Genealogical Society, 207

St. Louis Genealogical Society Quarterly, 42, 208, 222
St. Louis Magazine, 196, 199
St. Louis Public Radio, 130
St. Louis University, 124, 127, 197
St. Stanislaus Seminary, 224
St. Vrain, 72
Starbird, 125, 126, 220
Star-Times, 126
Ste. Genevieve, 166, 200, 201
steamboat, 70, 77, 78, 100, 106, 138, 143, 215
Stegall, 127
Steinmann, 145
Stellhorn, 94, 110, 111, 116, 117, 212, 213, 226
Stenger, 155
Stith, 201
Stone Industry, 225
Stovsky, 196, 205
Stroer, 100
Stuart, 54
Study & Farrar, 120
Sullivan, 42, 104, 143
Sunset Park, 199
Swanson, 73
syndic, 34, 50, 55

T

Taille de Noyer, 224
Talisman, 111
Tandy, 77
Teason, 179
Tegtmeye, 200
Temple, 90
Tennessee, 11
Texas, 41, 63, 104, 119
The History of St. Louis County, Missouri, 105
The Sinks, 10
Thomas, 25, 43, 48, 61, 63, 68, 90, 108, 207, 208, 220, 222
Thompson, 62, 70, 92, 107, 108, 109, 113, 139, 174, 177, 187, 193
Thorp, 108
Traad, 127
Trampe, 116
Treadway, 122
Triple C 4-H Club, 9, 109, 111
Troy, 180, 192
Trudeau, 42, 58, 87, 172
Tunstall, 34, 90
Tunstall-Douglass House, 17, 18, 37, 90, 101, 125, 126, 127
Turner, 178

Twillman, 193

U

Underground Railroad, 73, 112, 210
Underground Storage, 123, 140
Union, 15, 58, 88, 90, 110, 112, 113, 173, 185, 211
Union Boulevard, 126
Union Meeting House, 88, 90, 97, 98, 211, 219
United Methodist Church, 157
University of Missouri, 127, 220
Upper Louisiana, 170, 207, 209, 221
Urban League, 125

V

Vaile, 93, 94, 103, 104, 111, 128, 130, 153, 161, 162, 166, 190, 193
Valley Bistro Café, 130
Vandike, 136, 162, 163, 166, 168
Vanesco, 40
Veale, 91, 103, 104, 106, 114
Veiled Prophet Queen, 199
Vermont, 48, 49, 50
Village of Fours, 161
Vincent, 33, 36, 37, 69, 71, 85, 86, 89, 180, 181, 201
Vineyard, 162
Virginia, 39, 57, 59, 60, 61, 62, 71, 72
Visintine, 145
Vossenkemper, 91, 95
Vossenkemper School, 14, 89, 91, 94, 95, 110, 111, 140
Vouziers, 13, 73, 118, 119, 196, 197, 200, 205, 214

W

Wagner, 109
Waier, 120, 121, 147, 216, 226, 228
Waldbart Nursery, 154, 162
Wallace and Rees, 161
Walnut Landing, 69
Walsh, 178
Walters-Kroenke, 162
War of 1812, 23, 60, 84
Warren, 34, 40, 67, 71, 72, 73, 109, 139, 178, 187, 210, 226
Warsaw, 164
Washington County, 107, 207
Washington Redskins, 130
Washington University, 16, 121, 122, 123, 124, 126, 145, 202, 214
Watchman Advocate, 68, 205, 220

Watchman-Advocate, 170
WaterFurnace, 147
Webster Groves, 181
Wehmer, 89, 92, 93, 94, 106, 107, 108, 109, 111, 181, 190, 193, 212, 213, 219
Wehmer Estates, 108
Welch, 62, 108, 130
Wells, 43
Wentzville, 192
Werner, 201
West Alton, 75
Westlake Quarry, 108, 161, 192
Westphalia, 99, 100, 205, 212, 213, 219
Whistler, 61
White Hall, 49
Wickham, 174, 177
Wiese, 102
Wildwood, 20, 205, 206, 207, 222
Wilkinson, 33, 35, 36, 38, 67, 207
Williams, 125, 159
winery, 64
Winkler, 112, 184, 226
Witte, 111, 116, 117
Wittich, 74, 75, 174, 175
Wolferman, 220
Wolff, 106, 154
Women's Airforce Service Pilots, 127
Women's Auxiliary Ferrying Squadron, 127
Wood, 126
Woodland, 19, 21, 22, 142, 203
World War I, 10, 118, 121, 124, 197, 200, 204
World War II, 10, 17, 86, 126, 127, 144, 145, 153, 181, 204
World's Fair, 194
Wortmann, 64
WPA, 23, 164, 206, 218, 221
Wright, 220
Wright City, 192
Wyatt, 121

Y

Yaeger, 74
yellow fever, 101
Young, 53

Z

Zykan, 9, 129, 130
Zykan Brothers Hauling, 130, 139

Made in the USA
Lexington, KY
31 March 2017